FUNDAMENTALS OF PROGRAMMING

Mir Shehzad Ahmad

TAP

Toronto Academic Press

Fundamentals of Programming

Mir Shehzad Ahmad

Toronto Academic Press
224 Shoreacres Road
Burlington, ON L7L 2H2
Canada
www.tap-books.com
Email: orders@arclereducation.com

ISBN: 978-1-77469-757-3

ABOUT THE AUTHOR

Mir Shahzad Ahmad is an accomplished information security expert with over seven years of experience in the field. With a passion for cybersecurity and a drive to keep individuals and businesses safe from cyber threats, Mir has become a respected authority in his field. Mir's expertise lies in understanding the ever-changing landscape of cyber threats and developing effective strategies to mitigate risks. He has worked with a wide range of clients, from small businesses to multinational corporations, helping them to safeguard their data and systems. Throughout his career, Mir has developed a reputation for his ability to communicate complex cybersecurity concepts in a clear and concise manner. He has authored numerous articles on the subject and is a sought-after speaker at conferences and events. Mir is also an experienced educator, having trained a number of individuals and organizations on best practices in cybersecurity. He holds several certifications in the field, including CISSP, CEH, and CISM. Mir is dedicated to helping businesses and individuals stay ahead of the curve when it comes to cybersecurity. His insights and expertise make him a valuable resource for anyone looking to protect themselves from cyber threats.

Contents

5 Functions 107

6 Arrays 129

7 Control Structures 151

8 Fundamentals of Object-Oriented Programming 169

List of Figures

List of Tables

List of Abbreviations

AI	Artificial Intelligence
ANSI	American National Standards Institute
API	Application Programming Interface
ASCII	American Standard Code for Information Interchange
DBAs	Database Administrators
DRY	Don't Repeat Yourself
FLPL	Fortran List Processing Language
GUI	Graphical User Interface
IPL-1	Information Processing Language I
ISP	Internet Service Provider
JIT	Just-In-Time
JSP	Java Server Pages
JSTL	Java Server Pages Standard Tag Library
JVM	Java Virtual Machine
NP	Nondeterministic Polynomial
OOP	Object-Oriented Programming
RAM	Random-Access Machine
RIA	Rich Internet Applications
W3C	World Wide Web Consortium
WWW	World Wide Web
XML	Extensible Markup Language
XSLT	eXtensible Stylesheet Language

PREFACE

Programming refers to the process of creating software or computer programs that can perform specific tasks. It involves using programming languages such as Python, Java, C++, JavaScript, and others to write code that can be executed by a computer. Programming is used in a wide range of applications, including web development, mobile app development, game development, scientific computing, and data analysis. It can involve various programming paradigms, such as procedural, object-oriented, or functional programming. To write effective and efficient code, programmers need to understand programming concepts such as data types, functions, arrays, control structures, algorithms, and data structures. Programming can be a rewarding career and requires continuous learning and adaptation to keep up with the latest technologies and developments in the world.

The discussion of the book starts with the fundamentals of programming and software development lifecycle, followed by the evolution and evaluation of different programming languages. Also, the basic concept of algorithms and data structures, along with different data types used in programming, are described in detail in this book. The fundamental concept of functions and arrays in programming is also explained in detail. The concept of control structures, which refer to programming language constructs that allow programmers to manage the flow of program execution based on specific conditions, is described in the book. Lastly, the fundamentals of object-oriented programming (OOP) are described in detail at the end of this book.

This book comprises of eight-chapters; Chapter 1 discusses the fundamentals of programming with an emphasis on the history of programming and the life cycle of software development. Chapter 2 deals with the evolution and evaluation of major programming languages and provides an insight into the summary and history of major programming languages.

Chapter 3 is about the data types used in programming and describes the use of numeric and Boolean data types in different programming languages. Chapter 4 discusses the need for data structures and algorithms in programming, along with the issues solved by these concepts.

Chapter 5 describes the concept of functions in programming which is a block of code that performs a specific task and can be called or invoked from other parts of a program. Chapter 6 deals with the concepts of arrays in programming which is a data structure that stores a collection of elements, such as numbers or strings, in contiguous memory locations. Chapter 7 is about control structures and describes the use of else/if, case-control, and iteration control structures (loops) in programming, and Chapter 8 is about object-oriented programming and provides insight into features and different concepts applied in object-oriented programming.

This book has been written specifically for students and scholars to meet their needs in terms of knowledge and to provide them with a broad understanding of the fundamentals of programming. We aim for this book to be a resource for academics in many subjects since we believe it will provide clarity and insight for its readers.

—Author

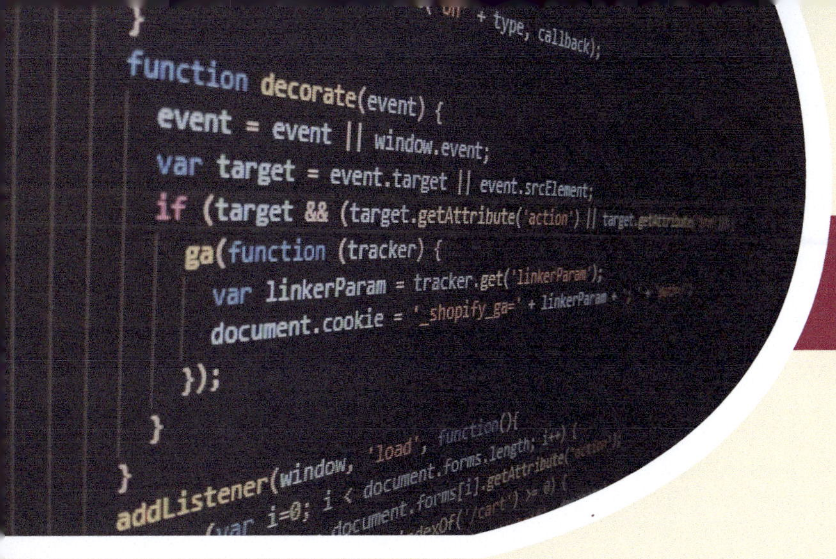

CHAPTER 1

INTRODUCTION TO PROGRAMMING

UNIT INTRODUCTION

These days, computers are indispensable. Everyone utilizes them to communicate, have fun, and solve challenging work-related problems and are used in various fields, including business, entertainment, telecommunications, and banking. It is hardly an exaggeration to argue that computers form the neurological network of our modern civilization, and it is hard to imagine life without them (Iverson, 1962).

Despite their widespread use, few individuals are familiar with how computers operate. The software that runs on the computers—not the computers themselves—matters. Computers are valuable to users because the software enables a wide range of services that improve our quality of life (Wirth, 1971).

Professionals use programming as a fundamental tool to design and build complicated software systems, automate tedious operations, and address challenging issues. In our digital age, a necessary ability is becoming increasingly significant. Numerous industries, like healthcare, finance, and entertainment, have been transformed through programming. Therefore, to become a successful developer or programmer, it is imperative to possess a firm understanding of the foundations of programming (Rosen, 1972).

Learning Objectives

Students are going to able to comprehend the following after reading this chapter:

- The fundamental idea of programming;
- Knowledge of information processing by computers;
- Computer programming history;
- Aspects of several programming languages;
- Software development lifecycle.

Key Terms

- Algorithms
- BASIC
- C++
- COBOL
- Computers
- FORTRAN
- Java
- Programming
- Python
- Script
- Software
- Testing

1.1. PROCESSING OF INFORMATION

To comprehend what it means to program, one can generally relate a computer or its operating system to a vast factory, including all its workshops, warehouses, and transportation. Visualizing the degree of complexity present in a modern computer using this basic comparison is simpler. A computer runs several of that correspond to a factory's workshops and production lines. The operational memory (RAM), the hard drive, and its contention s serve warehouses, while the various protocols serve as transportation systems for information input and output (Aho et al., 1979).

Did you Know?

Ada Lovelace created the initial computer program in the middle of the nineteenth century.

Different workshops produce the many goods that are produced at a factory. They use the warehouses' raw materials and keep their finished products there. The suppliers bring the finished goods from their warehouses to the outlets, while the warehouses deliver the raw materials to the warehouses. Different modes of transportation are employed to achieve this. Raw materials entering the plant undergo many processes and eventually emerge as finished goods. Each factory transforms unprocessed supplies into a finished good that may be consumed (Hosoya & Pierce, 2003).

A computer is a tool for processing information. In contrast to a manufacturing facility in our instance, information serves as the computer's raw material and final product. Most of the time, the input data is taken from one of the storage areas (files or RAM), where it was previously moved. It then goes through one or more procedures and transforms into a new product. A good example is web-based applications. Information processing often entails extracting content from databases and processing it for display in HTML. They employ HTTP for transferring raw materials and finished goods (Shaikhha et al., 2019).

1.2. MANAGING THE COMPUTER

Numerous levels of management are involved in the entire process of producing goods in a factory. Operators run the machinery and assembly lines, managers oversee the workshops, and general executives oversee the entire plant. They all exert control over various processes at various tiers. The lowest level of service providers are the machine operators, who use buttons and levers to operate the machines. The workshop managers will advance to the levels carried out, watching commands (Holsapple, 2005).

Computers and software have numerous levels of control and management, much like this. The simplest level is controlled by the processor and its registers (this is done by utilizing low-level machine programs); we can relate it to managing the equipment in the workshops. Are all under greater control of the operating system (Windows 7, for instance) – it can be compared to how many workshops and departments function in manufacturing. The application software is at the top of the hierarchy. It manages a large number of tasks that use a lot of processor activities. General executives operate the entire production at this level to optimize resource usage and deliver superior results (Hosoya & Pierce, 2003).

Did you Know?

IBM created FORTRAN, the initial high-level programming language, in the 1950s.

1.3. THE ESSENCE OF PROGRAMMING

The goal of a program is to manage every aspect of a computer's operation. The "orders" and "commands" provided by the programmer, referred to as programming instructions, are used to do this. To "program" is to arrange computer operations through a series of instructions. The computer (namely, the OS, the CPU, and peripheral devices) implicitly complies with these written orders (instructions). Writing a "program" refers to organizing a set of instructions to get a computer to do something. "computer programs" or "scripts" describes these sets of instructions (Wadler, 1992).

An algorithm is a series of processes to accomplish a goal, finish a task, or produce a specific outcome. This is why programming and algorithms relate to one another. Programming entails putting the desired action on the computer into a step-by-step or algorithmic description.

Computers are controlled by these instructions, which programmers make. These directives are referred to as programs. Many programs were written in a variety of programming languages. Each language targets different levels of computer control. There are languages designed for the lowest (machine) level of computation – for instance, an assembler. Others, like C, are most beneficial when used at the system level (when interfacing with the operating system). High-level languages are also employed in the development of application programs. Some examples of these languages are Java, Perl, C#, Visual Basic, Python, Ruby, PHP, C++, & JavaScript (Jones, 2005) (Figure 1.1).

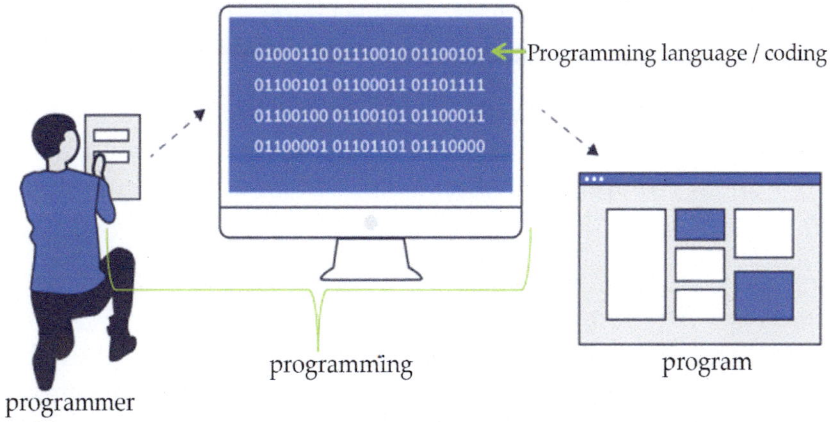

Figure 1.1. Illustration of relation between programmer, programming, and program.

Source: Wan Fazlini, Creative Commons License.

1.4. HISTORY OF PROGRAMMING

The earliest mechanical computers were developed in the early 1800s when programming began. These machines weren't programmable in the traditional sense; but were capable of rudimentary arithmetic calculations.

Ada Lovelace, a mathematician, wrote the very first computer program in the middle of the 19th century. It was intended to operate on Charles Babbage's Analytical Engine. Although Lovelace's program was never used, her work set the stage for subsequent programming projects (Bergin, 2007). Many significant computing tools, such as the Hollerith tabulating device, were created in the late 1800s and early 1900s and utilized for the 1890 US census. The Hollerith machine employed punch cards to represent data so that a machine could read it and automatically tally it. The idea of a universal machine that could be programmed to carry out any computation which could be defined algorithmically was created by mathematician Alan Turing in the 1930s. Turing's work was essential to advancing contemporary computing and established the groundwork for the 1940s that produced the first electronic computers (Sammet, 1972).

The circuitry in the initial electronic computers was made of vacuum tubes, which were big, expensive machines largely employed for scientific and military purposes, such as deciphering codes throughout World War II and calculating the yield of an atomic weapon. Programming languages were created in the 1950s and 1960s to facilitate software creation for these systems. To enable scientists and businesspeople to construct programs for scientific and commercial applications, languages like FORTRAN, COBOL, & BASIC were developed (Liskov, 1996).

Several programming languages were created in the 1970s and 1980s that emphasized various facets of programming. Systems programming was intended for C and Pascal, whereas advanced applications were intended for languages including Smalltalk and Lisp.

New programming languages, as well as frameworks, were developed in the 1990s and 2000s as a result of the growth of the internet and personal computing. For online development, languages like Java, Python, and Ruby gained popularity, while the proliferation of mobile devices sparked the creation of emerging mobile programming languages such as Swift and Kotlin (Liskov, 1996). Today, software powers anything from smartphones to automobiles to medical gadgets, making programming an essential part of contemporary civilization. New languages, frameworks, and tools are being developed to suit the increasing needs of modern computing as the area continues to advance quickly.

1.5. TYPES OF PROGRAMMING LANGUAGES

Programming languages may be generally categorized based on their traits and features. The following is a description of a few of the most popular types of programming languages (Ancona et al., 2016).

1.5.1. High-Level Programming Languages

These languages have been created to be simple enough for anybody to read and understand. In contrast to low-level programming languages, they frequently used English-like syntax and had a greater level of abstraction (Barnett & Greenes, 1970).

1.5.2. Low-Level Programming Languages

These languages provide a higher level of management of system resources and are intended to be more directly related to the technology of a system of computers. Low-level languages include assembly languages (Baillie, 2005).

1.5.3. Procedural Programming Languages

These languages are built around procedures and subroutines, standalone coding units that carry out particular functions. The most common procedural programming languages are C and Pascal.

1.5.4. Object-Oriented Programming (OOP) Languages

The foundation of these languages is the idea of objects of desire, data, and behavior. Examples include Java, Python, and C++ (Jordan et al., 2015).

1.5.5. Functional Programming Languages

Because functions are considered first-class citizens in these languages, they can be supplied like arguments, retrieved as values, and kept in variables. Functional programming languages include Haskell, Lisp, and Clojure (Hudak, 1989).

1.5.6. Scripting Languages

These languages are meant for quick and simple task automation and prototyping. They frequently have a dynamic type and trash collection and tend to be interpreted instead of compiled. Examples include JavaScript, Python, and Ruby (Xie & Aiken, 2006).

1.5.7. Markup Languages

Instead of specifying the functionality of software applications, these languages are employed to define the structure and display of texts. Markup languages include things like HTML, XML, and LaTeX (Vilhjálmsson et al., 2007).

1.5.8. Query Languages

These coding languages are employed to retrieve and modify data from databases. The most popular query language is SQL (Angles et al., 2017) (Figure 1.2).

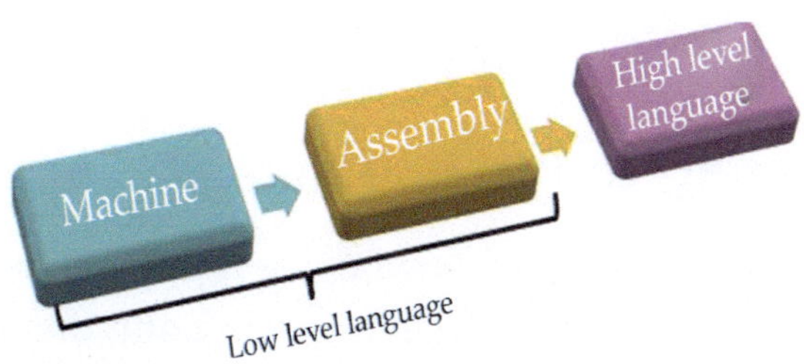

Figure 1.2. Image of different programming languages.

Source: Wan Fazlini, Creative Commons License.

1.6. STAGES IN SOFTWARE DEVELOPMENT

Software development can be extremely difficult and time consuming, requiring an extensive group of software engineers and additional experts. As a result, various techniques and procedures that simplify the work of programmers have been developed. The only thing that has similarities is that each software product passes through several stages during its development (Cysneiros & Kushniruk, 2003):

i. Assembling the task's requirements for the product;
ii. Planning and putting together the architecture and design;
iii. Implementation (which involves developing program code);
iv. Product evaluations (testing);
v. Deployment and use; and
vi. Support.

Most implementation, testing, deployment, and support tasks utilize programming (Smith & Woodside, 1999) (Figure 1.3).

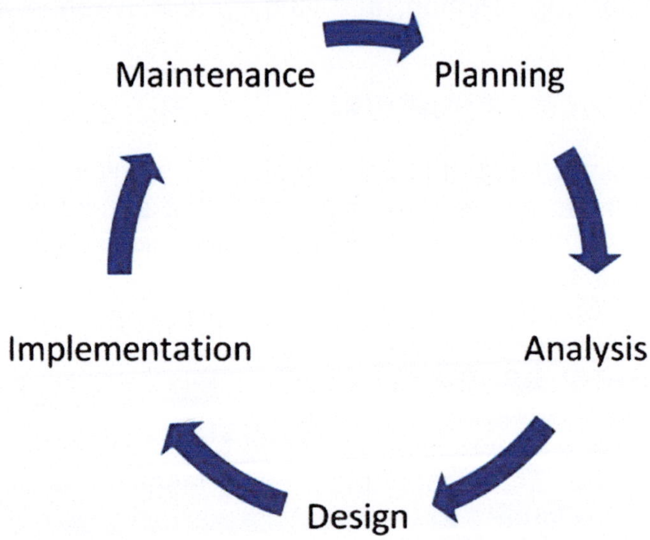

Figure 1.3. Representation of software development lifecycle.

Source: Kenneth Leroy, Creative Commons License.

1.6.1. Gathering the Requirements

Only the concept of a particular product is present at first. It provides a set of specifications that outline what both the user and the machine must do. In most cases, these actions simplify previously simple tasks; examples include calculating ballistic trajectories, generating salaries, and using Google Maps to find the shortest route. In many instances, the software adds functionality that wasn't there before, such as automating a certain task (Ruparelia, 2010).

The specifications for the good are typically given in writing, whether in English or another language. At this time, no programming has been done. Experts familiar with the issues in a particular field define the requirements. Additionally, may write them up so that coders can easily grasp them. These experts are typically called business analysts and not programming specialists (Saeed et al., 2019).

Did you Know?

Python, a computer language, was named after Monty Python's Flying Circus, a prominent 1970s British sketch comedy program.

1.6.2. Planning and Preparing the Architecture and Design

The planning stage is the next step after gathering all the information needed. A technical implementation strategy for the project is now developed, outlining the program's platforms, technologies, and first architectural (design). Software engineers with a lot of expertise do this step, which involves a lot of creative labor. Software architects are another name for them. The specifications select the following components (Zachman, 1987):

- The kind of application, such as console applications, desktop GUI applications, client-server applications, web applications, rich internet applications (RIA), mobile applications, peer-to-peer applications, or other applications;
- The software's architecture, such as its SOA architecture, multi-layer, single-layer, double-layer, and, or triple-layer architecture (Maranzano et al., 2005);
- The programming language, such as C#, Ruby, Python, PHP, Java, JavaScript, or C++, is most appropriate for the implementation;
- The technologies which will be used include the following: the platform (Microsoft.NET, Java EE, LAMP, or another), the database servers (Oracle, SQL Server, MySQL database, NoSQL database, or another), the user experience (Silverlight, Flash, Windows, JavaServer Faces, and the Eclipse program RCP, the ASP.NET Forms, WPF, or another), the data access (for example, Hibernate, JPA, or ADO.NET Entity Framework), the reporting (Zachman, 1999).

- The development frameworks, such as ASP.NET MVC (for.NET), Knockout.js (such as JavaScript), Rails (such as Ruby), Django (such as Python), and many others, will make development easier.
- The size and expertise of a development team (sizable, seasoned teams of developers complete huge, important projects) (Brancheau et al., 1989);
- The development plan divides functionality into phases and specifies resources and completion dates for each phase.
- Other factors (team size, location, communication techniques, etc.) (Sowa & Zachman, 1992). Although many principles make accurate analysis and planning easier, this stage still calls for a good bit of intuition and insight. This step already predetermines the next phase in the development process. At this point, just preparation is being done instead of programming.

1.6.3. Implementation

The phase that has the strongest ties to programming is the implementation phase. At this stage, a program (application) is carried out (written) by the specified task, design, and architecture. By creating the source code for the program, programmers take part. When building a small project, the other stages can be cut short or eliminated, but the implementation must always be included; otherwise, the procedure is not software development. This book describes the implementation skills needed to construct software programs, including developing a programmer's mindset and understanding how to use all the tools offered through the C# language and the .NET platform (Wulf, 1980).

1.6.4. Product Testing

Testing products is a crucial phase in the development of software. Its goal is to guarantee that all regulations are carefully followed. Although manual implementation of this process is an option, automated testing is preferred. Small programs are used in these studies to automate them as much as feasible. To check the accuracy of the code, product testing contains both automated and human procedures because some functionality is very difficult to automate (Stefik & Hanenberg, 2014).

QAs (Quality control engineers) implement the testing (trials) procedure. They collaborate closely with programmers to identify and fix software faults. Finding bugs in the code is a top priority, and hardly any new code is developed.

The testing phase typically uncovers many flaws and faults, returning the program to the implantation phase. Before a software product meets both requirements, thus is prepared for deployment. Therefore, the usage phases of the two preceding stages are closely related, and it is typical for any software product to flip between them repeatedly (Hailpern & Santhanam, 2002).

1.6.5. Deployment and Operation

The act of putting a certain software product into use is known as deployment. This phase may be the most time-consuming and expensive if the good is sophisticated and serves a large population. This is a quick and simple technique for smaller programs. The most typical scenario involves the creation of an installer—a specialized application. It guarantees the product's rapid and simple installation (Kontogiannis, 2008). Additional software for support is created specifically for the deployment if the product will be used in a big business with thousands of copies. The product is prepared for use when the installation is successfully finished. Training staff members to use it in the following stage (Fischer et al., 2012).

Did you Know?

Grace Hopper, an information technology scientist, develop the term "bug" to characterize a computer error after discovering a moth lodged in a single of her computer circuits.

Deployment of the latest edition of Microsoft Windows within the state government would serve as an illustration. This includes setting up and configuring the program and instructing staff members on utilizing it.

Typically, the software development team or certified deployment experts perform the deployment. Systems administrators, database administrators (DBAs), system engineers, specialized consultants, and other professionals can be among them. Nearly no new code is written, but the current code is tweaked and configured until it satisfies all the necessary conditions for a successful deployment (Dearle, 2007).

1.6.6. Technical Support

Inevitably, issues may arise during the exploitation process. They may be brought on by various things, such as software bugs, improper usage, or poor configuration, but most issues arise when users alter their requirements. These issues prevent the program from accomplishing the business task for which it was designed. The professionals in support and development must be more involved in this. No matter how amazing a software product is, the support process typically lasts the entire duration of its existence (Chakraborty et al., 2021).

The development team and specially trained support specialists provide the support. Numerous individuals may participate in the process based on the modifications made – administrators, executives, architects, programmers, quality assurance engineers, etc.When the tax legislation that affects the serviced accounting procedure changes, for instance, a software program that calculates salaries will need to be updated; if the end user's hardware is updated, for instance, the software will need to be set up and configured once more, necessitating the assistance of the support staff (Kert, 2011) (Figure 1.4).

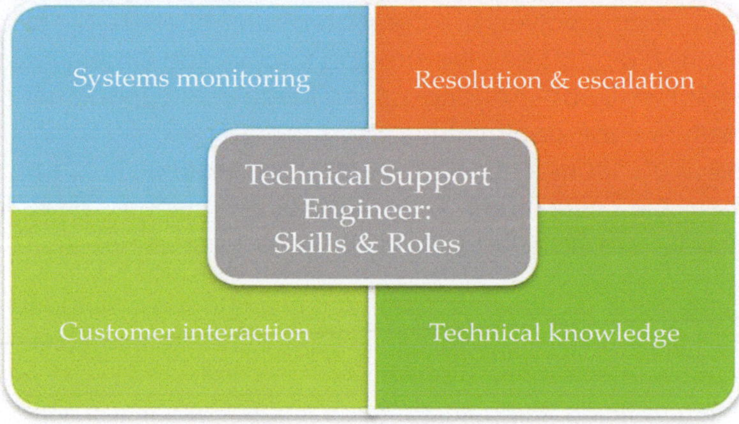

Figure 1.4. Illustration of skills and roles of technical support engineer.

Source: Chrissy Kid, Creative Commons License.

1.6.7. Documentation

The documentation stage runs concurrently with all the previous stages; it is not a distinct step. The goal of documentation, a crucial component of software development, is to transfer information among the various parties involved in creating and maintaining a software product. Both inside and outside of a single stage, information is transmitted. The people who develop programs (architects, programmers, QA engineers, and others) typically write the development documentation, a collection of documents (Yngve & Sammet, 1963).

1.7. SOFTWARE DEVELOPMENT IS MORE THAN JUST CODING

Software development involves many procedures besides merely writing code, including requirements evaluation, design, planning, testing, and support. These processes all call for a range of professionals known as software engineers. A tiny but crucial component of software development is programming (Sanner, 1999).

Because programming is the only one of the processes necessary for creating software, it will be the only topic covered in this book.

ACTIVITY 1.1:

i. Select a beginner-friendly programming language like Python, JavaScript, or Ruby. Setting up a development workspace and installing any required software.
ii. Create straightforward programs that do simple operations like computing a rectangle's area.

1.8. SUMMARY

The programming process is designing, developing, testing, and maintaining computer programs—sets of directions that computers follow to carry out specified tasks. Computer programs are created using programming languages. PHP, Ruby, Python, C++, Java, the PHP language, and many other programming languages are available. Each language has distinctive syntax, norms, and characteristics (Stamelos et al., 2002). Programmers build software applications, websites, and games with programming languages. In addition to IDEs and debugging tools, programmers use various other technologies and tools to create, test, and debug their programs.

REVIEW QUESTIONS

1. What is programming, and why is it important in today's world?
2. What are some popular programming languages? What are their unique features?
3. What is the software development life cycle? How does programming fit into it?
4. What are some potential challenges and ethical considerations regarding programming and technology?

MULTIPLE CHOICE QUESTIONS

1. What is programming?

a. Writing instructions for a computer to execute
b. Writing stories for a computer to read
c. Drawing pictures for a computer to see
d. All of the above

2. Which of the following is not a popular programming language?

a. Java
b. Python
c. Photoshop
d. None of the above

3. Which programming language was designed for building web applications?

a. C++
b. JavaScript
c. Ruby
d. All of the above

4. Who is considered to be the first computer programmer?

a. Ada Lovelace

b. Alan Turing

c. Charles Babbage

d. None of the above

5. Which of the following was the first high-level programming language?

a. FORTRAN

b. COBOL

c. BASIC

d. None of the above

Answers to Multiple Choice Questions

1. (a); 2. (c); 3. (b); 4. (a); 5. (a)

REFERENCES

1. Aho, A. V., Kernighan, B. W., & Weinberger, P. J., (1979). Awk—A pattern scanning and processing language. *Software: Practice and Experience, 9*(4), 267–279.
2. Ancona, D., Bono, V., Bravetti, M., Campos, J., Castagna, G., Deniélou, P. M., & Yoshida, N., (2016). Behavioral types in programming languages. *Foundations and Trends® in Programming Languages, 3*(2, 3), 95–230.
3. Angles, R., Arenas, M., Barceló, P., Hogan, A., Reutter, J., & Vrgoč, D., (2017). Foundations of modern query languages for graph databases. *ACM Computing Surveys (CSUR), 50*(5), 1–40.
4. Baillie, J. C., (2005). Urbi: Towards a universal robotic low-level programming language. In: *2005 IEEE/RSJ International Conference on Intelligent Robots and Systems* (pp. 820–825).
5. Barnett, G. O., & Greenes, R. A., (1970). High-level programming languages. *Computers and Biomedical Research, 3*(5), 488–494.
6. Bergin, T. J., (2007). A history of the history of programming languages. *Communications of the ACM, 50*(5), 69–74.
7. Brancheau, J. C., Schuster, L., & March, S. T., (1989). Building and implementing an information architecture. *ACM SIGMIS Database: The Database for Advances in Information Systems, 20*(2), 9–17.
8. Chakraborty, P., Shahriyar, R., Iqbal, A., & Uddin, G., (2021). How do developers discuss and support new programming languages in technical Q&A site? An empirical study of go, swift, and rust in stack overflow. *Information and Software Technology, 137*, 660-780.
9. Cysneiros, L. M., & Kushniruk, A., (2003). Bringing usability to the early stages of software development. In: *Proceedings. 11th IEEE International Requirements Engineering Conference, 2003* (pp. 359–360).

10. Dearle, A., (2007). Software deployment, past, present and future. In: *Future of Software Engineering (FOSE'07)* (pp. 269–284).
11. Fischer, J., Majumdar, R., & Esmaeilsabzali, S., (2012). Engage: A deployment management system. In: *Proceedings of the 33rd ACM SIGPLAN Conference on Programming Language Design and Implementation* (pp. 263–274).
12. Hailpern, B., & Santhanam, P., (2002). Software debugging, testing, and verification. *IBM Systems Journal, 41*(1), 4–12.
13. Holsapple, C. W., (2005). The inseparability of modern knowledge management and computer-based technology. *Journal of Knowledge Management, 9*(1), 42–52.
14. Hosoya, H., & Pierce, B. C., (2003). XDuce: A statically typed XML processing language. *ACM Transactions on Internet Technology (TOIT), 3*(2), 117–148.
15. Hudak, P., (1989). Conception, evolution, and application of functional programming languages. *ACM Computing Surveys (CSUR), 21*(3), 359–411.
16. Iverson, K. E., (1962). A programming language. In: *Proceedings of the May 1–3, 1962, Spring Joint Computer Conference* (pp. 345–351).
17. Jones, N. D., (2005). The essence of program transformation by partial evaluation and driving. *Logic, Language and Computation: Festschrift in Honor of Satoru Takasu*, 206–224.
18. Jordan, H., Botterweck, G., Noll, J., Butterfield, A., & Collier, R., (2015). A feature model of actor, agent, functional, object, and procedural programming languages. *Science of Computer Programming, 98*, 120–139.
19. Kert, S. B., (2011). The use of SMS support in programming education. *Turkish Online Journal of Educational Technology-TOJET, 10*(2), 268–273.
20. Kontogiannis, K., (2008). Challenges and opportunities related to the design, deployment and, operation of web services. *2008 Frontiers of Software Maintenance*, 11–20.
21. Liskov, B., (1996). A history of CLU. In: *History of Programming Languages—II* (pp. 471–510).
22. Maranzano, J. F., Rozsypal, S. A., Zimmerman, G. H., Warnken, G. W., Wirth, P. E., & Weiss, D. M., (2005). Architecture reviews: Practice and experience. *IEEE Software, 22*(2), 34–43.
23. Nance, R. E., (1996). A history of discrete event simulation programming languages. In: *History of Programming Languages—II* (pp. 369–427).
24. Rosen, S., (1972). Programming systems and languages 1965–1975. *Communications of the ACM, 15*(7), 591–600.
25. Ruparelia, N. B., (2010). Software development lifecycle models. *ACM SIGSOFT Software Engineering Notes, 35*(3), 8–13.
26. Saeed, S., Jhanjhi, N. Z., Naqvi, M., & Humayun, M., (2019). Analysis of software development methodologies. *International Journal of Computing and Digital Systems, 8*(5), 446–460.

27. Sammet, J. E., (1972). Programming languages: History and future. *Communications of the ACM, 15*(7), 601–610.
28. Sanner, M. F., (1999). Python: A programming language for software integration and development. *J Mol Graph Model, 17*(1), 57–61.
29. Shaikhha, A., Fitzgibbon, A., Vytiniotis, D., & PeytonJones, S., (2019). Efficient differentiable programming in a functional array-processing language. *Proceedings of the ACM on Programming Languages, 3*(ICFP), 1–30.
30. Smith, C. U., & Woodside, M., (1999). Performance validation at early stages of software development. *System Performance Evaluation: Methodologies and Applications,* 383–396.
31. Sowa, J. F., & Zachman, J. A., (1992). Extending and formalizing the framework for information systems architecture. *IBM Systems Journal, 31*(3), 590–616.
32. Stamelos, I., Angelis, L., Oikonomou, A., & Bleris, G. L., (2002). Code quality analysis in open source software development. *Information Systems Journal, 12*(1), 43–60.
33. Stefik, A., & Hanenberg, S., (2014). The programming language wars: Questions and responsibilities for the programming language community. In: *Proceedings of the 2014 ACM International Symposium on New Ideas, New Paradigms, and Reflections on Programming & Software* (pp. 283–299).
34. Vilhjálmsson, H., Cantelmo, N., Cassell, J., Chafai, N. E., Kipp, M., Kopp, S., & Van, D. W. R. J., (2007). The behavior markup language: Recent developments and challenges. In: *Intelligent Virtual Agents: 7th International Conference, IVA 2007 Paris, France, September 17–19, 2007 Proceedings 7* (pp. 99–111).
35. Wadler, P., (1992). The essence of functional programming. In: *Proceedings of the 19th ACM SIGPLAN-SIGACT Symposium on Principles of Programming Languages* (pp. 1–14).
36. Wirth, N., (1971). The programming language Pascal. *Acta Informatica, 1*, 35–63.
37. Wulf, W. A., (1980). Trends in the design and implementation of programming languages. *Computer, 13*(1), 14–25.
38. Xie, Y., & Aiken, A., (2006). Static detection of security vulnerabilities in scripting languages. In: *USENIX Security Symposium* (Vol. 15, pp. 179–192).
39. Yngve, V. H., & Sammet, J. E., (1963). Toward better documentation of programming languages: Introduction. *Communications of the ACM, 6*(3), 76.
40. Zachman, J. A., (1987). A framework for information systems architecture. *IBM Systems Journal, 26*(3), 276–292.
41. Zachman, J. A., (1999). A framework for information systems architecture. *IBM Systems Journal, 38*(2, 3), 454–470.

CHAPTER 2

EVALUATION OF MAJOR PROGRAMMING LANGUAGES

UNIT INTRODUCTION

This chapter explains how a group of programming languages evolved. It emphasizes on the capabilities of the language and the reasons for its evolution while also examining the environments in which it was created. The novel aspects that each language introduces are simply addressed, not the entire descriptions of the languages. The characteristics that most affected later languages or the discipline of computer science are of key significance (Backus, 1954; Arnold et al., 2006).

This chapter doesn't go into detail on any language characteristic or idea; that is reserved for later chapters. For journey through the evolution of these languages, brief, informal descriptions of traits will serve. This chapter covers a wide range of language ideas and languages that many readers will be unfamiliar with. These subjects are only covered in depth in later chapters. Those who consider this disturbing might wish to postpone studying this chapter till they have finished the entire book.

The selection of the languages to be discussed in this chapter was selective, and some of the readers will be disappointed that some or all of their favorites were omitted. To preserve this historical scope at a fair extent, though, it was essential to exclude some languages that are widely praised by some. The selections were determined on estimation of the significance of every language to linguistic evolution and the computing industry itself.

The chapter is structured as follows: Language's founding iterations are typically framed chronologically. Languages' following iterations, though, appear alongside their first iteration instead of in later parts. For instance, the part with Fortran I discusses Fortran 2003 (1956). Additionally, in some circumstances, auxiliary languages that are associated with a language that possesses its own part are included in that section. There are 14 complete example programs listed in this chapter, all in a distinct language. Various programs serve as examples of how programs in such languages appear; they aren't explained here. Except for the portions written in Lisp, Smalltalk, and COBOL, much of the code in such programs must be readable and understandable to readers who are acquainted with either of the popular programming languages (ACM, 1979, 1993).

Fortran, PL/I, Basic, ALGOL 60, Pascal, C, Java, Ada, JavaScript, and C# applications all tackle the same issue. Although most of the modern languages in the list above offer dynamic arrays, they weren't use in the instance programs due to the ease of the problem. Furthermore, in the Fortran 95 example, employing features were omitted that may have prevented the need of loops entirely, in section to keep the code simple and understandable, and in part to demonstrate the language's core loop structure (Aho et al., 1988).

Learning Objectives

After the chapter, students will be able to understand the following:

- Historical background and summary of Zuse's Plankalkul;
- Learn about pseudocodes in programming;
- Understanding the design process, historical background of Fortran, Lisp, COBOL, and SNOBOL programming languages;
- Knowledge about the object-oriented programming (OOP), mark-up programming and scripting languages.

Key Terms

- Ada
- ALGOL 60
- C#
- Data structures
- Dynamic arrays
- Fortran
- Iteration
- Lisp
- Pascal
- Pseudocodes
- Zuse's Plankalkul

2.1. ZUSE'S PLANKALKÜL

This chapter's 1st programming language is extremely odd in a number of ways. For starters, it was never put into practice. Additionally, while being created in 1945, its specification wasn't made public till 1972. Several of the language's capabilities didn't transfer to other languages till 15 years after its creation since just some people were acquainted with it (Aho et al., 2006) (Figure 2.1).

	V	V
V	1	2
K	1.3	0
A	8	9

Figure 2.1. Instance of Zuse's Plankalkul.

Source: Bram Bruines, Creative Commons License.

2.1.1. Historical Background

Konrad Zuse (called "Tsoozuh"), a German physicist, created a series of complicated and powerful computers out of electromechanical relays throughout 1936 and 1945. By 1945, Aerial bombardment had damaged all but one among his most recent models, the Z4, so he relocated to Hinterstein, a distant Bavarian town, and his study team members split up (Andrews & Schneider, 1983).

In 1943, Zuse began work on a thesis for his doctoral dissertation proposing the development of a language for describing calculations on the Z4. In 1947, he began work on the project independently. This language was given the name Plankalkül, which signifies program calculus. In the 1945 lengthy document that wasn't published till 1972 (Zuse, 1972), Zuse devised Plankalkül and developed algorithms in a language to address a range of problems.

Did you Know?

The first programming language, called Fortran, was developed in the 1950s by IBM.

2.1.2. Language Summary

With many of its most cutting-edge characteristics in the domain of data structures, Plankalkül was impressively comprehensive. The single bit was the most basic data format in Plankalkül. From the type of bit, the integer and floating-point numeric kinds were developed. The most important bit of the standardized fraction portion of the floating-point number wasn't stored since the two's-complement notation and hidden bit technique were utilized instead.

Plankalkül supported records and arrays further to the typical scalar kinds (known as structs in languages based on C). Nested records may be present in the records (Arden et al., 1961; ANSI, 1966).

Even though there was no clear goto, the language did contain a repetitive expression comparable to the *Ada for*. It also included the instruction *Fin* with a superscript indicating an escape from a set number of iterative loop nestings or the start of a novel iteration process. Plankalkül added a choice statement, but an *else* clause wasn't permitted.

The incorporation of mathematical equations depicting the existing connections amongst program variables was among the most intriguing aspects of Zuse's programming. These expressions indicated what might be valid during processing at the locations where they occurred in the code. These are nearly identical to axiomatic semantics and Java assertions statements. The programs in Zuse's paper were significantly more complicated than those developed before 1945. In it were programs for sorting arrays of data, testing the interconnection of a graph, performing integer and floating-point functions, incorporating square root, and performing syntax evaluation on logic formulas with 6° of priority for parentheses and operators. His 49 pages of codes for chess, a game in which he wasn't an adept, were by far his most astounding accomplishment (Backus, 1954, 1959).

Zuse's explanation of Plankalkül might have been difficult to execute as stated if it had been discovered by a computer engineer in the 1950s. That one component of the language was the notation. Here, 2 or 3 lines of code made up every statement. The declarations of modern languages were most reminiscent of the 1st sentence. The subscripts of array references in the 1st line were on the 2nd line, which was discretionary. In the mid-19th century, Charles Babbage wrote algorithms for the Analytical Engine using the same technique for signaling subscripts. The class names for the parameters stated in the 1st line were included in the last line of every Plankalkül statement. When first viewed, this notation might be rather frightening (Backus, 1978).

This syntax is demonstrated by the assignment statement in the instance below that allocates the value of the term A[4]+1 to A[5]. Subscripts are listed in the V-labeled row, while data types are listed in the S-labeled row. 1.n in this case denotes an integer with n bits:

```
  | A + 1 => A
V | 4 5
S | 1.n 1.n
```

If Zuse's approach had been universally recognized in 1945 or indeed 1950, one can only hypothesize about the path programming language creation would have followed. It is also intriguing to think how his work may have differed if he had conducted it in a calm setting accompanied by other scientists, as opposed to in Germany in absolute solitude (Backus et al., 1963; Bodwin et al., 1982).

2.2. PSEUDOCODES

First, keep in mind that this context uses the word pseudocode differently than that of nowadays. The languages covered in this section are referred to as pseudocodes since that is the term given to them when they were created and used. Therefore, it is obvious that these aren't pseudocodes in the modern sense (Bohm & Jacopini, 1966).

Computers of the 1940s and 1950s were significantly less useful than all of those accessible today. The machines of the time were computationally intensive due to the absence of supporting software, additional to being slow, inaccurate, costly, and having incredibly limited memories. Because there weren't any high-level languages or indeed assembly languages, programming had to be executed in machine code, which is time-consuming and error prone. One of its flaws is the usage of numeric codes to convey instructions. An ADD command, for instance, could be represented by the code 14 instead of a connotative textual term, even if just by a single letter. This makes reading programs extremely tough. Exact addressing is a much more critical issue that makes program updating time-consuming and error prone. Assume there is a machine language program preserved in memory (Brinch, 1975, 1977) (Figure 2.2).

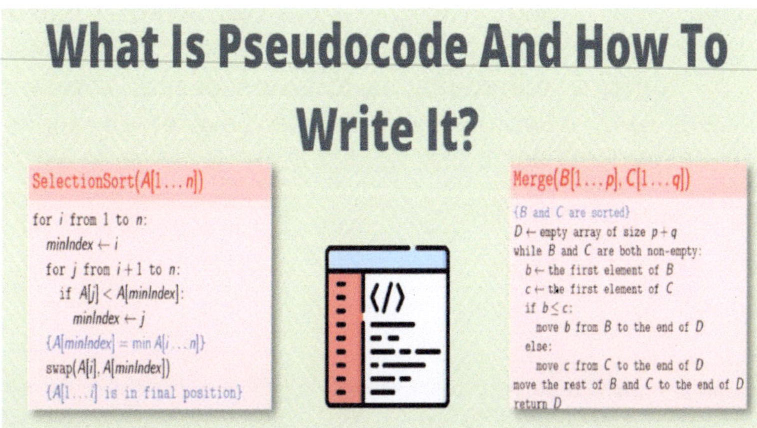

Figure 2.2. Instance of pseudocode.

Source: Digital Ocean, Creative Commons License.

Several of these instructions relate to other areas inside the program, typically to refer data or to specify the destinations of branch instructions. Since these addresses should be raised to accommodate the new command, the accuracy of any commands that relate to addresses outside the insertion point is compromised when an instruction is inserted anywhere besides at the end of the program. To correctly perform the addition, it is necessary to locate and modify all instructions that relate to locations following the addition. A similar issue happens when an instruction is deleted. In this instance, machine languages typically offer a no operation command that can substitute removed instructions, so averting the issue (Brinch, 1978).

These issues plague all machine languages uniformly, and they served as the main driving forces behind the creation of assemblers and assembly languages. The majority of programming issues at the time were numerical, necessitating the usage of floating-point arithmetic and some form of indexing in order to conveniently employ arrays. Nevertheless, neither of these features was built into the structure of the computers that were available in the 1940s and 1950s. The emergence of languages that are a little more advanced was a logical result of these shortcomings (Chomsky, 1956; Chambers & Ungar, 1991).

2.2.1. Short Code

John Mauchly created the 1st of these novel languages, dubbed Short Code, in the year 1949 for BINAC computer, the 1st practical stored-program electronic computer. Ultimately, Short Code was ported to a UNIVAC I computer (the 1st electronic computer marketed in the US) and served as among the principal programming languages for such machines for a number of years. A programming guide for UNIVAC I version of the initial Short Code survived, despite the fact that its comprehensive explanation wasn't ever published (Remington-Rand, 1952). It is reasonable to presume that the 2 versions were essentially identical (Chomsky, 1959; Clarke et al., 1980). The UNIVAC's own words I had 72 bits of memory, which were organized into 12 six-bit chunks. Short Code was made up of coded copies of mathematical equations to be assessed. The programs were byte-pair numbers, and a word might include several equations. The function codes listed below were included:

```
01 - 06 abs value 1n (n+2)nd power
02) 07 + 2n (n+2)nd root
03 = 08 pause 4n if <= n
04 / 09 (58 print and tab
```

Constants and variables were designated with byte-pair codes. A0 and B0 might be variables, for instance. The assertion would be represented as 00 A0 03 20 06 B0 in a word.

```
A0 = SQRT(ABS(B0))
```

The term was padded with the number 00 to make it longer. It's worth noting that there wasn't any multiplication code; rather, multiplication was easily signaled by aligning the 2 operands, like in algebra.

Short Code was executed with a pure operator instead of being transformed to machine code. This was known as automated programming at the time. The programming procedure was clearly reduced, but at the cost of processing time. Short code translation was roughly 50 times slower as compared to machine code translation (Cohen, 1981; Converse & Park, 2000).

Did you Know?

The programming language JavaScript was originally developed in just 10 days by Brendan Eich.

2.2.2. Speedcoding

Other locations were developing interpretative systems that broadened machine languages to incorporate floating-point computations. John Backus's Speedcoding system for IBM 701 is an instance of such system (Backus, 1954). The Speedcoding interpreter transformed the 701 into a 3-address virtual floating-point calculator. The system provided pseudo commands for the 4 floating-point arithmetic functions, along with square root, arc tangent, sine, logarithm, and exponent (Conway, 1963; Conway & Constable, 1976).

The virtual design also included input/output transformations, and unconditional and conditional branches. Observe that after loading the translator, there were only 700 words left in accessible memory, and that the add command took around 4.3 milliseconds to complete. This gives you a sense of the restrictions of such systems. However, Speedcoding also had a cutting-edge feature that automatically increased address registers. It wasn't till the UNIVAC 1107 computers in the year 1962 that this feature was implemented in hardware. These characteristics allowed matrix multiplication to be completed in 12 Speedcoding commands. Backus asserted that utilizing Speedcoding, issues that may take 2 weeks to design in machine code might be programmed in matter of hours (Deliyanni & Kowalski, 1979; Correa, 1992).

2.2.3. The UNIVAC Compiling System

During 1951 and 1953, a group headed by Grace Hopper at UNIVAC created the A-2, A-1, and A-0 compiling systems, which extended the pseudocode into machine code modules in almost the same manner that macros are extended into assembly language. Even though the pseudocode source for these compilers was still relatively basic, it was a significant advance over machine code since it made source programs considerably shorter. Wilkes (1952) proposed a similar approach separately.

2.2.4. Associated Work

Around the same time, other ways to make programming easier were being created. The difficulty of actual addressing was partially solved at Cambridge University in the year 1950 thanks to a technique devised by David J. Wheeler. Later, Maurice V. Wilkes expanded on the notion to create an assembly program that might integrate certain subroutines and assign storage (Wilkes et al., 1951, 1957). Certainly, this was a significant and essential advancement (DeRemer, 1971).

It is also worth noting that assembly languages, which are very distinct from the pseudocodes presented, emerged in the early 1950s. They had very little influence, however, on the architecture of high-level languages (Deutsch & Bobrow, 1976; DeRemer & Pennello, 1982).

2.3. IBM 704 AND FORTRAN

The release of IBM 704 in the year 1954 marked one of the most significant developments in computing, in large part since its characteristics encouraged the invention of Fortran. One might claim that if IBM hadn't introduced the 704 and Fortran, another company with a comparable machine and corresponding high-level language might have quickly followed. Nevertheless, IBM was the 1st company with the insight and resources to implement these innovations (Dijkstra, 1968).

2.3.1. Historical Background

The absence of floating-point architecture in the accessible computers from the 1940s to mid-1950s was among the main factors contributing to the acceptance of interpretive systems' speed. It took a long time to mimic every floating-point function in software. The cost of translation and the modeling of indexing were comparatively small due to the substantial amount of processor time that was dedicated to software floating-point computation. Interpretation was a reasonable cost as long as floating-point computation need to be done by software. Several more programmers at the time, though, avoided using interpretative systems in favor of manually written machine (or assembly) language, which they felt was more effective. The conclusion of the interpretative period, at least for scientific processing, was announced with the introduction of the IBM 704 system, which included indexing and floating-point commands in hardware. The hiding spot for the expense of translation was eliminated by the addition of floating-point hardware (Dijkstra, 1972, 1975).

Even though Fortran is frequently credited as the 1st created high-level language, the subject of who gets credit for designing the 1st such language is rather debatable. Alick E. Glennie's Autocode translator for the Manchester Mark I computer is credited to Pardo & Knuth (1977). Glennie created the translator at Royal Armaments Research Establishment at Fort Halstead, England. By September 1952, the translator was fully working. Conversely, Glennie's Autocode, as per John Backus (Wexelblat, 1981), was very low-level and machine focused that it must not be regarded a built system. Laning and Zierler of the MIT (Massachusetts Institute of Technology) are credited by Backus.

The Zierler and Laning system were the 1st algebraic interpretation system to be developed. By algebraic, it is meant that it interpreted arithmetic statements, employed subprograms to perform transcendental operations (such as logarithm and sine), and contained arrays. In 1952, an exploratory prototype version of the system was built on the MIT Whirlwind computer, and by May 1953, a more practical version had been developed. The translator created a subroutine call for every program formula or expression. Just one actual machine commands contained were for branching, which made the source language simple to comprehend. Even though this work-initiated Fortran development, it never left MIT.

Despite these earlier efforts, Fortran was the 1st extensively used compiled high-level language. The following parts provide a history of this significant advancement (Dijkstra, 1976; Dybvig, 2009).

2.3.2. Design Process

Fortran development began well before the 704 platform was unveiled in May 1954. In November 1954, IBM's John Backus and his team had completed the study "The IBM Mathematical Formula Translating System: FORTRAN" (IBM, 1954). This document describes the initial version of Fortran, known as Fortran 0, before it was implemented. It also declared confidently that Fortran will deliver the effectiveness of hand-coded systems as well as the simplicity of programming of interpretive pseudocode systems. Another rush of confidence was expressed in the text, which claimed that Fortran might remove coding errors and the troubleshooting procedure. The earliest Fortran translator had limited syntax error checking centered on this notion (Ellis & Stroustrup, 1990).

The following factors influenced the development of Fortran: (a) computers had limited memory, were slow, and were generally unreliable; (b) scientists used computers primarily for computational modelling; (c) there were no current efficient and productive ways to code computers; and (d) since computers were more expensive than programmers, the 1st Fortran compilers focused primarily on the speed of the created object code. This setting directly influences the features of the 1st Fortran versions (Farber et al., 1964).

2.3.3. Fortran I Overview

Throughout the execution period, which started in January 1955 and lasted until the compiler's launch in April 1957, Fortran 0 was updated. The developed language, which is referred as Fortran I, is documented in October 1956 edition of the original Fortran Programmer's Reference Manual (IBM, 1956). Fortran I supported input/output structuring, variable names with up to 6 characters, user-defined subroutines, despite the absence of the statement (Farrow, 1982; Fischer et al., 1984).

The 704 instructions served as the foundation for all Fortran I control commands. It is unclear if the creators of Fortran I recommended these commands to the designers of 704 or even whether the Fortran I designers mandated the architecture of control statement. The Fortran I language doesn't contain any statements for data-typing. All parameters were assumed to be of the floating-point type except those whose names started with I, J, K, L, M, or N. The letters chosen for this standard were centered on the point that engineers and scient at the period typically employed the letters I j, and k as variable subscripts. The 3 extra letters were included by the inventors of Fortran as a kind gesture (Flanagan, 2011). The boldest assertion made by the Fortran design team during the creation of language would be that the machine code generated by the translator would be approximately half as effective as code generated by hand. This, above all, made potential customers skeptical and prohibited a significant amount of attention in Fortran prior to its debut. To practically everyone's amazement, the Fortran design team came close to achieving its efficiency objective (Frege, 1892; Floyd, 1967). The 18 worker-years utilized to build the 1st compiler were mostly devoted to optimization, and the outcomes were very successful. The outcomes of a poll taken in April 1958 demonstrate the achievements of Fortran. Despite the pessimism of the majority of the software industry just a year earlier, at a certain time, nearly half of the program being created for 704s was being developed in Fortran (Friedl, 2006).

2.3.4. Fortran II

In 1958, the Fortran II translator was released. It corrected numerous flaws in the Fortran I translation system and included some important language characteristics, the most significant of which was the autonomous translation of subroutines. Without autonomous compilation, any modification to a program necessitated recompilation of the complete program. Fortran I's absence of independent-compilation ability, along with the 704's low stability, limited program length to around 300 to 400 lines (Wexelblat, 1981). Longer programs have a lower likelihood of being entirely generated before the failure of machine. The capability to include pre-compiled machine language variants of subprograms significantly simplified the compilation procedure and enabled the development of much large software systems (Fuchi, 1981; Goldberg & Robson, 1983).

2.3.5. Evaluation

The initial Fortran engineering team saw language development as merely a needed preamble to the essential task of translating. Moreover, it never appeared to the team that Fortran might be utilized on machines other than IBM's. Furthermore, since the replacement to 704, 709, was revealed before the 704 Fortran translator was released, they were compelled to investigate developing Fortran translators for other IBM machines. In view of the basic intentions of its founders, the impact of Fortran on computer usage, as well as the fact that all succeeding programming languages feel indebted to Fortran, is quite astonishing (Gordon, 1979; Goos & Hartmanis, 1983).

The fact that the kinds and memory for all of the variables are set before program execution was a characteristic of Fortran I including its predecessors prior to version 90 that allowed highly efficient compilers. Implementation couldn't assign any additional variables or room. Versatility was given up in favor of clarity and effectiveness.

It made it impossible to build data structures that expand or change shape continuously, and it precluded the notion of recursive subprograms. As compared to more contemporary software projects, the programs which were being developed at the time the first Fortran versions were developed were predominantly of a numerical character. Consequently, the sacrifice wasn't a big one (Griswold et al., 1971; Halstead, 1985).

It's difficult to overestimate Fortran's overall effectiveness. It fundamentally altered how computers are utilized today. In fact, a major factor in this is the fact that it was the first extensively utilized high-level language. Early iterations of Fortran fail in a number of ways when compared to ideas and languages created later, as is to be anticipated. Even so, it would be unfair to contrast the efficiency and service quality of the 2015 Ford Mustang with those of the 1910 Model T Ford. Nevertheless, despite Fortran's shortcomings, it has been in use for close to 60 years due, among other things, to the massive investment made in Fortran software (Hammond, 1983; Harbison et al., 2002).

2.4. FUNCTIONAL PROGRAMMING: LISP

The 1st functional programming language was created to give language characteristics for list computation, which arose from the earliest applications in the field of AI (artificial intelligence).

2.4.1. The Early Stages of AI and Processing of List

Midway through the 1950s, AI became a topic of interest in many countries. This interest originated in part from languages, in part from psychology, and in part from mathematics. Linguists were engaged in interpreting natural language. Psychologists were concerned in simulating the collection and storage of human information, along with other basic brain functions. Mathematicians were engaged in automating theorem proving and other intelligent operations. All of these studies led to the same ending: a way should be devised to enable computers to handle symbolic data in associated lists. At the time, majority of the processing was performed on arrays of numeric data (Hoare, 1973; Hogger, 1984) (Figure 2.3).

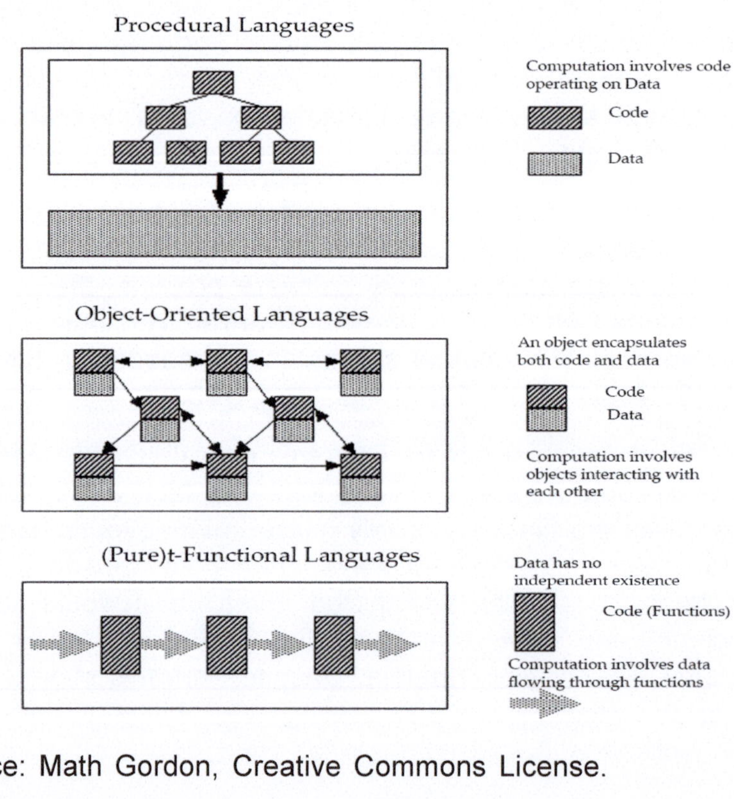

Figure 2.3. Illustration of programming languages.

Source: Math Gordon, Creative Commons License.

At RAND Corporation, J. C. Shaw, Herbert Simon and Allen Newell created the idea of list processing. The Logic Theorist, including some of the earliest AI systems, and the language in which it might be executed were first described in a famous work (Simon & Newell, 1956).

Information processing language I (IPL-1) was the name of the language, however it was never used. The following iteration, IPL-II, was put into practice using the RAND Johnniac computer. IPL was still being developed in the year 1960, the year that the IPL-V description was released (Tonge & Newell, 1960). The IPL languages weren't widely used because of their low-level. The execution of these languages on the mysterious Johnniac machine prevented them from becoming widely used; they were basically assembly languages for the theoretical computer, executed with an interpreter (Horn, 1951).

The IPL languages made significant contributions in list structure and demonstrating that list computation was viable and beneficial. In the 1950s, IBM got interested in AI and chose theorem demonstrating as a showcase area. The Fortran project was in progress at the time.

The expensive expenditure of the Fortran I compiler persuaded IBM that their list computation must be included into Fortran instead of as a separate language. As a result, FLPL (Fortran list processing language) was devised and executed as the Fortran extension. FLPL was utilized to build the theorem prover for plane geometry, which was previously thought to be the easiest subject for mechanical theorem proving (Huskey et al., 1963; Hughes, 1989).

2.4.2. Lisp Design Procedure

In the year 1958, John McCarthy of MIT accepted an internship with the IBM Information Research Department. His objective for the internship was to research symbolic calculations and construct a set of criteria for performing such computations. He selected differentiation of algebraic expressions as a pilot instance problem domain.

This research generated a set of language needs. Among these were mathematical operation control flow approaches, such as recursion and conditional formulations. Fortran I, the only accessible high-level language at the time, lacked both of these features (IEEE, 1985).

The necessity for constantly created linked lists and some sort of implied deallocation of discarded lists emerged from the symbolic-differentiation analysis as additional requirements. McCarthy might simply not permit his sophisticated differentiation algorithm to become overburdened with specific deallocation declarations (Jensen & Wirth, 1974; Johnson, 1975).

McCarthy realized that a novel language was required because FLPL didn't enable recursion, dynamic storage management, conditional expressions, or implicit deallocation. Marvin Minsky and McCarthy created the MIT artificial intelligence Project with money from Research Laboratory of Electronics upon McCarthy's arrival to MIT in 1958. The project's initial significant endeavor was to develop the software system for processing of list. It was generally to be utilized primarily to execute the McCarthy-proposed Advice Taker scheme. This application inspired the creation of the language for processing of list, Lisp. It is frequently referred to as pure Lisp since it is a strictly functional language. Following is a description of the evolution of pure Lisp (Knuth, 1965; Kernighan & Ritchie, 1978).

Remember

The programming language Lisp, which was first developed in the late 1950s, is still used today in many artificial intelligence and machine learning.

2.4.3. Data Structures

Atoms and lists are the only 2 types of data structures available in pure Lisp. Atoms can be literal numbers or symbols that take the shape of identifiers. IPL-II made utilization of the logical idea of storing symbolic data in associated lists. Such structures permit entries and removals at any time, which were previously believed to be essential elements of list processing. Conversely, it was later discovered that these procedures are infrequently needed by Lisp applications.

Parentheses are used to separate the elements of lists. Simple lists with only atoms as elements have the following structure:

```
(A B C D)
```

Parentheses are also used to specify nested list structures. Consider the following list is made up of four elements:

```
(A (B C) D (E (F G)))
```

The 1st is atom A; the 2nd is sublist (B C); the 3rd is atom D; the 4th is sublist (E (F G)), which possesses as its 2nd element the sublist (F G). Fundamentally, lists are maintained as single-linked list architectures, for each node representing a list element and containing 2 pointers. The initial pointer of a node comprising an atom point to a description of the atom, including its symbol or numerical value, or a link to the sublist. The initial pointer of node for the sublist element points to the 1st node of the sublist. In both instances, the 2nd pointer of the node points to following list item. The initial element of a list is referred via a pointer.

Figure 2.4 shows the internal descriptions of the 2 lists that were previously displayed. Keep in mind that a list's components are displayed horizontally. The last member in a list hasn't any successors, thus its linkage is NIL, which is shown in Figure 2.4 as an element with a diagonal line. Sub-lists are displayed in the same format (Knuth, 1974, 1981).

2.4.4. Procedures in Functional Programming

As the functional programming language, Lisp was created. In a strictly functional program, all processing is done by applying operations to arguments. In operational language programs, neither assignment statements nor variables are required, as they are in imperative language systems. Moreover, recurring operations can be expressed via recursive function calls, eliminating the need for iteration. Functional programming differs greatly from imperative programming due to these fundamental notions (Kowalski, 1979; Kochan, 2009).

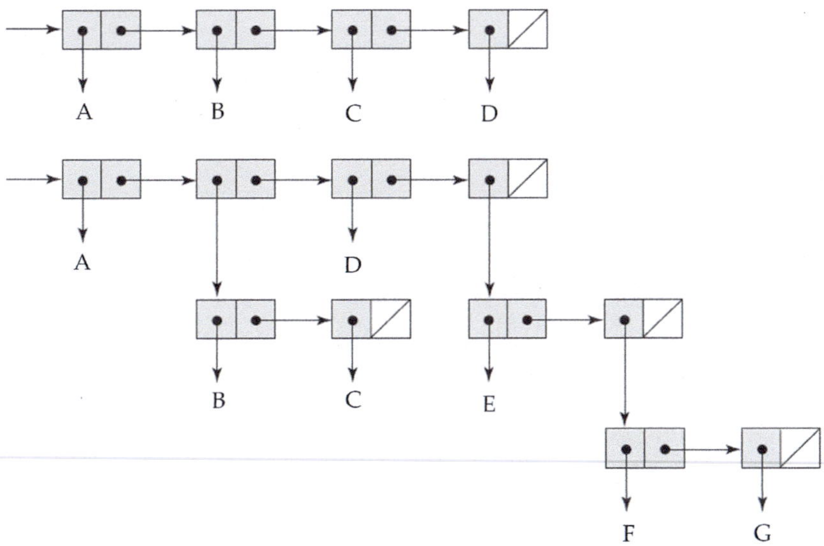

Figure 2.4. Internal demonstration of two Lisp lists.

Source: Lisp2D, Creative Commons License.

2.4.5. The Syntax of Lisp

Lisp is extremely distinct from imperative languages, since it is the functional programming language and as Lisp programs vary considerably in structure from those written in languages such as Java and C++. For instance, Java's syntax is a complex combination of algebra and English, but Lisp's syntax is a paradigm of clarity. The format of program code and data is identical: parenthesized lists. Consider once more the list:

```
(A B C D)
```

It appears as the list of 4 elements when taken as data. When considered as code, it is the 3 parameters B, C, and D being applied to the function A.

2.4.6. Evaluation

Lisp has ruled AI applications over the past few decades. Much of what gave Lisp its image for inefficiency has been eradicated. Many modern executions are generated, and the implementing algorithms is far faster than interpreting the source code. Additional to its achievements in AI, Lisp was a leader in functional programming, a field of programming language research that has demonstrated to be vibrant. Many academics in programming languages consider that functional programming is a superior method for developing software as compared to procedural programming with the help of imperative languages.

2.4.7. Two Successors of Lisp

Scheme and Standard Lisp are two of the most widespread dialects of Lisp today. These are explained briefly in subsections.

2.4.7.1. Scheme

MIT developed the Scheme programming language in 1970s. It is compact in size, using static framing exclusively, and treats procedures as first-class objects. Scheme operations, as first-class objects, can be allocated to variables, supplied as parameters, and retrieved as the results of function applications. They can also serve as list components. Initial version of Lisp lacked all of these features and didn't employ static scoping. Scheme, a tiny language with simple linguistic structure, is well-suited for instructional applications, like functional programming programs and general programming presentations (Laning & Zierler, 1954; Ledgard & Marcotty, 1975).

2.4.7.2. Common Lisp

Many distinct dialects of Lisp were created and utilized throughout the 1970s and early 1980s. As a result, the issue of portability across programs written in different dialects emerged, which is a well-known issue. Graham (1996) proposed Standard Lisp as a solution to this problem. The characteristics of numerous Lisp dialects created in early 1980s, notably Scheme, were combined to create Common Lisp. Standard Lisp is a fairly vast and sophisticated language due to its amalgamation. Conversely, because it is based entirely on Lisp, its syntax, basic operations, and core structure are all inspired by that language (Liskov et al., 1981; Lischner, 2000).

2.5. COMPUTERIZING BUSINESS RECORDS

In a way, the history of COBOL is the antithesis of that of ALGOL 60. COBOL has little influence on the architecture of later programming languages, with the exception of PL/I. It might still be the most extensively used language, but it is hard to say with certainty. As of COBOL's debut, some have tried to build a modern language for business applications. This is perhaps the most significant reason for COBOL's lack of impact. This is due in large part to the suitability of COBOL's abilities to its application domain. Small firms have experienced a considerable deal of development in business computers during the past three decades. Such little software advancement has occurred in these companies. Rather, the majority of software is bought off the shelf for a variety of typical commercial applications (Lomet, 1975; Lutz, 2013).

2.5.1. Historical Background

The origins of COBOL are kind of comparable to those of ALGOL 60 in that the syntax was created by a group of individuals who met for very brief intervals of time. When Fortran was just being developed, in 1959, the condition of business computing was comparable to the level of scientific computing at the time. FLOW-MATIC, a built language for commercial applications, had been introduced in the year 1957, but it was exclusive to UNIVAC and was created for their machines. The United States Air Force also employed AIMACO, but it was really a slight variant of FLOW-MATIC. IBM had created COMTRAN, a language for commercial applications, but it hadn't yet been put into use. Other language structure initiatives were also in the works (MacLaren, 1977).

2.5.2. FLOW-MATIC

FLOW-MATIC was the main ancestor of COBOL, therefore its roots are at least deserving of a brief examination. In December 1953, Grace Hopper of Remington-Rand UNIVAC authored a truly prescient suggestion. It proposed that mathematical programs must be expressed in mathematical notation and data processing algorithms must be written using English language (Wexelblat, 1981). However, it was hard in 1953 to persuade non-programmers that the computer might be programmed to comprehend English language. It wasn't till 1955 that a comparable idea had a chance of being financed by UNIVAC administration, and anyway, a prototype system was required to make the final case. A step in this selling procedure entailed developing and running a simple software that used English, German, and French keywords in that order. The UNIVAC administration thought this presentation was outstanding, which was a key factor in them approving Hopper's suggestion (McCarthy, 1960; Marcotty et al., 1976).

2.5.3. COBOL Design Procedure

On May 28–29, 1959, the Pentagon hosted the 1st formal meeting on the topic of a universal language for commercial applications, which was funded by the Department of Defense. The committee reached a conclusion that the language, dubbed Common Business Language CBL at the time, must possess the following basic features: The majority agreed that as much English as feasible must be used, while a few pushed for a much more mathematical language. To increase the number of people who can program computers, the language should be simple to use, even if that means being less effective. Additional to making the language easier to use, it was anticipated that managers might be able to read programs written in English. Finally, the architecture shouldn't be excessively constrained by execution issues.

Did you Know?

COBOL which is still used today in many business applications was originally developed in 1959.

One of the committee's main interests was that actions to build this global language be taken promptly, as much work was being done to build other commercial languages. Sylvania and RCA were developing their respective commercial application languages additional to the existing ones. It was obvious that the more it took to create a global language, the harder it should be to spread the language. On this logic, it was agreed that current languages must be studied quickly. The Short-Range Committee was constituted for this purpose (McCracken, 1961, 1970).

Initial decisions were made to divide the language's statements into two groups – data description and computational operations—and to place the statements from each category in discrete sections of programs. The Short-Range Committee debated whether or not to include subscripts. Subscripts, according to numerous committee members, were too complicated for those working in processing of data, who were regarded to be uneasy with mathematical notation. Comparable debates surrounded the inclusion of mathematical expressions. The language that would ultimately be known as COBOL 60 was detailed in the Short-Range Committee's final report, which was finished in December 1959 (Meyer, 1990; Metcalf et al., 2004).

The language description for COBOL 60 was classified as initial when it was issued by the Government Printing Office in April 1960. The publication of modified versions occurred in 1961 and 1962. ANSI (American National Standards Institute) formalized the terminology in 1968. ANSI certified the subsequent 3 iterations in 1974, 1985, and 2002. Today, the language keeps evolving (Milos et al., 1984).

2.5.4. Evaluation

Numerous innovative concepts were created by the COBOL language, most of which later emerged in other languages. For instance, the 1st high-level language structure for macros was the DEFINE verb from COBOL 60. More significantly, COBOL was the first programming language to execute hierarchical data structures, which were introduced in Plankalkül. The majority of the languages created since then have them included. Due to its support for extended names and word-connector characters, COBOL was also the first programming language to permit names to have true figurative meanings (hyphens) (Naur, 1960; Mitchell et al., 1979).

Generally, the data partition of COBOL's architecture is powerful, but the process division is somewhat weak. The data partition defines each variable in detail, such as the amount of decimal digits and the placement of the assumed decimal point. This degree of information is also used to define file records, as well as lines to be sent to a printer, making COBOL excellent for producing accounting reports. The absence of functions was the most significant flaw of the initial procedure division. Editions of COBOL before to the 1974 version also didn't support parameterized subprograms (Nilsson, 1971; Ousterhout, 1994).

The last point on COBOL: It was the 1st programming language for which the Department of Defense ordered its use (DoD). COBOL wasn't built expressly for the Department of Defense, therefore this necessity occurred after its inception. Without this requirement, COBOL undoubtedly wouldn't have survived despite its advantages. Poor performance of initial compilers rendered the language prohibitively expensive. Gradually, compilers grew more effective, and computers become significantly faster, inexpensive, and had higher memory capacities. Together, these elements contributed to COBOL's success within and beyond the DoD. Its introduction led to the digital mechanization of accounting, a significant advance by any standard (Pagan, 1981; Paepcke, 1993).

2.6. THE EARLY STAGES OF TIMESHARING

One more programming language that has seen extensive utilization, but little recognition is Basic (Waite & Mather, 1971). It has been generally disregarded by computer scientists, much like COBOL. Such as COBOL, it was also clunky and had a small number of control expressions in its early iterations. In 1970s and 1980s, Basic was widely used on microcomputers. This was a direct result of 2 of the primary features of initial versions of Basic. It was simple to learn for novices, particularly those who weren't science-oriented, and its smaller languages might be executed on computers with very little memory. As the capability of microcomputers increased and alternative programming languages were created, Basic's usage declined. In the early 1990s, Visual Basic (Microsoft, 1991) sparked a comeback in the popularity of the Basic programming language.

2.6.1. Design Procedure

Two mathematicians, Thomas Kurtz and John Kemeny, created the first version of Basic at Dartmouth College in New Hampshire in 1960s. At the time, they were working on compilers for a number of ALGOL 60 and Fortran dialects. The majority of their students had no issue picking up or utilizing such languages during their courses.

Dartmouth, conversely, was predominantly a liberal arts college with just around 25% of the student body being scientific and engineering majors. In 1963, it was determined to create a brand-new language specifically for liberal arts students. Terminals might be the means of computer access for this novel language. The system had the following objectives:

i. It should be simple for non-science students to study and use;
ii. It should be amusing and friendly;
iii. It should offer rapid improvement for homework;
iv. It should permit free and remote access;
v. It should contemplate user time more significant as compared to computer time.

The final objective was a radical idea. It was founded at least in part on the assumption that computers might become much less expensive over time, which was indeed the case. Combining the 2nd, 3rd, and 4th objectives resulted in the timesharing feature of Basic. In 1960s, these objectives might be attained with unique access via terminals by a large number of concurrent users.

Utilizing remote access to the GE 225 computer, Kemeny started work on the translator for the original version of Basic in 1963. In the winter of 1963, the architecture and programming of operating system for Basic commenced. At 4 in the morning on May 1, 1964, the 1st time-shared basic program was entered and executed. The amount of terminals on the system increased to 11 in June and 20 by the fall (Perlis & Samelson, 1958; Peyton, 1987).

2.6.2. Language Overview

The first variant of Basic was incredibly compact and weirdly non-interactive: There wasn't any method for a program that was running to receive input from the user. Programs were entered by hand, compiled, and then executed in the batch-oriented fashion. Only 14 distinct statement kinds and one data type—floating-point—were accessible in the 1st version of Basic. The type was designated to as numbers since it was thought that some of the potential consumers might understand the distinction amongst integer and floating-point types. It was a fairly restricted language altogether, but it was also very simple to learn (Pratt, 1984).

2.6.3. Evaluation

The most significant characteristic of the initial Basic was that it was generally the 1st extensively utilized language that could be accessed via terminals linked to remote computers. At the time, terminals had just become accessible. Before that though, the majority of computer programs were submitted using paper tape or punched cards. The syntax of ALGOL 60 had a little impact on the architecture of Basic, which was largely influenced by Fortran. Later, it expanded in a number of ways, with no standardization effort. ANSI published the Minimal Basic standard (ANSI, 1978b); however, this reflected the minimal amount of linguistic characteristics. In fact, the first version of Basic closely resembled Minimal Basic (Richards, 1969; Robbins, 2005).

Even though it might come as a surprise, Digital Equipment Corporation wrote a big section of its biggest operational system for PDP-11 minicomputers, RSTS, in 1970s using a pretty complex variant of Basic called Basic-PLUS.

Basic has been chastised for, among many other things, the poor architecture of software written in it. According to the grading criteria, notably accessibility and consistency, the language performs very poorly. Obviously, the initial stages of the language weren't intended for, and shouldn't have been utilized for, large-scale systems. Newer versions are far more suitable for such jobs (Roussel, 1975; Rubin, 1987).

2.7. TWO INITIAL DYNAMIC LANGUAGES: SNOBOL AND APL

This section's structure differs from those of the other segments since the languages described here are rather distinct. Both APL and SNOBOL had no significant impact on subsequent popular languages. SNOBOL and APL are very distinct from one another in both appearance and intent. However, they have two things in common: dynamic typing and dynamic storage assignment. Both languages have fundamentally untyped variables. A variable takes on the kind of the value it is given when it is given a value, at which point it gets a type. A variable only receives storage when a value is given to it since there isn't any way to predict how much storage will be required in advance (Rutishauser, 1967; Sammet, 1969).

2.7.1. Origins and Features of APL

Kenneth E. Iverson created APL (Brown et al., 1988) at IBM about 1960. It was initially supposed as a language for defining computer design, not as the programming language for implementation. APL was 1st defined in the book A Programming Language, from whence it derives its name (Iverson, 1962). IBM created the initial execution of APL in 1960s.

It was difficult for implementors to use APL since it includes so many strong operators that are stated with so many symbols. APL was originally used with IBM terminals of printing.

These terminals included unique additional print balls that offered the peculiar character set the language demanded. APL offers a lot of unit functions on arrays, which is one cause why it has so many operators. For instance, any matrix can be transposed using just one operator. Although the huge operator library offers extremely high expressivity, it also renders APL programs challenging to read. As a result, people believe that APL is best suited for throw-away programming (Schorr & Waite, 1967; Schneider, 1999).

While it is possible to write programs rapidly, they should be destroyed after utilization since they are hard to maintain. APL has existed for 50 years and is still in use today, albeit in a limited capacity. In addition, it hasn't altered over its lifespan.

2.7.2. Origins and Features of SNOBOL

Farber, Polonsky, & Griswold (1964) created SNOBOL (Griswold et al., 1971) at Bell Laboratories in 1960s. It was designed especially with text processing in mind. A set of potent functions for string pattern recognition makes up the core of SNOBOL. Text editors for composing were among SNOBOL's early uses. SNOBOL isn't utilized for such projects since its dynamic nature makes it sluggish than other languages. Nevertheless, SNOBOL is still a fully functional and recognized language that is applied to a wide range of text-processing activities across numerous application domains (Scott & Strachey, 1971; Sebesta, 1991).

2.8. OBJECT-ORIENTED PROGRAMMING (OOP): SMALLTALK

The first computer language to completely enable object-oriented programming (OOP) was Smalltalk. Thus, it is an essential component of any debate regarding the origin of programming languages (Figure 2.5).

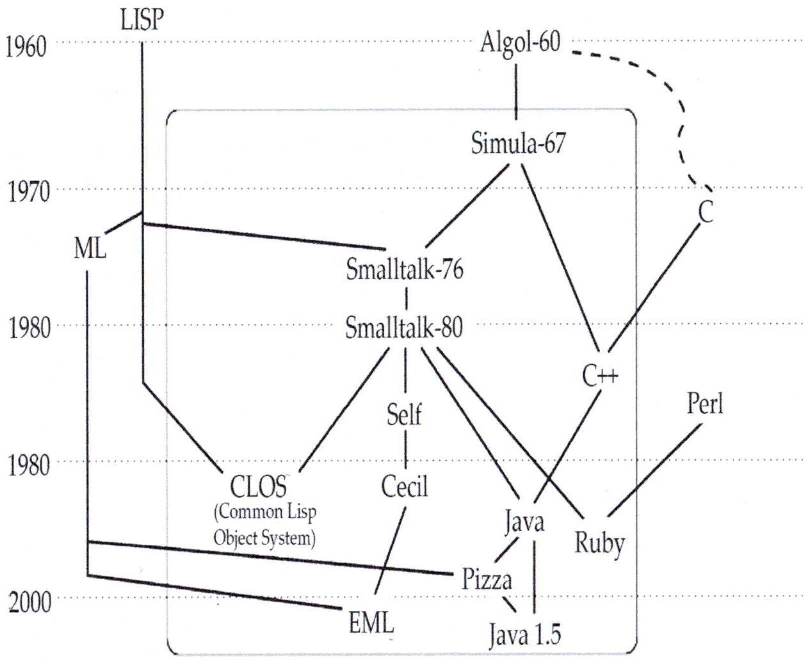

Figure 2.5. Illustration of Smalltalk's DAG family and associated languages.

Source: Courses.cs, Creative Commons License.

2.8.1. Design Procedure

Alan Kay's PhD thesis at the University of Utah in 1960s laid the groundwork for the foundation of the Smalltalk programming language (Kay, 1969). Kay possessed exceptional foresight to foresee the emergence of sophisticated desktop computers in the future. Remember that the 1st microcomputer systems didn't become commercially available till the 1970s, and they were just distantly similar to the machines envisaged by Kay, which were expected to implement a million or more commands per second and had numerous MB megabytes of memory. In 1980s, these machines, in the shape of workstations, became commonly accessible (Shaw, 1963; Sommerville, 2010). Kay anticipated that non-programmers would utilize desktop computers, necessitating the necessity for extremely potent human-interface capabilities. Computers in 1960s were batch-oriented and only utilized by scientists and experienced programmers. Kay reasoned that a computer might need to be extremely interactive and have complex visuals in its user interface in order for nonprogrammers to utilize it. Some of the graphical ideas were inspired by Seymour Papert's LOGO expertise, which used visuals to help kids utilize computers (Papert, 1980).

Initially, Kay conceived a system he termed Dynabook, which was intended to be a general-purpose information processor. It was partially centered on the Flex programming language, which he had assisted develop. Flex was mostly centered on SIMULA 67. Dynabook utilized the standard desk model, which consists of a number of barely obscured pages. The emphasis is frequently on the top sheet, with the others briefly out of sight. Utilizing screen windows to signify the numerous pieces of paper on desktop, Dynabook's display might mimic this image. The interaction between the user and such a display evolved from Smalltalk. Object-oriented software development approaches and programming languages are by far the most influential today. Even though some of the concepts of object-oriented languages originated in SIMULA 67, they matured in Smalltalk. It is evident that Smalltalk's influence on the computing industry is vast and will last for a long time (Stoy, 1977; Steele, 1990).

2.9. MERGING IMPERATIVE AND OBJECT-ORIENTED CHARACTERISTICS

Bjarne Stroustrup at Bell Laboratories made the initial transition from C to C++ in the year 1980. The early changes to C indulged the inclusion of type verification and conversion for function argument values as well as, more importantly, classes that are comparable to those in Smalltalk and SIMULA 67. Also included were buddy classes, destructor, and constructor procedures, private/public access management of inherit modules, and derived classes. Inline functions, basic parameters, and the assignment operator overloading were all implemented in the year 1981. The final language, known as C with Classes, is detailed in Stroustrup (1983).

It is worthwhile to examine some C with Classes objectives. The fundamental objective was to create the language in which codes could be structured similarly to SIMULA 67, with classes and heredity. The 2nd significant objective was to have minimal, or no performance disadvantage compared to C. For instance, array index range verification wasn't explored since it would outcome in a considerable performance loss compared to C. 3rd objective of C with Classes was that it might be used for all applications for which C might be used, therefore essentially neither of C's characteristics, including those deemed hazardous, would be deleted (Suzuki, 1982; Syme et al., 2010).

Virtual techniques, which offer dynamic linking of approach calls to particular method descriptions, name of method and operator overloading, and types of reference, were added to this language in the year 1984. The name of this language variant was C++. In Stroustrup, it is mentioned (1984). The first accessible execution, known as Cfront, which converted C++ code into C programs, debuted in the year 1985. Release 1.0 refers to both the variant of Cfront and C++ that it executed. In Stroustrup, it is mentioned (1986).

Throughout 1985 and 1989, C++ underwent further development, particularly in response to user feedback on the initial distributed execution. Release 2.0 is the name of the ensuing version. In June 1989, the Cfront execution of it was released. Functionality for several inheritance and abstract classes, as well as the few additional improvements, were the two most significant innovations included to C++ Release 2.0.

C++ Version 3.0 emerged throughout 1989 and 1990. Templates that offer parameterized kinds and exception management were introduced. ISO describes the existing variant of C++, which was specified in 1998. Microsoft announced its .NET computing system in the year 2002, which contained the latest edition of C++ known as Managed C++ or MC++. MC++ enhances C++ to enable access to the .NET Platform's features. Capabilities, delegates, interfaces, and the reference type for garbage-gathered objects are among the additions (Teitelman, 1975; Tenenbaum et al., 1990).

2.9.1. Language Summary

Since C++ enables algorithmic and OOP, it has both methods and functions. In C++, operators may be saturated, allowing the user to add new operators to replace those that already appear on user-defined types. Additionally, C++ methods can be "overloaded," which allows the user to declare many methods with about the same name as long as their argument types or numbers change.

Virtual methods in C++ offer dynamic binding. These techniques offer type-dependent operations inside a set of classes that are associated via inheritance by employing overloaded methods. A pointer to an object of class A could also point to objects of classes that share an ancestor with class A. When this pointer is pointed to an overridden virtual technique, the method of the existing type is dynamically selected.

Classes and methods can be designed, allowing them to be parameterized. For instance, a method can be built as a functionalized method in order to support several parameter types. Classes have the same level of flexibility. C++ allows for various inheritance.

2.9.2. Evaluation

The popularity of C++ has continued to grow. The accessibility of good and affordable translators is one of the reasons for its growth. The point that it is almost entirely fully compatible with C (which means that C algorithms can be converted into C++ programs with little modification), and that C++ code can typically be linked with C code makes it reasonably simple for numerous C programmers to learn C++. Last but not least, C++ was the only language that was accessible at the time it initially arose and when OOP started to get considerable interest. On the downside, since C++ is such a vast and difficult language, it obviously has limitations comparable to PL/I. It absorbed most of C's flaws, making it less secure than languages like Ada and Java (Thompson, 1999; Thomas et al., 2013).

2.9.3. An Associated Language: Objective-C

Objective-C is a mixed language with object-oriented and imperative elements (Kochan, 2009). Tom Love and Brad Cox created Objective-C in 1980s. Originally, it was composed of C and Smalltalk's classes and message forwarding. Objective-C seems to be the only computer language built by providing features for OOP to the imperative language using the Smalltalk syntax for this assistance.

The NeXT computer software was created using Objective-C, which Steve Jobs acquired when he left Apple and started NeXT. Together with the NeXTstep programming environment and a collection of tools, NeXT also launched its Objective-C translator. Following the failure of the NeXT project, Apple purchased NeXT and utilized Objective-C to create MAC OS X. All iPhone software is written in Objective-C, which illustrates why it gained prominence so quickly after the iPhone debuted (Turner, 1986; Ullman, 1998). The flexible binding of messages to objects is an attribute that Objective-C borrowed from Smalltalk. This means that messages aren't checked statically. If the message is delivered to an object and object is incapable of responding, it isn't known till runtime, when an anomaly is thrown. Apple introduced Objective-C 2.0 in the year 2006, which provided a garbage gathering method and a novel syntax for specifying properties. Consequently, the iPhone runtime doesn't support trash collection. Objective-C is a tight superset of C, so most of that language's vulnerabilities are available in Objective-C as well (van Wijngaarden et al., 1969).

2.10. AN IMPERATIVE-CENTERED OBJECT-ORIENTED LANGUAGE: JAVA

Java's developers began with C++, then eliminated some constructs, altered others, and introduced a few more. The resultant language has much of C++'s strength and versatility, but it is smaller, easier, and safer. Java has evolved significantly since that first design.

2.10.1. Design Procedure

Along with many other programming languages, Java was created for a specific purpose for which there didn't seem to be a suitable prevailing language. Sun Microsystems decided in the year 1990 that a programming language was required for embedded consumer electronics, including toasters, microwaves, and interactive TV systems. One of the main objectives with such a language was dependability. It might not appear like a crucial aspect of the software for a gas oven might be dependability. If software in an oven malfunctioned, it's unlikely that it would endanger anyone seriously or result in expensive lawsuits. Unfortunately, it might be expensive to recall a specific model if it turned out to have flawed software after a million copies had been produced and sold. As a result, software reliability is a key feature of consumer electronics goods (Wadler, 1998).

After evaluating C and C++, it was determined that none were suitable for software development for consumer electronic products. Even though C was a compact programming language, it lacked assistance for OOP, which they thought essential. C++ enabled OOP, and it was deemed too vast and difficult since it allowed procedural programming. Also, it was assumed that C or C++ nor Java had been developed. It was created with the core objective of delivering greater clarity and dependability than C++ was thought to provide.

User electronics were the primary inspiration for Java, so even though neither of the early items that utilized it were ever commercialized. Java was discovered to be a helpful tool for Web programming beginning in the year 1993, when the WWW (world wide web) started to become extensively utilized, and partly due of the novel graphical browsers (Warren et al., 1979).

Particularly, Java applets swiftly grew in popularity in the mid to late 1990s. Java applets are comparatively short Java algorithms that are processed in Web browsers but whose results can be indulged in visible Web documents. The Web was Java's most widely used application during its early years of prominence. James Gosling, who also created the UNIX emacs operator and the NeWS window-based system, led the Java design department.

2.10.2. Language Outline

As already said, Java is centered on C++, but was meant to be smaller, cheaper, and more dependable. Java, like C++, contains classes and primitive kinds. Java arrays are examples of an already defined class, while C++ arrays aren't; however, several C++ users create wrapper classes for arrays to add functionality such as index range verification, which is explicit in Java.

Although Java lacks pointers, its reference types nonetheless offer some of the features of pointers. These identifiers are employed to identify instances of classes. The heap is used to generate all items. When appropriate, references are still effectively dereferenced. They therefore act more like common scalar variables. Java features a built-in primitive Boolean type called Boolean that is mostly utilized for control expressions in control statements (like while and if). Arithmetic expressions can't be utilized as control expressions, contrasting C and C++ (Wegner, 1972; Watt, 1979).

Java, unlike several of its contemporaries that enable OOP, such as C++, doesn't permit the creation of independent subprograms. Most Java subprograms are expressed as methods within classes. Additionally, methods can only be accessed via a class or object. As a result, C++ allows object-oriented and procedural programming, whereas Java solely facilitates OOP.

The fact that C++ permits several inheritances explicitly in its class definitions is another significant distinction among C++ and Java. Java primarily allows for a single class's inheritance, but its interface structure allows for some of the advantages of multiple inheritance. Structures and unions are two C++ constructs that weren't translated into Java. Through the synchronized modifier, which can be present on methods and blocks, Java supports a rather basic type of concurrency control. It results in a lock being connected in either situation. The lock makes guarantee that access or implementation are strictly exclusive. Concurrent processes, often known as threads in Java, are rather simple to construct (Weissman, 1967; Wegner, 1972).

Java objects utilize implicit memory deallocation, commonly known as garbage collection. This eliminates the necessity for the programmer to remove objects manually when they aren't any longer required. Programs built in languages that lack garbage gathering frequently suffer from memory leakage, which occurs when storage is generated but never removed. This will inevitably result in the exhaustion of all accessible storage space.

Java only supports assignment kind coercions (automatic type conversions) if they are expanding (moving from smaller type to the bigger type), in contrast to C and C++. Therefore, coercions from int to float are performed throughout the assignment operator, and not from float to int.

2.10.3. Evaluation

The developers of Java did an excellent job of removing unnecessary or hazardous C++ functionality. For instance, the deletion of 50% of C++'s assignment coercions were unquestionably a step toward higher certainty. Index range verification for array accesses also increases the safety of the language. The introduction of multitasking and the class libraries for GUIs, database access, and networking expand the range of programs that may be created in the language.

The adaptability of Java, particularly in intermediate step, has sometimes been ascribed to the language's architecture, but this isn't the case. Every language can be transformed to an intermediate step and run on any system that offers that intermediate form's virtual machine. The cost of adaptability is the price of translation, which has generally been several orders of magnitude higher as compared to the cost of machine code implementation. The original Java interpreter, known as JVM (Java virtual machine), was really at least 10 times slower as compared to equivalent compiled C programs. Conversely, utilizing JIT (just-in-time) compilers, several Java programs are transformed to machine program before being run. This puts Java programs on par with programs written in traditional compiled languages like C++, particularly when array index range verification is ignored (Wheeler, 1950; Weissman, 1967).

Java's popularity grows rapidly as compared to every other programming language. This was first owing to its usefulness in programming dynamic Web content. Obviously, one of several reasons for Java's rapid ascent to popularity is that programmers enjoy its structure. Some programmers believed that C++ was too vast and complicated to be useful and secure. Java provided them with a powerful alternative to C++, but in a cheaper, safer language. A further argument is that the compiler system for Java is available for free and may be downloaded from the Internet. Java is currently utilized in a range of application domains.

Year 2014 saw the release of Java SE8, the latest version of Java. The language has gained important characteristics since the original iteration. A novel iteration construct, generics, lambda expressions, enumeration class, and various class libraries are among them (Wheeler, 1950).

2.11. MARKUP-PROGRAMMING HYBRID LANGUAGES

In this language some elements, like control flow and calculation, can express programming activities. Following are descriptions of two hybrid languages, JSP and XSLT.

2.11.1. XSLT

The metamarkup language is XML (extensible markup language). The definition of markup languages is done using this language. The markup languages that describe XML data documents are derived from XML. Even though XML documents can be read by humans, machines process them. Occasionally, this processing consists just of conversions into different forms that could be successfully shown or printed. These modifications are frequently made to HTML, which the web browser may display. In other instances, the document's data is processed in the same way as other types of data files are (Wirth, 1971, 1973).

One more markup language, XSLT (eXtensible stylesheet language) transforms, is used to convert XML files to HTML files. XSLT allows you to express programming-like actions. As a result, XSLT is a hybrid markup-programming language. W3C (World Wide Web Consortium) developed XSLT in 1990s.

A program that accepts input an XML data file and XSLT file is an XSLT processor. Using the alterations indicated in the XSLT file, the XML data file is changed into another XML file, 21 during this procedure. The XSLT file provides transformations by specifying templates, which seem to be data patterns the XSLT processor might find in XML input document. Every template in the XSLT file is accompanied by its translation commands, which explain how the matching data should be converted prior to being included in an output file. The templates so function as subprograms that are "run" when the XSLT processor detects a pattern fit in the XML file's data (Wirth, 1988; Wilson, 2005).

Lower-level programming constructs are also present in XSLT. A looping component, for instance, enables the selection of repeated sections of the XML file. A sorting procedure is also present. These more basic constructions are described by XSLT elements like <for-each>.

2.11.2. JSP

The main portion of JSTL (Java Server Pages Standard Tag Library) is one more markup-programming hybrid language, albeit with a different shape and function than XSLT. It is required to teach servlets and JSP (Java server pages) prior to discussing JSTL. A servlet is the Java class example that sits on and is implemented by a Web server.

A markup document that is being shown by the web browser requests the implementation of a servlet. The HTML document representing the servlet's output is delivered to requesting browser. A servlet container is a software that runs within the Web server procedure and manages the implementation of servlets. Form computation and database access are prominent applications of Servlets. A group of technologies known as JSP was created to assist dynamic Web content and meet additional processing requirements. When the browser requests a JSP file, which frequently combines Java and HTML, the JSP processor algorithm, which is installed on the Web server system, turns the content to a servlet. The servlet receives a copy of the embedded Java code from the document. In Java print commands, the plain HTML is captured and output in its original form. The processing of the JSTL markup found in the JSP file is covered in the paragraph that follows.

The servlet container runs the servlet generated by the JSP processor. The JSTL describes a set of XML action components that govern the processing of JSP documents on a Web server. These items have the same structure as other XML and HTML elements. The JSTL control step element if, which defines a Boolean expression as such an attribute, is among the most often used. The body of the if element is HTML program that will only be used for the output document if a Boolean expression examines to true. The if element corresponds to the #if preprocessor command in C/C++. Similarly, to whether the C/C++ preprocessor computes C and C++ code, the JSP container handles the JSTL portions of JSP documents. The preprocessor instructions are commands that tell the preprocessor how to build the output file from the input document. Likewise, JSTL control action items are directives that guide the JSP processor on how to construct the XML output document from the XML input document (Wirth & Hoare, 1966).

The if element is frequently used to validate form data that users of browsers have contributed. The JSP processor has accessibility to form data, which may be evaluated to see if it is logical data using the if element. If not, the output file's if element may include an error code for the user.

ACTIVITY 2.1:

Choose two programming languages and compare them based on their performance, ease of use and community support.

JSTL includes choose, when, and else elements for various selection controls. JSTL also offers a forEach element that iterates across collections, which are often client-provided form values. Begin, end, and step properties can be used with the forEach element to govern its repetitions.

2.12. SCRIPTING LANGUAGES

Over the last 35 years, scripting languages have progressed. These languages were first employed by placing a collection of commands, known as a script, in a document to be translated. The earliest of these languages, sh (for shell), started out as a tiny set of instructions that were translated as calls to system subprograms that executed utility duties like file handling and simple filtering of file. With the addition of variables, functions, control flow statements, and several other capabilities, a comprehensive programming language was created. David Korn created among the most effective and well-known of these languages, ksh (Korn & Bolsky, 1995), which is among the most generally recognized. One other scripting language is awk, which was created at Bell Laboratories by Al Aho, Peter Weinberger, and Brian Kernighan (Aho et al., 1988). Initially, awk was a report-generation language, but it has now evolved into a more common language.

2.13. SUMMARY

Programming languages are evaluated on several criteria, including their performance, ease of use, availability of libraries and frameworks, community support and scalability. The evaluation of a programming language is subjective and depends on the purpose for which it is being used. Java is a popular programming language that is used for developing enterprise-level applications. It is known for its performance, scalability, and security features. C# is a modern OOP language developed by Microsoft and is commonly used for developing windows applications and games. PHP is a server-side scripting language that is commonly used for developing dynamic web applications. It is known for its ease of use and scalability.

REVIEW QUESTIONS

1. What are the main criteria used to evaluate programming languages?
2. How does Java compare to other programming languages in terms of performance and security?
3. What advantages does python offer for data analysis and machine learning?
4. What are some of the limitations of using certain programming languages and how can developers work around them?
5. How do emerging programming languages fit into the landscape of established programming languages and how should developers evaluate these new options?

MULTIPLE CHOICE QUESTIONS

1. Which of the following is not typically considered when evaluating programming languages?

a. Performance
b. Ease of use
c. Compatibility with existing systems
d. Availability of popular memes

2. Which programming language is commonly used for developing enterprise-level applications?

a. Python
b. JavaScript
c. Java
d. PHP

3. Which programming language was designed for building web applications?

a. C++

b. JavaScript
c. Ruby
d. All of the above

4. **Which of the following is not typically considered when evaluating the scalability of a programming language?**
   a. Performance
   b. Ease of use
   c. Community support
   d. Compatibility with existing systems

5. **Which programming language is commonly used for data analysis and machine learning?**
   a. JavaScript
   b. Python
   c. C#
   d. Ruby

Answers to Multiple Choice Questions

1. (d); 2. (c); 3. (b); 4. (c); 5. (b)

REFERENCES

1. ACM, (1979). "Part A: Preliminary Ada reference manual" and part B: Rationale for the design of the Ada programming language. *SIGPLAN Notices, 14*(6).
2. ACM, (1993a). History of programming language conference proceedings. *ACM SIGPLAN Notices, 28*(3).
3. ACM, (1993b). High performance FORTRAN language specification part 1. *FORTRAN Forum, 12*(4).
4. Aho, A. V., Kernighan, B. W., & Weinberger, P. J., (1988). *The AWK Programming Language* (Vol. 14, pp. 6–9). Addison-Wesley, Reading, MA.
5. Aho, A. V., Lam, M. S., Sethi, R., & Ullman, J. D., (2006). *Compilers: Principles, Techniques, and Tools* (2nd edn. Vol. 18, pp. 15–18). Addison-Wesley, Reading, MA.
6. Andrews, G. R., & Schneider, F. B., (1983). Concepts and notations for concurrent programming. *ACM Computing Surveys, 15*(1), 3–43.
7. ANSI, (1966). *American National Standard Programming Language FORTRAN* (pp. 5–16). American National Standards Institute, New York.
8. Arden, B. W., Galler, B. A., & Graham, R. M., (1961). *MAD at Michigan* (Vol. 7, No. 12, pp. 27, 28). Datamation.

9. Backus, J., (1954). The IBM 701 speedcoding system. *J. ACM, 1*, 4–6.
10. Backus, J., (1959). The syntax and semantics of the proposed international algebraic language of the Zurich ACM-GAMM conference. *Proceedings International Conference on Information Processing* (pp. 125–132). UNESCO, Paris.
11. Backus, J., (1978). Can programming be liberated from the von Neumann style? A functional style and its algebra of programs. *Commun. ACM, 21*(8), 613–641.
12. Backus, J., Bauer, F. L., Green, J., Katz, C., McCarthy, J., Naur, P., Perlis, A. J., et al., (1963). Revised report on the algorithmic language ALGOL 60. *Commun. ACM, 6*(1), 1–17.
13. Bodwin, J. M., Bradley, L., Kanda, K., Litle, D., & Pleban, U. F., (1982). Experience with an experimental compiler generator based on denotational semantics. *ACM SIGPLAN Notices, 17*(6), 216–229.
14. Bohm, C., & Jacopini, G., (1966). Flow diagrams, Turing machines, and languages with only two formation rules. *Commun. ACM, 9*(5), 366–371.
15. BrinchHansen, P., (1975). The programming language concurrent-Pascal. *IEEE Transactions on Software Engineering, 1*(2), 199–207.
16. BrinchHansen, P., (1977). *The Architecture of Concurrent Programs*. Prentice-Hall, Englewood Cliffs, NJ.
17. BrinchHansen, P., (1978). Distributed processes: A concurrent programming concept. *Commun. ACM, 21*(11), 934–941.
18. Chambers, C., & Ungar, D., (1991). Making pure object-oriented languages practical. *SIGPLAN Notices, 26*(1), 1–15.
19. Chomsky, N., (1956). Three models for the description of language. *IRE Transactions on Information Theory, 2*(3), 113–124.
20. Chomsky, N., (1959). On certain formal properties of grammars. *Information and Control, 2*(2), 137–167.
21. Clarke, L. A., Wileden, J. C., & Wolf, A. L., (1980). Nesting in Ada is for the birds. *ACM SIGPLAN Notices, 15*(11), 139–145.
22. Cohen, J., (1981). Garbage collection of linked data structures. *ACM Computing Surveys, 13*(3), 341–368.
23. Converse, T., & Park, J., (2000). *PHP 4 Bible* (pp. 12–15). IDG Books, New York.
24. Conway, M. E., (1963). Design of a separable transition-diagram compiler. *Commun. ACM, 6*(7), 396–408.
25. Conway, R., & Constable, R., (1976). *PL/CS—A Disciplined Subset of PL/I* (Vol. 1, pp. 7, 8). Technical Report TR76/293. Department of Computer Science, Cornell University, Ithaca, NY.
26. Correa, N., (1992). Empty categories, chain binding, and parsing. In: Berwick, R. C., Abney, S. P., & Tenny, C., (eds.), *Principle-Based Parsing* (pp. 83–121). Kluwer Academic Publishers, Boston.

27. Deliyanni, A., & Kowalski, R. A., (1979). Logic and semantic networks. *Commun. ACM, 22*(3), 184–192.
28. DeRemer, F., & Pennello, T., (1982). Efficient computation of LALR (1) look-ahead sets. *ACM TOPLAS, 4*(4), 615–649.
29. DeRemer, F., (1971). Simple LR(k) grammars. *Commun. ACM, 14*(7), 453–460.
30. Deutsch, L. P., & Bobrow, D. G., (1976). An efficient incremental automatic garbage collector. *Commun. ACM, 11*(3), 522–526.
31. Dijkstra, E. W., (1968a). Goto statement considered harmful. *Commun. ACM, 11*(3), 147–149.
32. Dijkstra, E. W., (1968b). Cooperating sequential processes. In: Genuys, F., (ed.), *Programming Languages* (pp. 43–112). Academic Press, New York.
33. Dijkstra, E. W., (1972). The humble programmer. *Commun. ACM, 15*(10), 859–866.
34. Dijkstra, E. W., (1975). Guarded commands, nondeterminacy, and formal derivation of programs. *Commun. ACM, 18*(8), 453–457.
35. Dijkstra, E. W., (1976). *A Discipline of Programming* (Vol. 3, No. 5, pp. 7–12). Prentice-Hall, Englewood Cliffs, NJ.
36. Dybvig, R. K., (2009). *The Scheme Programming Language* (4th edn., Vol. 1, No. 2, pp. 10–13). MIT Press, Boston.
37. Ellis, M. A., & Stroustrup, B., (1990). *The Annotated C++ Reference Manual* (Vol. 1, pp. 10–15). Addison-Wesley, Reading, MA.
38. Farber, D. J., Griswold, R. E., & Polonsky, I. P., (1964). SNOBOL, a string manipulation language. *J. ACM, 11*(1), 21–30.
39. Farrow, R., (1982). LINGUIST 86: Yet another translator writing system based on attribute grammars. *ACM SIGPLAN Notices, 17*(6), 160–171.
40. Fischer, C. N., & LeBlanc, R. J., (1977). *UW-Pascal Reference Manual* (Vol. 3, No. 1, pp. 11–16). Madison Academic Computing Center, Madison, WI.
41. Fischer, C. N., & LeBlanc, R. J., (1980). Implementation of runtime diagnostics in Pascal. *IEEE Transactions on Software Engineering, SE-6*(4), 313–319.
42. Fischer, C. N., & LeBlanc, R. J., (1991). *Crafting a Compiler in C* (Vol. 1, No. 5, pp. 1–5). Benjamin/Cummings, Menlo Park, CA.
43. Fischer, C. N., Johnson, G. F., Mauney, J., Pal, A., & Stock, D. L., (1984). The Poe language-based editor project. *ACM SIGPLAN Notices, 19*(5), 21–29.
44. Flanagan, D., (2011). *JavaScript: The Definitive Guide* (6th edn., Vol. 1, No. 1, pp. 5–8). O'Reilly Media, Sebastopol, CA.
45. Floyd, R. W., (1967). Assigning meanings to programs. In: Schwartz, J. T., (ed.), *Proceedings Symposium Applied Mathematics. Mathematical Aspects of Computer Science*. American Mathematical Society, Providence, RI.
46. Frege, G., (1892). Über sinn und bedeutung. *Zeitschrift für Philosophie und Philosophisches Kritik*, *100*, 25–50.

47. Friedl, J. E. F., (2006). *Mastering Regular Expressions* (3rd edn.). O'Reilly Media, Sebastopol, CA.
48. Friedman, D. P., & Wise, D. S., (1979). Reference counting's ability to collect cycles is not insurmountable. *Information Processing Letters, 8*(1), 41–45.
49. Fuchi, K., (1981). Aiming for knowledge information processing systems. *Proceedings of the International Conference on Fifth Generation Computing Systems*. Japan Information Processing Development Center, Tokyo. Republished (1982) by North-Holland Publishing, Amsterdam.
50. Gehani, N., (1983). *Ada: An Advanced Introduction*. Prentice-Hall, Englewood Cliffs, NJ.
51. Gilman, L., & Rose, A. J., (1983). *APL: An Interactive Approach* (3rd edn.). John Wiley, New York.
52. Goldberg, A., & Robson, D., (1983). *Smalltalk-80: The Language and Its Implementation*. Addison-Wesley, Reading, MA.
53. Goldberg, A., & Robson, D., (1989). *Smalltalk-80: The Language*. Addison-Wesley, Reading, MA.
54. Goodenough, J. B., (1975). Exception handling: Issues and proposed notation. *Commun. ACM, 18*(12), 683–696.
55. Goos, G., & Hartmanis, J., (1983). The programming language Ada reference manual. American national standards institute. ANSI/MIL-STD-1815A-1983. *Lecture Notes in Computer Science 155*. Springer-Verlag, New York.
56. Gordon, M., (1979). *The Denotational Description of Programming Languages, An Introduction*. Springer-Verlag, New York.
57. Graham, P., (1996). *ANSI Common LISP*. Prentice-Hall, Englewood Cliffs, NJ.
58. Gries, D., (1981). *The Science of Programming*. Springer-Verlag, New York.
59. Griswold, R. E., & Griswold, M. T., (1983). *The ICON Programming Language*. Prentice-Hall, Englewood Cliffs, NJ.
60. Griswold, R. E., Poage, F., & Polonsky, I. P., (1971). *The SNOBOL 4 Programming Language* (2nd edn.). Prentice-Hall, Englewood Cliffs, NJ.
61. Halstead, R. H. Jr., (1985). Multilisp: A language for concurrent symbolic computation. *ACM Transactions on Programming Language and Systems, 7*(4), 501–538.
62. Halvorson, M., (2013). *Microsoft Visual Basic 2013 Step by Step*. Microsoft Press, Redmond, WA.
63. Hammond, P., (1983). *APES: A User Manual. Department of Computing Report 82/9.* Imperial College of Science and Technology, London.
64. Harbison, III. S. P., & Steele, G. L. Jr., (2002). *A. C. Reference Manual* (5th edn.) Prentice-Hall, Upper Saddle River, NJ.
65. Henderson, P., (1980). *Functional Programming: Application and Implementation*. Prentice-Hall, Englewood Cliffs, NJ.

66. Hoare, C. A. R., & Wirth, N., (1973). An axiomatic definition of the programming language Pascal. *Acta Informatica, 2*, 335–355.
67. Hoare, C. A. R., (1969). An axiomatic basis of computer programming. *Commun. ACM, 12*(10), 576–580.
68. Hoare, C. A. R., (1972). Proof of correctness of data representations. *Acta Informatica, 1*, 271–281.
69. Hoare, C. A. R., (1973). Hints on programming language design. *Proceedings ACM SIGACT/SIGPLAN Conference on Principles of Programming Languages.* Also published as technical report STAN-CS-73-403, Stanford University Computer Science Department.
70. Hoare, C. A. R., (1974). Monitors: An operating system structuring concept. *Commun. ACM, 17*(10), 549–557.
71. Hoare, C. A. R., (1978). Communicating sequential processes. *Commun. ACM, 21*(8), 666–677.
72. Hoare, C. A. R., (1981). The emperor's old clothes. *Commun. ACM, 24*(2), 75–83.
73. Hogger, C. J., (1984). *Introduction to Logic Programming.* Academic Press, London.
74. Hogger, C. J., (1991). *Essentials of Logic Programming.* Oxford Science Publications, Oxford, England.
75. Holt, R. C., Graham, G. S., Lazowska, E. D., & Scott, M. A., (1978). *Structured Concurrent Programming with Operating Systems Applications.* Addison-Wesley, Reading, MA.
76. Horn, A., (1951). On sentences which are true of direct unions of algebras. *J. Symbolic Logic, 16*, 14–21.
77. Hudak, P., & Fasel, J., (1992). A gentle introduction to Haskell. *ACM SIGPLAN Notices, 27*(5), T1–T53.
78. Hughes, J., (1989). Why functional programming matters. *The Computer Journal, 32*(2), 98–107.
79. Huskey, H. K., Love, R., & Wirth, N., (1963). A syntactic description of BC NELIAC. *Commun. ACM, 6*(7), 367–375.
80. IBM, (1954). *Preliminary Report, Specifications for the IBM Mathematical Formula Translating System, FORTRAN.* IBM Corporation, New York.
81. IBM, (1956). *Programmer's Reference Manual, The FORTRAN Automatic Coding System for the IBM 704 EDPM.* IBM Corporation, New York.
82. IBM, (1964). *The New Programming Language.* IBM UK Laboratories, Hursley, England.
83. Ichbiah, J. D., Heliard, J. C., Roubine, O., Barnes, J. G. P., Krieg-Brueckner, B., & Wichmann, B. A., (1979). Part B: Rationale for the design of the Ada programming language. *ACM SIGPLAN Notices, 14*(6).

84. Ierusalimschy, R., (2006). *Programming in Lua* (2nd edn.). Lua.org, Rio de Janeiro, Brazil.

85. INCITS/ISO/IEC, (1997). *1539-1-1997, Information Technology— Programming Languages— FORTRAN, Part 1: Base Language*. American National Standards Institute, New York.

86. Ingerman, P. Z., (1967). Panini-Backus form suggested. *Commun. ACM, 10*(3), 137.

87. ISO, (1982). *ISO7185:1982, Specification for Programming Language Pascal*. International Organization for Standardization, Geneva, Switzerland.

88. ISO, (1998). *ISO14882-1, ISO/IEC Standard – Information Technology— Programming Language— C++*. International Organization for Standardization, Geneva, Switzerland.

89. ISO, (1999). *ISO/IEC 9899:1999, Programming Language C*. American National Standards Institute, New York.

90. ISO/IEC, (1996). *14977:1996, Information Technology— Syntactic Metalanguage— Extended BNF*. International Organization for Standardization, Geneva, Switzerland.

91. ISO/IEC, (2002). *1989:2002, Information Technology— Programming Languages— COBOL*. American National Standards Institute, New York.

92. ISO/IEC, (2010). *1539-1, Information Technology— Programming Languages— Fortran*. American National Standards Institute, New York.

93. ISO/IEC, (2014). *8652/2012(E), Ada 2012 Reference Manual*. Springer-Verlag, New York.

94. Iverson, K. E., (1962). *A Programming Language*. John Wiley, New York.

95. Jensen, K., & Wirth, N., (1974). *Pascal Users Manual and Report*. Springer-Verlag, Berlin.

96. Johnson, S. C., (1975). *Yacc— Yet Another Compiler*. Computing Science Report 32. AT&T Bell Laboratories, Murray Hill, NJ.

97. Jones, N. D., (1980). *Semantic-Directed Compiler Generation: Lecture Notes in Computer Science,* (Vol. 94). Springer-Verlag, Heidelberg, FRG.

98. Kay, A., (1969). *The Reactive Engine*. PhD Thesis. University of Utah, September.

99. Kernighan, B. W., & Ritchie, D. M., (1978). *The C Programming Language.* Prentice-Hall, Englewood Cliffs, NJ.

100. Knuth, D. E., & Pardo, L. T., (1977). Early development of programming languages. In: Holzman, G., & Kent, A., (eds.), *Encyclopedia of Computer Science and Technology* (Vol. 7, pp. 419–493). Dekker, New York.

101. Knuth, D. E., (1965). On the translation of languages from left to right. *Information & Control, 8*(6), 607–639.

102. Knuth, D. E., (1967). The remaining trouble spots in ALGOL 60. *Commun. ACM, 10*(10), 611–618.

103. Knuth, D. E., (1968a). Semantics of context-free languages. *Mathematical Systems Theory, 2*(2), 127–146.

104. Knuth, D. E., (1968b). *The Art of Computer Programming* (2nd edn., Vol. I). Addison-Wesley, Reading, MA.

105. Knuth, D. E., (1974). Structured programming with GOTO statements. *ACM Computing Surveys, 6*(4), 261–301.

106. Knuth, D. E., (1981). *The Art of Computer Programming* (2nd edn., Vol. II). Addison-Wesley, Reading, MA.

107. Kochan, S. G., (2009). *Programming in Objective-C 2.0.* Addison-Wesley, Upper Saddle River, NJ.

108. Kowalski, R. A., (1979). *Logic for Problem Solving: Artificial Intelligence Series* (Vol. 7). Elsevier-North Holland, New York.

109. Laning, J. H. Jr., & Zierler, N., (1954). *A Program for Translation of Mathematical Equations for Whirlwind I.* Engineering memorandum E-364. Instrumentation Laboratory, Massachusetts Institute of Technology, Cambridge, MA.

110. Ledgard, H. F., & Marcotty, M., (1975). A genealogy of control structures. *Commun. ACM, 18*(11), 629–639.

111. Ledgard, H., (1984). *The American Pascal Standard.* Springer-Verlag, New York.

112. Lischner, R., (2000). *Delphi in a Nutshell.* O'Reilly Media, Sebastopol, CA.

113. Liskov, B., & Snyder, A., (1979). Exception handling in CLU. *IEEE Transactions on Software Engineering, SE-5*(6), 546–558.

114. Liskov, B., Atkinson, R. L., Bloom, T., Moss, J. E. B., Scheffert, C., Scheifler, R., & Snyder, A., (1981). *CLU Reference Manual.* Springer, New York.

115. Lomet, D., (1975). Scheme for invalidating references to freed storage. *IBM Journal of Research and Development, 19*, 26–35.

116. Lutz, M., (2013). *Learning Python* (5th edn.). O'Reilly Media, Sebastopol, CA.

117. MacLaren, M. D., (1977). Exception handling in PL/I. *ACM SIGPLAN Notices, 12*(3), 101–104.

118. Marcotty, M., Ledgard, H. F., & Bochmann, G. V., (1976). A sampler of formal definitions. *ACM Computing Surveys, 8*(2), 191–276.

119. Mather, D. G., & Waite, S. V., (1971). *Basic* (6th edn.). University Press of New England, Hanover, NH.

120. McCarthy, J., (1960). Recursive functions of symbolic expressions and their computation by machine, part I. *Commun. ACM, 3*(4), 184–195.

121. McCarthy, J., Abrahams, P. W., Edwards, D. J., Hart, T. P., & Levin, M., (1965). *LISP 1.5 Programmer's Manual* (2nd edn.). MIT Press, Cambridge, MA.

122. McCracken, D., (1961). *Guide to FORTRAN Programming.* John Wiley & Sons, Inc., New York.

123. McCracken, D., (1970). *Whither APL* (pp. 53–57). Datamation.

124. Metcalf, M., Reid, J., & Cohen, M., (2004). *Fortran 95/2003 Explained* (3rd edn.). Oxford University Press, Oxford, England.

125. Meyer, B., (1990). *Introduction to the Theory of Programming Languages*. Prentice-Hall, Englewood Cliffs, NJ.

126. Meyer, B., (1992). *Eiffel: The Language*. Prentice-Hall, Englewood Cliffs, NJ.

127. Milner, R., Harper, R., & Tofle, M., (1997). *The Definition of Standard ML-Revised*. MIT Press, Cambridge, MA.

128. Milos, D., Pleban, U., & Loegel, G., (1984). Direct implementation of compiler specifications. *POPL '84 Proceedings of the 11th ACM SIGACT-SIGPLAN Symposium on Programming Languages* (pp. 196–202).

129. Mitchell, J. G., Maybury, W., & Sweet, R., (1979). *Mesa Language Manual, Version 5.0, CSL-79-3*. Xerox Research Center, Palo Alto, CA.

130. Moss, C., (1994). *Prolog++: The Power of Object-Oriented and Logic Programming*. Addison-Wesley, Reading, MA.

131. Moto-Oka, T., (1981). Challenge for knowledge information processing systems. *Proceedings of the International Conference on Fifth Generation Computing Systems*. Japan Information Processing Development Center, Tokyo. Republished (1982). by North-Holland Publishing, Amsterdam.

132. Naur, P., (1960). Report on the algorithmic language ALGOL 60. *Commun. ACM, 3*(5), 299–314.

133. Newell, A., & Simon, H. A., (1956). The logic theory machine— A complex information processing system. *IRE Transactions on Information Theory, IT, 2*(3), 61–79.

134. Newell, A., & Tonge, F. M., (1960). An introduction to information processing language V. *Commun. ACM, 3*(4), 205–211.

135. Nilsson, N. J., (1971). *Problem Solving Methods in Artificial Intelligence*. McGraw-Hill, New York.

136. Ousterhout, J. K., (1994). *Tcl and the Tk Toolkit*. Addison-Wesley, Reading, MA.

137. Paepcke, E., (1993). *Object-Oriented Programming: The CLOS Perspective*. MIT Press, Cambridge, MA.

138. Pagan, F. G., (1981). *Formal Specifications of Programming Languages*. Prentice-Hall, Englewood Cliffs, NJ.

139. Papert, S., (1980). *MindStorms: Children, Computers and Powerful Ideas*. Basic Books, New York.

140. Perlis, A., & Samelson, K., (1958). Preliminary report— International algebraic language. *Commun. ACM, 1*(12), 8–22.

141. Peyton, J. S. L., (1987). *The Implementation of Functional Programming Languages*. Prentice-Hall, Englewood Cliffs, NJ.

142. Pratt, T. W., & Zelkowitz, M. V., (2001). *Programming Languages: Design and Implementation* (4th edn.). Prentice-Hall, Englewood Cliffs, NJ.

143. Pratt, T. W., (1984). *Programming Languages: Design and Implementation* (2nd edn.). Prentice-Hall, Englewood Cliffs, NJ.

144. Remington-Rand, (1952). *UNIVAC Short Code*. Unpublished collection of dittoed notes., 12(1), 7-12.
145. Reppy, J. H., (1999). *Concurrent Programming in ML*. Cambridge University Press, New York.
146. Richards, M., (1969). BCPL: A tool for compiler writing and systems programming. *Proc. AFIPS SJCC, 34*, 557–566.
147. Robbins, A., (2005). *Unix in a Nutshell* (4th edn.). O'Reilly Media, Sebastopol, CA.
148. Robinson, J. A., (1965). A machine-oriented logic based on the resolution principle. *Journal of the ACM, 12*, 23–41.
149. Roussel, P., (1975). *PROLOG: Manual de Reference et D'utilization. Research Report*. Artificial Intelligence Group, University of Aix-Marseille, Luming, France.
150. Rubin, F., (1987). 'GOTO statement considered harmful' considered harmful (letter to editor). *Commun. ACM, 30*(3), 195–196.
151. Rutishauser, H., (1967). *Description of ALGOL 60*. Springer-Verlag, New York.
152. Sammet, J. E., (1969). *Programming Languages: History and Fundamentals*. Prentice-Hall, Englewood Cliffs, NJ.
153. Sammet, J. E., (1976). Roster of programming languages for 1974–75. *Commun. ACM, 19*(12), 655–669.
154. Schneider, D. I., (1999). *An Introduction to Programming Using Visual BASIC 6.0*. Prentice-Hall, Englewood Cliffs, NJ.
155. Schorr, H., & Waite, W., (1967). An efficient machine independent procedure for garbage collection in various list structures. *Commun. ACM, 10*(8), 501–506.
156. Scott, D. S., & Strachey, C., (1971). Towards a mathematical semantics for computer language. In: Fox, J., (ed.), *Proceedings, Symposium on Computers and Automation* (pp. 19–46). Polytechnic Institute of Brooklyn Press, New York.
157. Scott, M., (2009). *Programming Language Pragmatics* (3rd edn.). Morgan Kaufman, San Francisco, CA.
158. Sebesta, R. W., (1991). *VAX Structured Assembly Language Programming* (2nd edn.). Benjamin/ Cummings, Redwood City, CA.
159. Sergot, M. J., (1983). A query-the-user facility for logic programming. In: Degano, P., & Sandewall, E., (eds.), *Integrated Interactive Computer Systems*. North-Holland Publishing, Amsterdam.
160. Shaw, C. J., (1963). A specification of JOVIAL. *Commun. ACM, 6*(12), 721–736.
161. Smith, J. B., (2006). *Practical OCaml*. Apress, Springer-Verlag, New York.
162. Sommerville, I., (2010). *Software Engineering* (9th edn.). Addison-Wesley, Reading, MA.
163. Steele, G. L. Jr., (1990). *Common LISP The Language* (2nd edn.). Digital Press, Burlington, MA.

164. Stoy, J. E., (1977). *Denotational Semantics: The Scott-Strachey Approach to Programming Language Semantics.* MIT Press, Cambridge, MA.

165. Stroustrup, B., (1983). Adding classes to C: An exercise in language evolution. *Software—Practice and Experience, 13*, 139–161.

166. Stroustrup, B., (1984). Data abstraction in C. *AT&T Bell Laboratories Technical Journal, 63*(8), 1701–1732.

167. Stroustrup, B., (1986). *The C++ Programming Language.* Addison-Wesley, Reading, MA.

168. Stroustrup, B., (1988). What is object-oriented programming? *IEEE Software*, 10–20.

169. Sussman, G. J., & Steele, G. L. Jr., (1975). *Scheme: An Interpreter for Extended Lambda Calculus*. MIT AI Memo No. 349.

170. Suzuki, N., (1982). Analysis of pointer 'rotation.' *Commun. ACM, 25*(5), 330–335.

171. Syme, D., Granicz, A., & Cisternino, A., (2010). *Expert F# 2.0.* Apress, Springer-Verlag, New York.

172. Tanenbaum, A. S., (2005). *Structured Computer Organization* (5th edn.). Prentice-Hall, Englewood Cliffs, NJ.

173. Tatroe, K., MacIntyre, P., & Lerdorf, R., (2013). *Programming PHP* (3rd edn.). O'Reilly Media, Sebastopol, CA.

174. Teitelbaum, T., & Reps, T., (1981). The Cornell program synthesizer: A syntax-directed programming environment. *Commun. ACM, 24*(9), 563–573.

175. Teitelman, W., (1975). *INTERLISP Reference Manual.* Xerox Palo Alto Research Center, Palo Alto, CA.

176. Tenenbaum, A. M., Langsam, Y., & Augenstein, M. J., (1990). *Data Structures Using C.* Prentice-Hall, Englewood Cliffs, NJ.

177. Thomas, D., Hunt, A., & Fowler, C., (2013). *Programming Ruby 1.9 & 2.0: The Pragmatic Programmers Guide (The Facets of Ruby).* The Pragmatic Bookshelf, Raleigh, NC.

178. Thompson, S., (1999). *Haskell: The Craft of Functional Programming* (2nd edn.). Addison-Wesley, Reading, MA.

179. Turner, D., (1986). An overview of Miranda. *ACM SIGPLAN Notices, 21*(12), 158–166.

180. Ullman, J. D., (1998). *Elements of ML Programming*. ML97 Edition. Prentice-Hall, Englewood Cliffs, NJ.

181. Van, E. M. H., (1980). *McDermott on Prolog: A Rejoinder* (No. 72, pp. 19, 20). SIGART Newsletter.

182. Van, W. A., Mailloux, B. J., Peck, J. E. L., & Koster, C. H. A., (1969). Report on the Algorithmic language ALGOL 68. *Numerische Mathematik, 14*(2), 79–218.

183. Wadler, P., (1998). Why no one uses functional languages. *ACM SIGPLAN Notices, 33*(2), 25–30.

184. Warren, D. H. D., Pereira, L. M., & Pereira, F. C. N., (1979). *User's Guide to Dec*

System-10 Prolog. Occasional paper 15. Department of Artificial Intelligence, University of Edinburgh, Scotland.

185. Watt, D. A., (1979). An extended attribute grammar for Pascal. *ACM SIGPLAN Notices, 14*(2), 60–74.
186. Wegner, P., (1972). The Vienna definition language. *ACM Computing Surveys, 4*(1), 5–63.
187. Wexelblat, R. L., (1981). *History of Programming Languages.* Academic Press, New York.
188. Wheeler, D. J., (1950). Program organization and initial orders for the EDSAC. *Proc. R. Soc. London, Ser. A, 202*, 573–589.
189. Wilkes, M. V., (1952). Pure and applied programming. In: *Proceedings of the ACM National Conference* (Vol. 2, pp. 121–124). Toronto.
190. Wilkes, M. V., Wheeler, D. J., & Gill, S., (1951). *The Preparation of Programs for an Electronic Digital Computer, with Special Reference to the EDSAC and the Use of a Library of Subroutines.* Addison-Wesley, Reading, MA.
191. Wilkes, M. V., Wheeler, D. J., & Gill, S., (1957). *The Preparation of Programs for an Electronic Digital Computer* (2nd edn.). Addison-Wesley, Reading, MA.
192. Wilson, P. R. (2005, June). *Uniprocessor garbage collection techniques. In Memory Management: International Workshop IWMM 92 St. Malo, France, September 17–19, 1992* Proceedings, 1-42).
193. Wirth, N., & Hoare, C. A. R., (1966). A contribution to the development of ALGOL. *Commun. ACM, 9*(6), 413–431.
194. Wirth, N., (1971). The programming language Pascal. *Acta Informatica, 1*(1), 35–63.
195. Wirth, N., (1973). *Systematic Programming: An Introduction.* Prentice-Hall, Englewood Cliffs, NJ.
196. Wirth, N., (1975). On the design of programming languages. *Information Processing 74 (Proceedings of IFIP Congress 74)* (pp. 386–393). North Holland, Amsterdam.
197. Wirth, N., (1977). Modula: A language for modular multi-programming. *Software—Practice and Experience, 7,* 3–35.
198. Wirth, N., (1985). *Programming in Modula-2* (3rd edn.). Springer-Verlag, New York.
199. Wirth, N., (1988). The programming language Oberon. *Software— Practice and Experience, 18*(7), 671–690.
200. Wulf, W. A., Russell, D. B., & Habermann, A. N., (1971). BLISS: A language for systems programming. *Commun. ACM, 14*(12), 780–790.
201. Zuse, K., (1972). *Der Plankalkül. Manuscript Prepared in 1945.* Published in Berichte der Gesellschaft für Mathematik und Datenverarbeitung, No. 63 (Bonn, 1972); Part 3: English translation of all but (pp. 42–244, 285) No. 106 (Bonn, 1976).

CHAPTER 3

DATA TYPES

UNIT INTRODUCTION

A data type specifies both a set of data elements as well as a set of activities that may be performed upon these values in a predetermined order. Data is manipulated by computer software to get the desired results. The degree whereby the data types that are accessible in the language that is used are similar to the things that exist in the actual world that are being addressed by the challenge is an essential component in deciding how easily they will be capable to do this job. As a result, a programming language must enable an adequate assortment of data types. For example, in the past 60 years, there has been an evolution in the ideas that constitute modern data types. All challenge space structures would have to be represented in the first languages using just a select handful of the most fundamental data structures that were supported by those languages. Linked sets and branching trees, for instance, were both implemented using arrays in versions of Fortrans before 1990 (Liskov & Zilles, 1974; Mitchell, 1996).

In COBOL, the data models made the first step out from the Fortran I paradigm by enabling programmers to define the precision of numeric data value, as well as by offering an organized data form for recordings of information (Scott, 1976; Herlihy & Liskov, 1982). This was the first move away first from Fortran I paradigm. The capacity of precision specification has been enhanced by PL/I to include both integer and flying types. The developers of PL/I incorporated a vast number of data types only with intention of making the language suitable for a wide variety of applications. A more effective method, which was first presented in ALGOL 68, is to supply a small number of fundamental data types as well as a small number of flexible framework operators. This enables a programmer to create data structures that are tailored to every need (Donahue & Demers, 1985; Swierstra, 2008) (Figure 3.1).

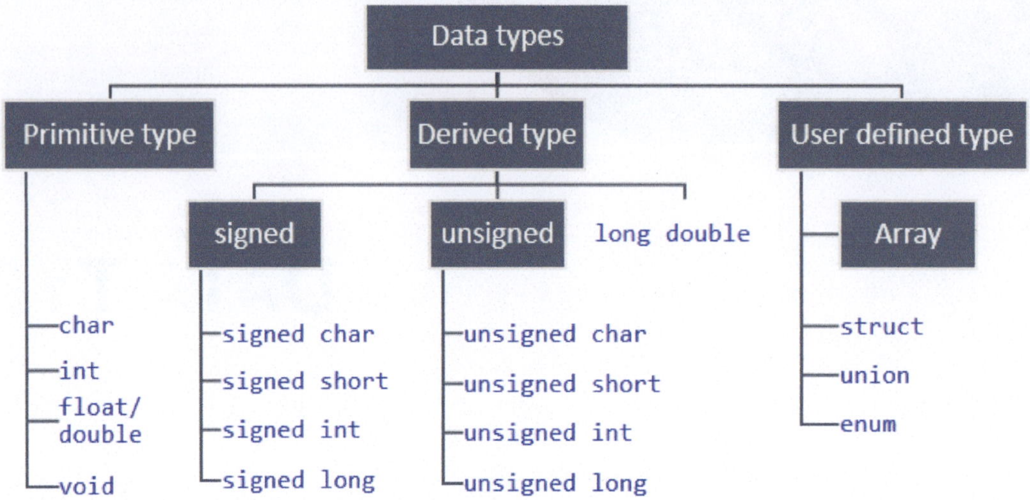

Figure 3.1. Illustration of informational hierarchy.

Source: Codeforwin, Creative Commons License.

Without a doubt, this was among the most significant advancements made in the process of data design style throughout time. Increased readability is another benefit of using user-defined types, which is achieved by giving each type a better explanation (Appleby & VandeKopple, 1991; Läufer & Odersky, 1994). They make it feasible to do types checking on the parameters of a certain category of usage, which would not have been possible in any other context. Another benefit of user-defined types is their contribution to the modifiability of such a program. For example, a programmer may alter the kind of categories of variables used in a software system by simply modifying a type of specification statement. When we take the idea of a user-defined type one step further, we arrived at the notion of abstract data. Abstraction types of data are being supported by the vast majority of computer languages produced since the middle of the 1980s (Myers, 1984; Morris & McKinna, 2019).

The core concept behind an abstract class would be that the interfaces of a category, which are visible to users, are isolated from the representations of the subtype values and also the set of activities that may be performed on those values. The user does not have access to this information. Abstractions are every one of the kinds that are made available by an elevated computer language. A computer language's category system may be used for a variety of purposes in various contexts. Error detection is the one that is most applicable in everyday life (Fegaras & Sheard, 1996; Almeida, 1997). The action of verifying types, as well as the benefits derived from doing so, is governed by the system based on the languages. The second way in which a system might be useful is in the way that it can facilitate the customization of a program. This is a consequence of the cross-module category verification that, among other things, guarantees that now the interfaces between modules are consistent (Garland & Guttag, 1988; Singh & Gulwani, 2016).

Manuals are also another other use for a system based. The type definitions in a program are used to record information about just the program's data, which then in turn reveals insight into the behavior of the program. A computer language's system is what determines how well a type is connected for each statement in that language. It also provides a set of rules for just how types may be equivalent to one another and how they can be compatible with one another. Knowing a computer language's data types is, without a doubt, among the most crucial steps involved in becoming familiar with the semantics of that language (Guttag, 1977; Kamin, 1983).

Clusters and records are indeed the two main prevalent structural (nonscalar) data types in programming languages; nevertheless, the use of associating arrays has substantially grown during the last several years. Since the introduction of the very first language of this kind in 1959, lists were an essential component of programming languages (Lisp). Since the beginning of this decade, programming has been more popular, which has resulted in lists being introduced to mostly imperative languages, including Python and C# (Cave & Pientka, 2012).

Category operators, also known as constructors, are what are used to build type statements, and they are what are being used to define all organized data types. For instance, arrays and pointers may be specified in C by using parenthesis and asterisks, respectively as category operators. Thinking about factors in terms of adjectives is a useful mental shortcut that is helpful on both a logical and a practical level. The assortment of properties that make up a variable is referred to as its descriptor. A descriptor is a section of memory that is used in an application to keep information on the characteristics of a variable. If all of the properties are static, then the descriptor is only needed during the compilation process. The compiler generates these descriptors, which are then used throughout the compilation process. They are often included as a component of the symbol table. However, to make use of dynamic characteristics, either a portion or the whole of the descriptor has to be kept throughout execution. In this particular instance, the run-time system makes use of the descriptor. In every circumstance, descriptors are utilized to carry out the correct method and the construction of code for allocations and deallocation procedures (Demers & Donahue, 1980).

When utilizing the word "variable," one has to exercise caution. Those who are solely familiar with classic imperative languages could believe identifiers to be variables; nevertheless, this line of thinking might cause difficulty when thinking about data types. In certain computer languages, names will not have types of data associated with them. It is important to keep in mind that names are only one of the many qualities that may be associated with a variable. The values of one variable and the amount of space that an item takes up are often connected with the term "object." However, we will only use the term "object" when referring to instances of consumer and vernacular abstract data all through this book. We will not use the term "object" when referring to the values of any predefined program variables (Mallgren, 1982; Atkinson & Buneman, 1987).

Many other forms of commonly used data will be covered in the sections that follow. For even the most part, design considerations that are unique to the type are mentioned. For each, a description is provided along with one or more examples of possible designs. One design problem is intrinsic to all datasets: How are the operations that are offered for variables of this kind described, and also what actions are available for them? (Bergstra & Tucker, 1983).

Learning Objectives

After the chapter, students will be able to understand the following:

- Basic concept of data types in programming;
- Learn about the numeric data types in programming;
- Understanding the Boolean data types used in different programming languages;
- Knowledge about the design process of character string data types.

Key Terms

- Arrays
- Boolean
- Characters
- Classes
- Data types
- Floating-point
- Integers
- Objects
- Programming
- Variables

3.1. PRIMITIVE DATA TYPES

Primitive types of data are those that have been not measured in terms of other kinds. A collection of basic data types is offered by almost all computer languages. The majority of the basic types, for instance, are essentially reflections of both the hardware. Others can be implemented with just a little amount of nonhardware assistance. The basic data kinds of languages are combined with one or more category constructors to describe the structured types (Bruce, 1996; Sekiyama et al., 2015) (Figure 3.2).

Data type	Size	Range	Description
char	1 byte	-128 to +127	A character
int	2 or 4 byte	-32,768 to 32,767 or -2,147,483,648 to +2,147,483,647	An integer
float	4 byte	1.2E-38 to 3.4E+38	Single precision floating point number
void	1 byte		void type stores nothing

Figure 3.2. Illustration of fundamental data types.

Source: Codeforwin, Creative Commons License.

3.1.1. Numeric Types

Primitive types in some earlier computer languages were merely numbers. Among some of the types offered by modern languages, numerical types continue to be at the center of things.

3.1.1.1. Integer

An integer is the most popular data type for basic numbers. Numerous systems' hardware allows integers in a variety of sizes. Some programmers offer these integer values as well as sometimes a few more. For instance, Java offers the bytes, short, int, and large verified integer types. Integer variable types, or types for decimal numbers without signed, are included in several languages, such as C++ and C#. Binary code often uses unsigned types. Computers store signed integer values as strings of bits, including one bit (usually the leftmost) serving as that of the sign. The hardware natively supports the majority of integer types (Bobrow & Raphael, 1974; Ernst & Ogden, 1980). The Python large integer type (F# also offers such integers) is one illustration of such an integer data type which is not funded either by hardware. This kind of value's length is unbounded. When doing integer multiplication in Python, numbers that are too big to be stored as int form values are instead stored as long integer value variables. Sign-intensity notation, wherein the sign bit is changed to signify negative, and the remaining bit of a binary string denotes the actual value of both numbers, may be used to store negative integers. But computer mathematics does not work well with the sign-magnitude language. Nowadays, the majority of systems store negative numbers using the twos complements notation since it makes additive inverse easier (Bobrow & Raphael, 1974). In addition to the rational complements of the positive's version of the numbers in two-digit notation, a negatives integer is represented. Some systems still utilize the individual's notation. The logical complements of an integer's exact amount are used to represent its negatives in the ones-complement format. The drawback of individual notation would be that it contains two interpretations of zero. For information on integer formats, see any textbook on assembler programming languages (Selinger, 2004; Liu et al., 2020).

Did you Know?

In JavaScript, the type of operator returns "object" for null values. This is a known quirk of the language.

3.1.1.2. Floating-Point

Actual figures are modelled by flying data types; however, the representations are simply an approximation of so many true values. For instance, the basic numbers p and e, which serve as the foundation for natural log, cannot be accurately expressed in floating-point format. No limited amount of memory storage can accurately represent any one of these values. The issue is made worse by the fact that floating-point values are often stored as binary on most systems. A limited amount of binary digits cannot, for instance, represent the numerical number 0.1. Accuracy loss during arithmetic is a further issue with floating-point types. Consult any textbook on numerical methods for further details on the issues with floating-point language (Guttag et al., 1978; Blanchette et al., 2015).

The form used to express floating-point numbers, which are taken from chemical equations, consists of fractions and exponents. Desktop computers represented floating-point numbers in several ways. Conversely, the IEEE Floating-Point Standards 754 format is used by the majority of more recent computers. The hardware-supported representation is used by language implementors. The two floating-point kinds most often seen in languages are float and double. The float type, which typically occupies four bytes of data, is the normal measurement. When greater fraction parts and/or a wider range of exponent are required, a double type is offered.

Variables with double precision often need twice quite so much memory as float parameters and offer at least four times as many fractional bits (Cleaveland, 1980; Leivant, 1983).

A floating-point subtype accuracy and ranges are used to specify the set of values it may represent. Precision, described as the number of bits, is the correctness of the fractional portion of a value. The range combines the range for the exponent and, more significantly, the range for fractions (Gries & Gehani, 1977).

The IEEE Floating-Point Standards 754 style for conventional single and double representations is seen in Figure 3.3 (IEEE, 1985). Tanenbaum provides information on the IEEE formats (2005).

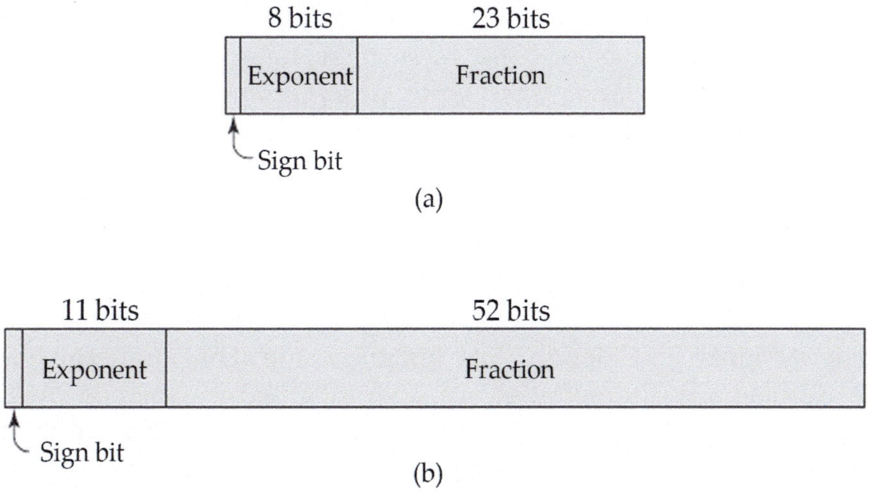

Figure 3.3. Illustration of single-precision and double-precision IEEE floating-formats.

Source: Ayusharma, Creative Commons License.

3.1.2. Boolean Types

Perhaps the most straightforward types are Boolean kinds. They only have two items in their value range: one is true and another false. Since their introduction in ALGOL 60, variables have been present in the majority of broad-sense languages created since that time. C89 is a well-known example of an exception when numerical expressions are utilized as conditional expressions. In these formulations, zero is regarded as false and all processing elements with nonzero numbers as true. Despite having a Boolean class, C99 and C++ also permit the usage of numerical expressions in the same manner as Booleans. In contrast, Java and C# are the next two languages (Demers et al., 1978; Hayward, 1986).

Programs frequently express switching or flags using Boolean types. The usage of Boolean types is much more understandable than using other kinds, including such integers, which could be used for these reasons. A Boolean meaning might well be represented bit, but since many computers could read a single bit of storage effectively, they are frequently kept inside the shortest cell of storage that can be addressed efficiently, generally a byte (Beeri & Ta-Shma, 1994).

Did you Know?

In some programming languages, one can use algebraic data types to define complex data structures that can hold multiple values of different types.

3.1.3. Character Types

Computers save textual data as numerical codings. The 8-bit ASCII (American Standard Code for Information Interchange) code, which employs the numbers 0 to 127 to represent 128 distinct characters, was historically the most widely used encoding. Another 8-bit character code is ISO 8859-1, although this one support 256 distinct characters. The ASCII character set was no longer sufficient for globalization of the commerce and the requirement for computers to interact with one another globally. In 1991, the Unicode Consortium released the UCS-2 standard, a 16-bit character set, as a reaction. This character set is sometimes known as Unicode. The majority of natural languages spoken in the world have symbols in Unicode. For instance, the Thai numerals and the Serbian Cyrillic alphabet are both included in Unicode. ASCII and Unicode have the same first 128 characters. The very first language to utilize the Unicode coding system was Java. Since then, it has migrated into Perl, JavaScript, and Python (Deschamp, 1982; Jansson & Jeuring, 1997).

3.2. CHARACTER STRING TYPES

A characters string category is one whose values are collections of individual characters. All types of data are frequently entered and produced in form of strings, and characters and strings variables are used to name the output. Naturally, character strings are also a crucial type for any applications that work with characters (Ambler & Hoch, 1977; Kaki et al., 2019).

3.2.1. Design Issues

The following are the two most significant design considerations that are particular to characters string types:

i. Should string be treated as a basic type or a specific class of character arrays? and
ii. Should string lengths be static or dynamic?

3.2.2. Strings and Their Operations

Assignments, catenation, substring referencing, comparing, and pattern recognition are the most used string actions. A connection to just a substring of the given text is known as a segment reference. In the broader context of an array, in which the string references are referred to as sliced, substring references are explored. In general, the availability of string arithmetic operations with variable lengths makes assignments and comparison procedures on special characters more challenging. What occurs, for instance, whenever a longer string gets allocated to a smaller string or the other way around? Even though these decisions are often straightforward and reasonable, programmers frequently have problems remembering these (Weihl, 1989; Egi & Nishiwaki, 2018).

Pattern matching is just a function that certain languages natively provide. In others, a method or class library offers it. String data is often kept in an array of individual characters and referred to as being in the language if strings aren't declared as basic types. This is the method used by C and C++ for storing strings in character arrays.

These languages' native libraries include several programming constructs. The tradition that character strings be ended with such a special character, null, which would be represented by zero, is used by many consumers of strings and also many utility functions (Lewis & Rosen, 1973). This is an option for keeping track of string variable lengths. The library functions just continue till the string being worked on contains the null character. Frequently, library methods that generate strings provide the null character. The compiler additionally includes the null characters within-characters string regular expressions that are created. Think about the statement that follows, for instance:

```
char str[] = “apples”;
```

In this case, apples0, wherein 0 is the null symbol, is a member of the char array str. The most popular library features for character strings throughout C and C++ include strcpy, which also moves strings, a line indicating, which catenates person provided string onto the other, strcmp, which also lexicographically relates two given strings (by the sequence of their personality codes), and strlen, which gives the total set of characters inside the text sequence, excluding null characters. Many string processing functions use char references that refer to char arrays as their arguments and results of the tests. String literals are another kind of parameter (Musser, 1980; Jones et al., 2019).

The Conduction mechanism library's string manipulating routines, which are also accessible in C++, are intrinsically unsafe and also have caused a lot of programming mistakes. The issue would be that this library's methods for moving data types do not prevent the destination from overflowing. Think about the strcpy call strcpy(dest, source); for instance.

Strcpy would write from over 30 bytes after dest if dest is 20 bytes long and src is 50 bytes long. The issue is that because strcpy is unable to find the size of the dest, it cannot guarantee that the storage after it won't be overwritten. Several additional functions in the C string package are susceptible to the same issue. C++ provides strings in addition to C-style strings via its regular economy library, which is comparable to Java's. C++ developers should utilize the string classes from the standard library instead of char arrays as well as the C string library due to the weaknesses of a C string library (Morris, 1973; LaLonde, 1989).

The String type in Java, which contents are fixed characters, and the StringBuffer class, which values are variable and much more like arrays containing individual characters, both support strings. The StringBuffer group's methods are used to provide these values. String types in C# and Ruby are comparable to those who are in Java. Python offers operations like substring referencing, catenation, and indexes to access different personalities, as well as techniques for finding and replacements. Strings are also included as a basic type. A feature association procedure is also available for strings. Thus, even though Python's strings are basic types, they behave just like character arrays for characters as well as substring accesses. But unlike Java's String class objects, Python strings are permanent. Strings are a class in F#. Access to and not a modification of single Unicode UTF-16 characters is possible (MacLennan, 1982; Broy et al., 1987).

The + operator may be used to join strings together. A string is a basic unchanging type in ML. It has methods for accessing substrings and determining a string's size, so it employs the catenation operator. Pattern-matching procedures are built into Perl, JavaScript, Ruby, and PHP (Dahlhaus & Makowsky, 1986; Yakushev et al., 2009).

The pattern-matching phrases in such languages are partially based on prepared statements in mathematics. In reality, regular expressions are a common name for them. To become a component of the UNIX shell languages, they developed from the first UNIX line editing, ed. They eventually developed into their present-day sophisticated form. At least one comprehensive book is available on these pattern-matching phrases (Friedl, 2006). Through two rather straightforward examples, we provide a quick overview of the structure of these phrases in just this section. Think about the following pattern:

```
/[A-Za-z][A-Za-z\d]+/
```

This pattern resembles (or describes) the traditional programming language naming form. Character classes are enclosed in brackets. All letters are provided in the first symbol class, as well as all letters and numerals are defined in the second (a digit is specified with the abbreviation \d). We would be unable to stop a name from starting with a number if just the second characters type was present. The second category's addition operator indicates that there should be either one of the items in the group. The entire pattern, therefore, matches sequences that start with a letter and then include one or more additional letters or numbers (Gruver et al., 1984; Weihl & Liskov, 1985).

Now have a look at the next pattern expression:

```
/\d+\.?\d*|\.\d+/
```

This pattern corresponds to literal numbers. The literal decimal point is shown by the 0.3 and what follows is quantified by the question mark as appearing either once or not at all. Two options in the entire pattern are separated by a vertical bar (|). The second choice matches strings that start with such a decimal place, following through one or even more digits. The very first alternative matching strings that include one or even more digits, perhaps followed by such a decimal place, followed by zero or even more digits. Regular expressions have been used to match patterns in the libraries and tools of C++, Java, Python, C#, and F# (Pratt et al., 1984; Mehlhorn & Näher, 1989).

ACTIVITY 3.1:

Create a program that demonstrates the difference between an integer and a float/ double data type. Write a program that performs some arithmetic operations on integer and float values and observes the difference in the output.

3.3. SUMMARY

In programming, data types refer to the different types of data that can be used in a program. They determine the values that a variable can take and the operations that can be performed on those values. Integer is a data type that represents whole numbers without whole numbers. Float/Double data types represent real numbers with decimal points. Boolean data type is commonly used in conditional statements and loops and represents a value that is either true or false. Character represents a single character and array represents a collection of values of the same data type. Object is a data type that represents an instance of a class, which is a user-defined data type that contains data members and member functions.

REVIEW QUESTIONS

1. What is a data type in programming?
2. What are some common types in programming?
3. What is the difference between an integer and a float/double data type?
4. What is a Boolean data type used for?
5. What is the difference between a character and a string data type?
6. What happens if you try to perform an operation on values with incompatible data types?

MULTIPLE CHOICE QUESTIONS

1. Which data type represents whole numbers without any decimal points?

a. Float
b. Double
c. Integer
d. Character

2. Which data type represents real numbers with decimal points?

a. Integer
b. String
c. Float
d. Object

3. Which data type represents a value that is either true or false?

a. Integer
b. Boolean
c. String
d. Character

4. Which data type represents an instance of a class?

a. Integer

b. String

c. Object

d. Float

Answers to Multiple Choice Questions

1. (c); 2. (c); 3. (b); 4. (c)

REFERENCES

1. Almeida, P. S., (1997). Balloon types: Controlling sharing of state in data types. In: *European Conference on Object-Oriented Programming* (pp. 32–59). Springer, Berlin, Heidelberg.
2. Ambler, A. L., & Hoch, C. G., (1977). A study of protection in programming languages. *ACM SIGOPS Operating Systems Review, 11*(2), 25–40.
3. Appleby, D., & VandeKopple, J. J., (1991). *Programming Languages* (Vol. 3). Tata McGraw-Hill.
4. Atkinson, M. P., & Buneman, O. P., (1987). Types and persistence in database programming languages. *ACM Computing Surveys (CSUR), 19*(2), 105–170.
5. Beeri, C., & Ta-Shma, P., (1994). Bulk data types, a theoretical approach. In: *Database Programming Languages (DBPL-4)* (pp. 80–96). Springer, London.
6. Bergstra, J. A., & Tucker, J. V., (1983). Hoare's logic for programming languages with two data types. *Theoretical Computer Science, 28*(1, 2), 215–221.
7. Blanchette, J. C., Popescu, A., & Traytel, D., (2015). Witnessing (co) datatypes. In: *European Symposium on Programming Languages and Systems* (pp. 359–382). Springer, Berlin, Heidelberg.
8. Bobrow, D. G., & Raphael, B., (1974). New programming languages for artificial intelligence research. *ACM Computing Surveys (CSUR), 6*(3), 153–174.
9. Broy, M., Wirsing, M., & Pepper, P., (1987). On the algebraic definition of programming languages. *ACM Transactions on Programming Languages and Systems (TOPLAS), 9*(1), 54–99.
10. Bruce, K. B., (1996). Progress in programming languages. *ACM Computing Surveys (CSUR), 28*(1), 245–247.
11. Cave, A., & Pientka, B., (2012). Programming with binders and indexed data-types. In: *Proceedings of the 39th Annual ACM SIGPLAN-SIGACT Symposium on Principles of Programming Languages* (pp. 413–424).

12. Cleaveland, J. C., (1980). Programming languages considered as abstract data types. In: *Proceedings of the ACM 1980 Annual Conference* (pp. 236–245).
13. Dahlhaus, E., & Makowsky, J. A., (1986). The choice of programming primitives for SETL-like programming languages. In: *European Symposium on Programming* (pp. 160–172). Springer, Berlin, Heidelberg.
14. Demers, A. J., & Donahue, J. E., (1980). Data types, parameters and type checking. In: *Proceedings of the 7th ACM SIGPLAN-SIGACT Symposium on Principles of Programming Languages* (pp. 12–23).
15. Demers, A., Donahue, J., & Skinner, G., (1978). Data types as values: Polymorphism, type-checking, encapsulation. In: *Proceedings of the 5th ACM SIGACT-SIGPLAN Symposium on Principles of Programming Languages* (pp. 23–30).
16. Deschamp, P., (1982). Perluette: A compilers producing system using abstract data types. In: *International Symposium on Programming* (pp. 63–77). Springer, Berlin, Heidelberg.
17. Donahue, J., & Demers, A., (1985). Data types are values. *ACM Transactions on Programming Languages and Systems (TOPLAS), 7*(3), 426–445.
18. Egi, S., & Nishiwaki, Y., (2018). Non-linear pattern matching with backtracking for non-free data types. In: *Asian Symposium on Programming Languages and Systems* (pp. 3–23). Springer, Cham.
19. Ernst, G. W., & Ogden, W. F., (1980). Specification of abstract data types in MODULA. *ACM Transactions on Programming Languages and Systems (TOPLAS), 2*(4), 522–543.
20. Fegaras, L., & Sheard, T., (1996). Revisiting catamorphisms over datatypes with embedded functions (or, programs from outer space). In: *Proceedings of the 23rd ACM SIGPLAN-SIGACT Symposium on Principles of Programming Languages* (pp. 284–294).
21. Garland, S. J., & Guttag, J. V., (1988). Inductive methods for reasoning about abstract data types. In: *Proceedings of the 15th ACM SIGPLAN-SIGACT Symposium on Principles of Programming Languages* (pp. 219–228).
22. Gries, D., & Gehani, N., (1977). Some ideas on data types in high-level languages. *Communications of the ACM, 20*(6), 414–420.
23. Gruver, W. A., Soroka, B. I., Craig, J. J., & Turner, T. L., (1984). Industrial robot programming languages: A comparative evaluation. *IEEE Transactions on Systems, Man, and Cybernetics*, (4), 565–570.
24. Guttag, J. V., Horowitz, E., & Musser, D. R., (1978). Abstract data types and software validation. *Communications of the ACM, 21*(12), 1048–1064.
25. Guttag, J., (1977). Abstract data types and the development of data structures. *Communications of the ACM, 20*(6), 396–404.
26. Hayward, V., (1986). Compared anatomy of the programming languages Pascal and C. *ACM SIGPLAN Notices, 21*(5), 50–60.

27. Herlihy, M. P., & Liskov, B., (1982). A value transmission method for abstract data types. *ACM Transactions on Programming Languages and Systems (TOPLAS), 4*(4), 527–551.

28. Jansson, P., & Jeuring, J., (1997). PolyP—A polytypic programming language extension. In: *Proceedings of the 24th ACM SIGPLAN-SIGACT Symposium on Principles of Programming Languages* (pp. 470–482).

29. Jones, M. P., Morris, J. G., & Eisenberg, R. A., (2019). Partial type constructors: Or, making ad hoc datatypes less ad hoc. *Proceedings of the ACM on Programming Languages, 4*(POPL), 1–28.

30. Jorrand, P., (1971). Data types and extensible languages. *ACM Sigplan Notices, 6*(12), 75–83.

31. Kaki, G., Priya, S., Sivaramakrishnan, K. C., & Jagannathan, S., (2019). Mergeable replicated data types. *Proceedings of the ACM on Programming Languages, 3*(OOPSLA), 1–29.

32. Kamin, S., (1983). Final data types and their specification. *ACM Transactions on Programming Languages and Systems (TOPLAS), 5*(1), 97–121.

33. LaLonde, W. R., (1989). Designing families of data types using exemplars. *ACM Transactions on Programming Languages and Systems (TOPLAS), 11*(2), 212–248.

34. Läufer, K., & Odersky, M., (1994). Polymorphic type inference and abstract data types. *ACM Transactions on Programming Languages and Systems (TOPLAS), 16*(5), 1411–1430.

35. Leivant, D., (1983). Structural semantics for polymorphic data types (preliminary report). In: *Proceedings of the 10th ACM SIGACT-SIGPLAN Symposium on Principles of Programming Languages* (pp. 155–166).

36. Lewis, C. H., & Rosen, B. K., (1973). Recursively defined data types: Part 1. In: *Proceedings of the 1st Annual ACM SIGACT-SIGPLAN Symposium on Principles of Programming Languages* (pp. 125–138).

37. Liskov, B., & Zilles, S., (1974). Programming with abstract data types. *ACM Sigplan Notices, 9*(4), 50–59.

38. Liu, Y., Parker, J., Redmond, P., Kuper, L., Hicks, M., & Vazou, N., (2020). Verifying replicated data types with type class refinements in liquid Haskell. *Proceedings of the ACM on Programming Languages, 4*(OOPSLA), 1–30.

39. MacLennan, B. J., (1982). Values and objects in programming languages. *ACM SIGPLAN Notices, 17*(12), 70–79.

40. Mallgren, W. R., (1982). Formal specification of graphic data types. *ACM Transactions on Programming Languages and Systems (TOPLAS), 4*(4), 687–710.

41. Mehlhorn, K., & Näher, S., (1989). LEDA a library of efficient data types and algorithms. In: *International Symposium on Mathematical Foundations of Computer Science* (pp. 88–106). Springer, Berlin, Heidelberg.

42. Mitchell, J. C., (1996). *Foundations for Programming Languages* (Vol. 1, pp.1-5). Cambridge: MIT press.
43. Morris, J. G., & McKinna, J., (2019). Abstracting extensible data types: Or, rows by any other name. *Proceedings of the ACM on Programming Languages, 3*(POPL), 1–28.
44. Morris, Jr. J. H., (1973). Protection in programming languages. *Communications of the ACM, 16*(1), 15–21.
45. Musser, D. R., (1980). On proving inductive properties of abstract data types. In: *Proceedings of the 7th ACM SIGPLAN-SIGACT Symposium on Principles of Programming Languages* (pp. 154–162).
46. Myers, E. W., (1984). Efficient applicative data types. In: *Proceedings of the 11th ACM SIGACT-SIGPLAN Symposium on Principles of Programming Languages* (pp. 66–75).
47. Pratt, T. W., Zelkowitz, M. V., & Gopal, T. V., (1984). *Programming Languages: Design and Implementation* (No. 04; QA76. 7, P8 1984.). Englewood Cliffs, NJ: Prentice-Hall.
48. Scott, D., (1976). Data types as lattices. *Siam Journal on Computing, 5*(3), 522–587.
49. Sekiyama, T., Nishida, Y., & Igarashi, A., (2015). Manifest contracts for datatypes. In: *Proceedings of the 42nd Annual ACM SIGPLAN-SIGACT Symposium on Principles of Programming Languages* (pp. 195–207).
50. Selinger, P., (2004). A brief survey of quantum programming languages. In: *International Symposium on Functional and Logic Programming* (pp. 1–6). Springer, Berlin, Heidelberg.
51. Singh, R., & Gulwani, S., (2016). Transforming spreadsheet data types using examples. In: *Proceedings of the 43rd Annual ACM SIGPLAN-SIGACT Symposium on Principles of Programming Languages* (pp. 343–356).
52. Swierstra, W., (2008). Data types à la carte. *Journal of Functional Programming, 18*(4), 423–436.
53. Weihl, W. E., (1989). Local atomicity properties: Modular concurrency control for abstract data types. *ACM Transactions on Programming Languages and Systems (TOPLAS), 11*(2), 249–282.
54. Weihl, W., & Liskov, B., (1985). Implementation of resilient, atomic data types. *ACM Transactions on Programming Languages and Systems (TOPLAS), 7*(2), 244–269.
55. Yakushev, A. R., Holdermans, S., Löh, A., & Jeuring, J., (2009). Generic programming with fixed points for mutually recursive datatypes. *ACM Sigplan Notices, 44*(9), 233–244.

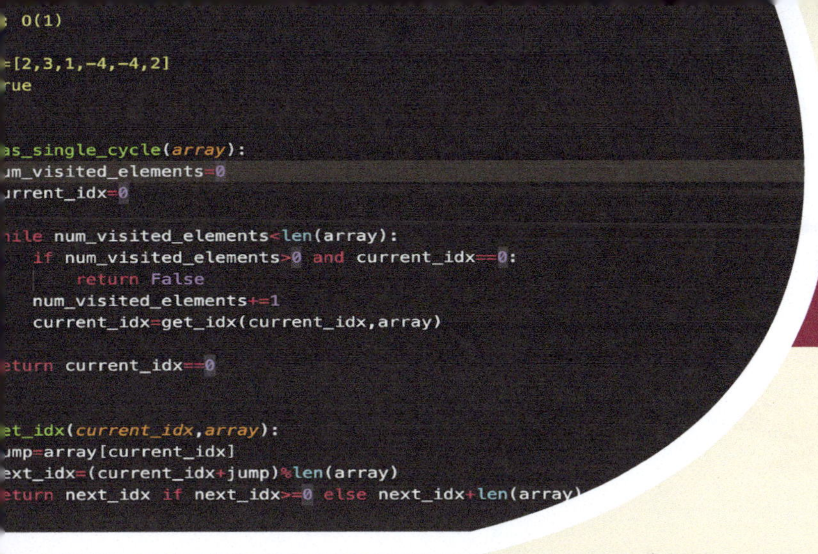

CHAPTER 4

ALGORITHMS AND DATA STRUCTURES IN PROGRAMMING

UNIT INTRODUCTION

An algorithm is a well-described computational process that accepts every value, or set of values, as input and outputs any value or set of values. As a result, an algorithm is a set of computing procedures that changes any input into an output. A further way to think about an algorithm is as a tool for solving a well-defined computing issue (Aggarwal & Vitter, 1988; Agrawal et al., 2004). Generally, the issue description presupposes the intended relationship between outputs and inputs, but the algorithm specifies a specific computing procedure for attaining that relationship.

Sorting is considered a basic step in computer science since it is helpful as an intermediary step in many applications. As a result, access to a huge variety of effective sorting algorithms is available (Ahuja & Orlin, 1989; Ahuja et al., 1989). The best algorithm for any specific application is determined by various factors, including the different items to be organized, the degree whereby the items are slightly organized, the computer architecture, potential item value limitations, and the kind of storage devices to be utilized: disks, main memory, or tapes.

When an algorithm halts with the appropriate output for each input example, it is thought to be appropriate. A proper algorithm solves the stated computing issue. An erroneous algorithm, on either side, cannot halt at all on certain input examples, or it can halt with an inaccurate response (Ahuja et al., 1989; Courcoubetis et al., 1992). In contrast to assumptions, erroneous algorithms may occasionally be advantageous if the rate of mistake may be controlled. Therefore, only accurate algorithms will be of concern (Szymanski & Van Wyk, 1983; King, 1995; Didier, 2009) (Figure 4.1).

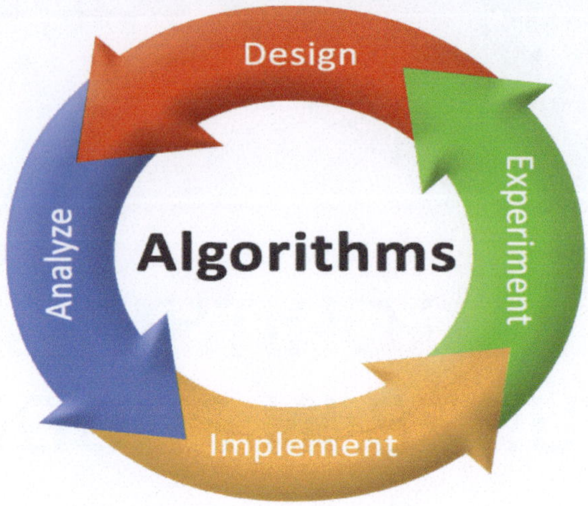

Figure 4.1. Illustration of algorithms' basic structure and overview.

Source: Tim Roughgarden, Creative Commons License.

An algorithm may be written in English, in the format of a computer program, or even as a hardware design. The only criterion is that the problem definition must include a clear description of the computational procedure to be used (Snyder, 1984). The following are the features of an algorithm:

- Each instruction should take an indefinite amount of time to complete.
- Almost every instruction should be explicit and accurate, that is, each instruction must have just one meaning.
- The consumer must get the expected outcomes after following the directions.
- There must be no unlimited repeating of a single or several instructions, implying that the algorithm must eventually finish.

Data structure is how data is organized in a computer's memory (or sometimes on a disk). Data structures include hash tables, binary trees, linked lists, and stacks. Structures' data are manipulated by algorithms in a variety of ways, for as, by adding new data items, looking for certain items, and sorting the items. An algorithm is similar to a recipe in that it contains a thorough set of directions for performing a task.

What kinds of issues can be resolved with this knowledge? Roughly categorize the instances in which they are helpful into three categories:

- Storage of real-world data;
- Tools for programmers; and

- Modeling.

The structure of data is a methodical strategy to arrange data so that it can be used effectively. Fundamental terms of the data structure are as follows:

- **Interface:** Each data structure has a respective interface. An interface shows the set of operations a data structure can perform, and the data structure is capable of performing. An interface specifies the supported operations, parameter types, and return types for each supported operation.
- **Implementation:** It provides the inner representation of a data structure. The implementation also describes the algorithms used for the data structure operations.

Learning Objectives

Readers will have the chance to understand the following by the chapter's conclusion:

- Understand the fundamental concepts of data structures and algorithms;
- Learn about the issues solved by algorithms and the need for data structures;
- Advantages and disadvantages of different data structures;
- Learn about analyzing algorithms and data structures.

Key Terms

- Algorithms
- Array
- Data item
- Data structures
- Entity
- Field
- File
- Group item
- Linked list
- Queues
- Stacks
- Trees

4.1. ISSUES SOLVED BY ALGORITHMS

Scientists have devised algorithms for a variety of computer problems, including sorting. Algorithms have a broad range of practical usage across the world. The following are certain such instances:

Did you Know?

The origins of algorithms can be traced back to ancient Babylonians, who used mathematical algorithms to solve problems related to commerce, trade and taxation.

i. The Human Genome Project are made tremendous progress in recent years toward the goal of classifying all 1,00,000 genes found in the DNA of humans, specifying the sequences of the 3 billion chemical base pairs that make up human DNA, storing this massive amount of information in databases, and developing data analysis techniques. Each procedure necessitates the use of complex algorithms. Several strategies for solving such biological challenges use various principles, allowing scientists to complete jobs while maximizing resource use (Aki, 1989; Akra & Bazzi, 1998). We may obtain more data from laboratory procedures, which saves us time, both machine and human, and money (Regli, 1992; Ajtai et al., 2001).

ii. The internet allows individuals worldwide to swiftly access and recover vast amounts of data. Various websites on the Internet handle and utilize this massive amount of data with the help of intelligent algorithms. Identifying effective paths for data to go and utilizing a search engine that may rapidly identify sites with our exact necessary information are two instances of challenges that fundamentally make utilization of various algorithms (Alon, 1990).

iii. It allows to negotiate and electronically trade services and things, which is a major advantage of electronic commerce. It is reliant upon the confidentiality of personal data such as details of credit card, keywords, and statements of bank to function properly. Public-key cryptography and digital signs are two of the essential technologies which are used in electronic commerce, and they are both important. Numerical algorithms and numeral theory are the foundations of such technologies (Andersson & Thorup, 2000; Bakker et al., 2012).

iv. Manufacturing and a variety of other commercial activities occasionally demand the allocation of scarce sources in the most advantageous manner. For example, an oil firm would want to determine where it must locate its wells to maximize the amount of profit it expects to make. Assigning crews to flights in the most cost-effective way feasible while ensuring that every trip is covered and that all applicable government laws regarding the scheduling of the crew are met is something an airline would aspire to do (Ramadge & Wonham, 1989; Amir et al., 2006). Certain political candidates may be faced with the decision of where to spend their money when purchasing campaign advertising to increase their chances of winning the election. An ISP (internet service provider) may be interested in knowing where they might put extra resources to better satisfy their customers' needs. All of the issues are instances of problems that may be handled by applying linear programming techniques (Dengiz et al., 1997; Berger & Barkaoui, 2004) (Figure 4.2).

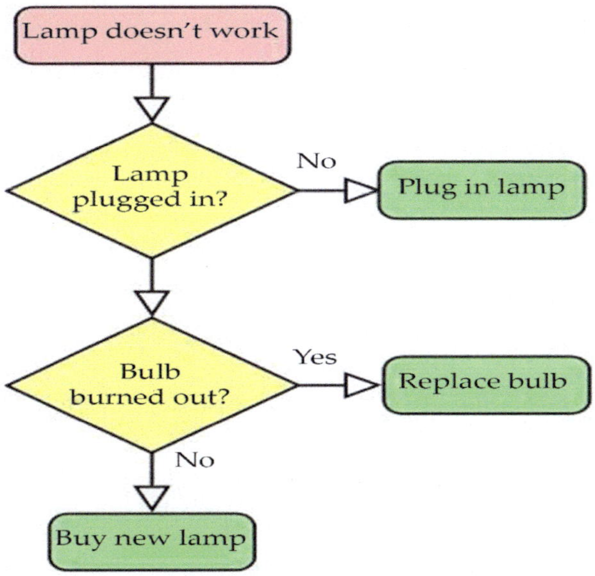

Figure 4.2. Flowchart of algorithm application.

Source: JT Newsome, Creative Commons License.

The basic approaches that imply to such difficulties and problem regions will be discussed. We'll look at ways to tackle a variety of specific issues, such as the ones listed below:

i. Assume there exists a detailed plan with the distance among each set of two intersections noted, and the quickest path from one intersection to the next needs to be discovered. Even if we ban routes from crossing over themselves, there might be a tremendous number of viable paths (Festa & Resende, 2002; Zhu & Wilhelm, 2006). How do you pick the fastest of all the available paths in this scenario? In this case, the plan will be described as a graph and then seek the shortest path between the graph's vertex points.

ii. Suppose that there are 2 systematic orders of symbols, X= $(x_1, x_2..., x_m)$ and Y= $(y_1, y_2, ..., y_n)$ as well as the largest communal subsequence of 'Y' and 'X' is to be discovered. A subsequence of 'X' would comprise 'X' minus with some (or all) of its components removed. One subsequence of (A, B, C, D, E, F, G, H, I) is, for example (B, C, E, G). The length of shared subsequence of 'X' and 'Y' determines the degree of similarity between the 2 sequences. For instance, if the 2 orders under consideration are basic pairs in the strands of DNA, they can be chosen to consider the same because a lengthy ordinary subsequence is shared. If 'X' has m symbols and 'Y' has n symbols, then there are 2^m and 2^n possible subsequences for 'X' and 'Y,' correspondingly. Unless both m and n are very tiny, choosing all probable subsequences of 'X' and 'Y' and then by matching it can take an excessive amount of time (Wallace et al., 2004; Wang, 2008).

iii. We are presented with a mechanical design for a library of components. Every component may include examples of other components, and we are obligated to mention the components in the order in which they are used so that every component appears before any other component that includes that component (Maurer, 1985; Smith, 1986). Assuming that the design has n pieces, then there would be nŠ alternative ordering, where the number nŠ represents the factorial function of the design. Since the factorial function increases more quickly as compared to an exponential function, this is not viable for us to produce every potential order and afterwards carry out its validation inside that order in such a way that every component comes before the components that are utilizing it. A problem of this nature is an example of topological sorting (Herr, 1980; Stock & Watson, 2001).

iv. In this case, let us suppose we have been given n points in the plane, and we want to discover the convex hull of such points, which is the small convex polygon encompassing the points in the plane. Immediately, we may believe of every point as being distinguished by the presence of a nail penetrating through a piece of cardboard. The convex hull will be indicated through a tight rubber band that surrounds all of the nails at this point. In the convex hull, every nail about which the rubber band makes a turn is represented by one of its vertices. As a result, every of the 2^n subsets of the points may be used as the vertices of the convex hull. Knowing the points that are vertices of the convex hull is not sufficient in this case; we also require to be familiar with the sequence in which they occur on the convex hull. Because of this, a variety of options for the convex hull vertices are accessible to the user (Price, 1973; Berry & Howls, 2012).

These lists have two characteristics with a wide range of exciting algorithmic problems:

i. They have many potential solutions, a large percentage of which fail to fix the problem. Identifying the "best" solution or the one that addresses the problem might be difficult (Arora, 1994).

ii. The majority of them have real-world applicability. Finding the shortest route was the simplest of the issues described above. Any transport organization, including a shipping company or a railroad, has a financial incentive to locate the shortest route via a road or a rail network because shorter routes result in cheaper labor and fuel costs (Bellare & Sudan, 1994; Friedl & Sudan, 1995). A routing node on the Internet, for example, could want to find the quickest way by the network so that a message can be routed quickly. Alternatively, someone going from Washington to Chicago may choose to get driving directions from a reliable website or use his or her GPS while driving (Sudan, 1992; Arora & Lund, 1996).

iii. It isn't required for every issue to be addressed by algorithms because a collection of contender solutions may be easily discovered. Consider the case when we are given a set of numerical figures that show signal specimens. We'd want to calculate the discrete DFT of such data right now (Fredman & Willard, 1993; Raman, 1996). The DFT translates the domain of time into the domain of frequency by creating a set of numeric coefficients, allowing us to specify the intensity of distinct frequencies in the sampled signal. Apart from being at the heart of signal processing, DFT has extensive applications in the compression of data, and multiplication of huge integers and polynomials (Polishchuk & Spielman, 1994; Thorup, 1997).

Did you Know?

The concept of data structures can be traced back to the 1940s, when John von Neumann introduced the concept of a stored program computer.

4.2. DATA STRUCTURES

A data structure is a method of storing and arranging information to make it easier to modify and access. No one data structure generally works fine for all applications, therefore it's significant to understand the benefits and drawbacks of some of them (Brodnik et al., 1997). The following are the features of data structures:

1. **Correctness:** A data structure must implement its interface correctly.
2. **Time Complexity:** The execution of data structure operations must be as brief as possible.
3. **Space Complexity:** A data structure action should use the least memory available.

4.2.1. Data Structure's Need

As applications become increasingly complex and data-rich, they frequently encounter three problems.

i. Consider a store's inventory that contains 1 million (106) items. The application has to browse over 1 million (106) items each time an item has to be searched, thus slowing the process of searching. As the data amount increases, the search will get slower.

ii. Processor speed – although the CPU can handle billions of data records, its speed is restricted.

iii. Multiple requests – due to numerous data queries of tens of thousands of users on a web server, even a speedy server will occasionally fail.

Data structures come to the rescue to address the issues mentioned above. Searching through every item in the data structure may not be necessary because the necessary data can be found fairly immediately.

4.2.2. Execution Time Cases

Three scenarios are typically used to compare the relative execution times of different data structures:

1. **Worst Case:** A data structure action uses all its available processing power. An operation requires no more compared to (n) time if the worst-case duration is (n), in which (n) is a function of n.
2. **Average Case:** This illustrates how long the data structure operation usually takes. If an operation requires n seconds to complete, then m operations will require m × n seconds.
3. **Best Case:** This is when an operation on a data structure is executed quickly. When an operation takes n seconds to complete, the total time required for the procedure could be as high as n (n).

4.2.3. Basic Terminologies

Following are definition of some of the terminologies used in data structures:

1. **Data:** It is a value and collection of values.
2. **Data Item:** It refers to a distinct element of values.
3. **Group Items:** The data object is broken down into smaller things.
4. **Elementary Items:** Non-splitable data elements are elementary objects.
5. **Entity and Attribute:** Entity has specific properties or characteristics that can have values applied to them.

6. **Entity Set:** It comprises entities with related attributes.
7. **Field:** A single basic informational unit that represents a property of an entity.
8. **Record:** It groups a particular entity's field values.
9. **File:** It is a collection of documents for entities in a particular entity set.

4.2.4. Overview of Data Structures

Considering data structures in terms of their advantages and disadvantages is another perspective. The key data storage structures covered are summarized in a table in this section. This is a birds-eye perspective of a terrain that will be explored later from the ground. The benefits and drawbacks of all of the data structures discussed in this book are shown in Table 4.1.

Table 4.1. Benefits and Drawbacks of Different Data Structures

Data Structure	Advantages	Disadvantages
Array	Quick insertion and access if the index are known.	Slow deletion, slow search, and fixed size.
Ordered array	Quicker than an unsorted array for searching.	Fixed-size, slow deletion, an insertion.
Stack	Access is last-in, first-out.	Accessing other objects slowly.
Queue	Gives access on a first-in, first-out basis.	Accessing other objects slowly.
Linked list	Quick addition and deletion.	Search slowly.
Binary tree	Quick insertion, search, and deletion (if the tree remains balanced).	Complex deletion algorithm.
Hash table	Fast access if the key is known. Speedy insertion.	Slow deletion, sluggish access if the key is unknown, and inefficient memory consumption.
Heap	Access to the largest item and quick insertion and deletion.	Accessing other objects slowly.

Source: Robert Lafore, Creative Commons License.

4.2.5. Hard Problems

Talking when it comes to efficient algorithms, the most commonly used metric for efficiency is speed, which is defined as the amount of time it takes for an algorithm to output its consequence. Furthermore, there have been a few situations for which there is ineffective solution at any given point in time. It is considered worthwhile to study problems with NP (nondeterministic polynomial time) solutions for 2 main reasons (Phillips & Westbrook, 1993; Ciurea & Ciupala, 2001). Firstly, even if there has not yet been discovered an efficient algorithm for an NP-complete issue, no single individual has ever demonstrated that an efficient algorithm for this problem can't be discovered. Nobody knows whether or whether not there are any effective algorithms available for NP-complete problems, which is a true statement. As a second point, there is an interesting feature of a collection of NP-complete problems in that if an efficient algorithm emerges for any one of them, then such an effective algorithm would exist for all of them as well (Cheriyan & Hagerup, 1989, 1995). Because of the link among NP-complete issues and the absence of effective solutions, the lack of effective solutions becomes even more frustrating. Third, multiple NP-complete problems are comparable to each other, but they are not similar to the issues for which we already have effective algorithms. Computer professionals are fascinated by the fact that a slight modification in the issue description may result in a significant difference in the competency of the most well-known algorithm in the world (Cheriyan et al., 1990, 1996).

It is important to be conversant with NP-complete issues since certain of them emerge unexpectedly frequently in real-world applications. Given the fact that you have been tasked with developing an effective algorithm for any NP-complete issue, it is likely that you would waste a significant amount of time in an unproductive pursuit. If on either side, you may demonstrate that the issue is NP-complete, you may devote your attention instead to inventing a proficient algorithm that delivers a decent, but the inefficient solution (Leighton, 1996; Roura, 2001; Drmota & Szpankowski, 2013). Consider the case of a delivery company with a main depot, which is already in existence. Throughout the day, its delivery vehicles are loaded at the depot and then dispatched to different locations to deliver items to customers. Every truck is expected to return to the depot before the end of the day so that it may be prepared for loading the following day's loads (Bentley et al., 1980; Chan, 2000; Yap, 2011). Specifically, the corporation desires to pick a series of delivery stops that results in the shortest total distance travelled by every vehicle to reduce prices. In this issue, which is known as the "travelling-salesman problem," the NP-completeness of the solution has been established. It doesn't have a fast algorithm to work with. Furthermore, given some specific assumptions, we may identify effective algorithms that provide an average distance that is not more than the shortest feasible distance (Shen & Marston, 1995; Verma, 1997).

4.2.6. Parallelism

Over many years, we had been able to depend upon the speed of processor clock increasing at a consistent pace. Even though physical restrictions provide an eventual impediment to ever-increasing clock speeds, the following is true: as with the clock's speed, power density increases super-linearly; as a result, chips are at risk of melting once their clock speeds reach a certain threshold (Meijer & Akl, 1987, 1988). We build circuits with many processing cores to conduct more computations per second and so achieve higher throughput. Such multicore computers may be compared to a large number of sequential computers on a single chip, or we may refer to them as a form of "parallel computer," depending upon your perspective. To get the maximum potential performance out of multicore machines, we should design algorithms with parallelism in mind while developing them. Algorithms that use several cores, like "multithreaded" algorithms, are particularly advantageous. From a theoretical standpoint, this sort of model has significant advantages, and as a result, it serves as the foundation for a large number of successful computer systems (Wilf, 1984).

4.3. ALGORITHMS LIKE A TECHNOLOGY

Assume that computers had been significantly faster than they were now, and their memory had been completely free. May you imagine every other cause to be interested in algorithms at this point? We would still like to explain that our solution ends and does so with an accurate result, therefore the answer remains affirmative. Given the high speed with which computers operate, any exact approach of problem-solving would be rendered ineffective (Igarashi et al., 1987; Park & Oldfield, 1993). You most likely will want your software execution to fall inside the limits of good software engineering practice (for instance, your execution must be well recorded and well designed), although, you are more than likely going to use whatever method is the quickest and most straightforward to put into action (Glasser & Austin Barron, 1983).

Computers can be extremely fast, but they are not capable of becoming indefinitely fast. Similar to that, while their memory can be cheap, it's not completely free. Time for computation is, thus, a finite source, just as memory is a finite resource. It is important to make effective use of such resources, and algorithms that are effective in terms of space or time may assist us in doing so (Wilson, 1991; Buchbinder et al., 2010).

Efficiencies of different algorithms that are created for the solution of the same issue frequently differ significantly in terms of their effectiveness. When compared to the variations resulting from hardware and software, such changes might be far more noticeable (Vanderbei, 1980; Babaioff et al., 2007; Bateni et al., 2010). For greater understanding, consider 2 alternate sorting methods. The 1st is known as insertion sort, and it takes about equivalent to c_1n^2 to sort n items; where c_1 is a constant that is independent of n; this implies that it takes roughly proportionate to n^2. The 2nd technique is known as merge sort, and it takes roughly the same amount of time as $c_2n\lg n$, wherein lgn represents $\log_2 n$ and c_2 is another constant that is independent of n. Insertion sort often is a small constant variable as compared to merge sort, like c_1 is smaller than c_2. We'll see that constant variables have a far less influence on the running duration than the reliance upon the input size n (Aslam, 2001; Du & Atallah, 2001; Eppstein et al., 2005). If we represent the running time of insertion sort as c1n n and the running time of the merge sort algorithm as $c_2n\lg n$, we can see that although insertion sort has a factor of n in its running time, merge sort has a factor of lgn, which is significantly less. Even though insertion sort is normally quicker than merge sort for smaller input sizes, once the size of input n grows large enough, merge sort's benefit of lgn versus n would greater than compensate for the dissimilarity in constant variables. There would always be a crossover point outside of which merge sort is quicker, irrespective of how much smaller c_1 is relative to c_2 (Sardelis &Valahas, 1999; Dickerson et al., 2003).

Did you Know?

The world's first computer algorithm was written by Ada Lovelace, a mathematician and computer programmer who is widely regarded as the world's first computer programmer.

Consider the following scenario: a faster computer (designated as computer A) is conducting insertion sort besides a slower computer (designated as computer B) that is doing merge sort. Every one of them should sort a 10-million-number array that has been given to them. (Although 10 million digits can sound high, given that the numbers are 8-byte integers, the input would only take up around 80 megabytes, which is more than enough space for even a low-cost laptop computer's memory to be filled several times over.) Take, for example, the assumption that computer A is capable of processing 10 billion instructions for one second, while computer B is capable of processing just 10 million instructions per second; this makes computer A one thousand times more powerful than computer B in terms of raw computing capacity (Goodrich et al., 2005). Let us assume that the world's most cunning programmer writes insertion sort for computer A in machine language, and the resultant code needs $2n^2$ instructions to arrange n integers, to emphasize the drastic difference. Furthermore, consider the following scenario: an average programmer applies merge sort by utilizing a higher-level language and an ineffective compiler, and the resultant code requires 50nlgn instructions. Thus, computer A would require the following resources to sort 10 million numbers:

$$\frac{2 \cdot (10^7)^2 \text{ instructions}}{10^{10} \text{ instructions/second}} = 20{,}000 \text{ seconds (more than 5.5 hours)}$$

On the other hand, computer B would take:

$$\frac{50 \cdot 10^7 \lg 10^7 \text{ instructions}}{10^7 \text{ instructions/second}} \approx 1163 \text{ seconds (less than 20 minutes)} .$$

Yet with a poor compiler, computer B would be greater than 17th times quicker than computer Through utilizing an algorithm that running time increases more gradually. When sorting 100 million values, the benefit of merge sort becomes even more apparent: insertion sort would take more than 23 days, but merge sort would take less than 4 hours. Generally, the relative advantage of merge sorting decreases as the size of the problem grows (Eppstein et al., 2008; Acar, 2009).

4.4. ALGORITHMS AND OTHER TECHNOLOGIES

The preceding case demonstrates that algorithms, such as the hardware of computer, must be considered technology. The system's overall performance is determined by both the use of effective algorithms and the use of fast hardware. Algorithms are making fast development in the same way that other computer technologies are (Amtoft et al., 2002; Ausiello et al., 2012). You could wonder if algorithms are genuinely that is significant on modern computers when other sophisticated technologies are taken into account, such as:

- Intuitive, simple graphical user interfaces (GUIs);
- Advanced computer architectures and production technologies;
- Object-oriented systems and object-oriented programming (OOP);
- Wireless and wired networking that is quick;
- Web technologies which are integrated.

Yes, it is correct. Although some programs (such as simple web-based apps) may not need algorithmic content at the utilization level, many others do. Suppose a Web-based service that explains how to go from one area to another (Szymanski, 1975; Aslam, 2001). Such service's implementation will be reliant on a GUI, wide-area networking, fast hardware, and, most likely, object orientation. However, algorithms will be required for specific activities like identifying routes (most likely utilizing a shortest-path method), interpolating addresses, and displaying maps (Bach, 1990; Avidan & Shamir, 2007).

Furthermore, even an application that doesn't need algorithmic data at the application level is heavily reliant on algorithms. Because the application requires fast hardware and the design hardware utilize algorithms. Moreover, the program makes utilize GUIs, which are created using algorithms (Winograd,

1970; Bach & Shallit, 1996). Furthermore, the application might depend on networking, and routing in networks is mostly based on algorithms. If the program is written in a language apart from machine language, it should be processed through a compiler, assembler, or interpreter, each of which employs a variety of algorithms. As a result, we may determine that algorithms are at the heart of nearly all computer technology today (Bailey et al., 1991; Baswana et al., 2002).

Furthermore, with computers' ever-increasing capabilities, we are using them to solve more complicated issues than ever before. As may be observed from the comparison of insertion sort and merge sort, the variations in performance among algorithms become more noticeable in the bigger problem (Bayer, 1972; Arge, 2001; Graefe, 2011). One identifying characteristic that distinguishes professional programmers from newbies is having a firm foundation of algorithmic knowledge and technique. Since we may do a few things with the aid of contemporary computer technologies without knowing anything about algorithms, we may accomplish a lot more with a solid understanding of algorithms (Blasgen et al., 1977).

4.5. ANALYZING DATA STRUCTURES AND ALGORITHMS

We must forecast the resources required by an algorithm during evaluating it. We are often concerned with sources like computer hardware or communication bandwidth, memory, because most of the time, we want to quantify computational time (Frigo et al., 1998; Blumofe & Leiserson, 1999). Identifying the most effective contestant algorithm for a topic is usually done by analyzing multiple contestant algorithms. This form of assessment may reveal more than one feasible candidate; although, we may typically eliminate weaker algorithms throughout the process (Blelloch & Gibbons, 2004).

We need to have an implementation technology model in place before we may perform an algorithm analysis. This model should take into account the technology's resources and its costs. Regarding the implementation technique, we'll use a generic one-processor or the random-access machine (RAM) model of computing. Furthermore, our algorithms would be implemented as computer programs. Every instruction in the RAM model is performed once a time, with no concurrent operations (Brent, 1974; Buhler et al., 1993; Brassard & Bratley, 1996).

The RAM model's instructions, and their charges, should be precisely defined. This effort would not only be arduous but would also provide limited insight into the algorithm's analysis and design. However, extreme caution must be exercised to avoid abusing the RAM model. For instance, if a RAM has a sort of instruction, we may arrange with just one instruction. Moreover, such a RAM is impractical as practical computers lack these instructions (Chen & Davis, 1990; Prechelt, 1993). As a result, we shall concentrate on the design of actual computers. The RAM model incorporates data transfer (store, copy, load,), arithmetic (such as division, multiplication, addition, subtraction, remainder, floor, ceiling, and so on), and control instructions that are commonly found in actual computers (subroutine call and return conditional and unconditional branch). Every instruction requires a set amount of time to complete.

4.5.1. Order of Growth

We may improve our study of the INSERTION-SORT easier by using a few simplifying assumptions. The real cost of every statement may be ignored as a 1st step by utilizing the constants c_i to denote such costs. Afterwards, we'll see that even such constants supply us with more information than we require. The worst-case running time was defined in the preceding sections as an^2 = b n+ C for certain constants a, b, and c that is based on the statement costs c_i. As a result, we may disregard both the abstract costs c_i and the real statement costs.

The sequence or rate of increase of the running time, which we are interested in, is another simplifying assumption that may be created. As a result, we only analyze the leading component of the formula (which is an^2), because the lower-order terms are fairly irrelevant for high values of n. In addition, the constant coefficient of the leading term is ignored since it is less relevant as compared to the rate of increase in finding computing effectiveness for large inputs. In the situation of insertion sort, we only have the n^2 factor from the leading word after discarding the constant coefficient of the leading term and the lower-order terms.

4.5.2. Insertion Sort Analysis

The time needed by the INSERTION-SORT method is mostly dependent on the input: sorting 1,000 numbers, for example, would take significantly longer than sorting 3 numbers. Furthermore, based upon how much each input sequence has been sorted, INSERTION-SORT might take a varied amount of time to arrange 2 input sequences of the similar size. Usually, the time needed by an algorithm grows in proportion to the size of the input, thus it is common to express program execution time as a function of input size. To do so, we need to be more careful in our definitions of "size of input" and "runtime."

The optimum estimate for the amount of the input is based upon the problem under analysis. The most common measure for a variety of issues, like sorting or calculating DFT, is the number of items in the input, for instance, n is the size of the array for arrangement. The whole number of bits necessary to indicate the input in conventional binary notation is the most ideal measure of the size of the input for various additional issues, such as the multiplication of two numbers. Sometimes, it is more appropriate to use two integers rather than one to express the input size. For instance, if an algorithm's input is a graph, the number of vertices and edges in the graph may be used to define the size of the input. For each of the difficulties we've looked at, we'll note to you which input size measures are being used.

The primitive operations or the number of executed steps determines an algorithm's *running time* for a given input. It is necessary to define the step idea in such a way that it is machine independent. Let us adopt the following viewpoint for the time being. A fixed sum of time is needed to implement every line of our pseudocode. Even though the time necessary to execute one line can vary from the time needed to execute another, we would suppose that every implementation of the ith line takes a constant amount of time equivalent to c_i. Such viewpoint is consistent with the RAM model, and it also illustrates how pseudo is implemented on the vast majority of real computers.

The next demonstration looks at the progression of the equation that is utilized to calculate the INSERTION-SORT running time. From a complicated formula that makes usage of all of the statement costs (that is, c_i) to a simplified representation that is brief and easier to manipulate, the expression progresses through the stages. This straightforward language makes it easier to measure the effectiveness of a specific algorithm in comparison to other algorithms. The demonstration of the INSERTION-SORT method in terms of the "cost" associated with every statement time and the number of times it is attempted to execute the statement.

For every j = 2, 3, 4, ... n, wherein n = *length*. A denotes the number of tries the 'while loop' experiment in line 5 is performed for that specific value of j. A 'for' or 'while' statement that exits conventionally (that is, because of a test in a looping header) has its execution performed once more than the body of the loop that exited conventionally. It is considered that comments are non-executable statements that don't spend any time when they are executed (Table 4.2).

Table 4.2. Illustration of Insertion Sort for Different Times and Cost

SL. No.	Times	Cost	INSERTION SORT (A)
.1	n–1	0	//Insertion of A[j] into an arranged sequence a[1 ... j–1]
.2	n–1	0	\\feeding addition of value in A[i]

.3	n	c1	for j=2 to length.A
.4	n–1	c2	key=A[j]
.5	n–1	c4	i = j–1
.6	$\sum_{j=2}^{n} t_j$	c5	while A[i]>key and i>0
.7	$\sum_{j=2}^{n} (t_j - 1)$	c6	A[i+1]=A[i]
.8	$\sum_{j=2}^{n} (t_j - 1)$	c7	i =i–1
.9	n–1	c8	A[i+1]=key

Source: Tim Roughgarden, Creative Commons License.

The phenomenon has several complexities. In most cases, computational steps defined in English are versions of a technique that takes longer than the expected (set) amount of time. For example, " the sorting of the points by x-coordinates" usually takes longer than the time allocated. It's also worth noting that a statement that invokes a subroutine spends the same amount of time, even if the function takes longer. As a result, for this sort of phenomenon, we identify the calling process. The overall running time of an algorithm is the addition of the running times of all the statements that have been performed. Every statement which is executed in c_i steps and is executed n times in total will contribute $c_i n$ to the overall running time. We add the multiplication of the times and cost columns to get the overall running time of INSERTION-SORT on an input consisting of n values, indicated by T(n), and we get:

$$\begin{aligned} T(n) &= c_1 n + c_2(n-1) + c_4(n-1) + c_5 \sum_{j=2}^{n} t_j + c_6 \sum_{j=2}^{n} (t_j - 1) \\ &\quad + c_7 \sum_{j=2}^{n} (t_j - 1) + c_8(n-1)\,. \end{aligned}$$

Although when dealing with known-size inputs, an algorithm's execution time can be influenced through which input of that size is specified. The best-case situation in INSERTION-SORT, for example, is when the arrangement is already ordered. Whenever the initial value of i is j–1, we receive A[i]≤key in line 5 for the values of j = 2, 3, ..., n. Consequently, t_j = 1 for j= 2, 3, ..., n and the running time of the best-case is:

$$\begin{aligned} T(n) &= c_1 n + c_2(n-1) + c_4(n-1) + c_5(n-1) + c_8(n-1) \\ &= (c_1 + c_2 + c_4 + c_5 + c_8)n - (c_2 + c_4 + c_5 + c_8)\,. \end{aligned}$$

For constants a and b, this running time may be represented as +b. Because a and b are both based upon the statement costs ci, n is a *linear function*.

The worst-case situation happens when the array is sorted in reverse order, that is, in decreasing order. Then, every element A[j] should be compared to each element in the entire sorted sub-array A[1... j–1], and consequently t_j = j for j = 2, 3, ..., n. Remember that:

$$\sum_{j=2}^{n} j = \frac{n(n+1)}{2} - 1$$

and

$$\sum_{j=2}^{n} (j-1) = \frac{n(n-1)}{2}$$

The running time of INSERTION-SORT in the situation of worst-case is:

$$\begin{aligned} T(n) &= c_1 n + c_2(n-1) + c_4(n-1) + c_5\left(\frac{n(n+1)}{2} - 1\right) \\ &\quad + c_6\left(\frac{n(n-1)}{2}\right) + c_7\left(\frac{n(n-1)}{2}\right) + c_8(n-1) \\ &= \left(\frac{c_5}{2} + \frac{c_6}{2} + \frac{c_7}{2}\right)n^2 + \left(c_1 + c_2 + c_4 + \frac{c_5}{2} - \frac{c_6}{2} - \frac{c_7}{2} + c_8\right)n \\ &\quad - (c_2 + c_4 + c_5 + c_8)\,. \end{aligned}$$

For constants a, b, and c, the running time of such worst-case may be represented as $an^2 = bn + c$. Because these constants are dependent on the statement costs c_i, it is a quadratic function of n.

In the Insertion sort scenario, an algorithm's running time is usually set for every specific input; while there have been some "randomized" algorithms whose behavior varies even for a fixed input.

4.5.3. Analysis of Worst-Case and Average-Case

To better understand the insertion sort, we have studied both cases: the best scenario, in which the input arrangement has already been categorized, and the worst situation, in which the arrangement has already been categorized in the opposite direction. All of our attention is focused solely on the worst-case, which is the longest possible running time for every input of size n. The following are the three most important causes for this perspective:

- By calculating the running time for the worst-case of an algorithm, we may obtain an upper bound on the running time of every input. Understanding the upper bound assures that the algorithm would not take much longer than it has been estimated to take. As a result, it removes the need for us to make an informed judgment, and we may safely trust that things would not become much worse.
- The worst-case scenario occurs fairly frequently for certain algorithms.

Whenever we check any database to discover certain particular data, we would frequently come into the worst-case scenario of the searching algorithm, which occurs when the data we seek is not there in the information.

- The "average case" is almost always just as dreadful as the "worst-case" scenario. Consider the following scenario: we randomly select n integers and then apply insertion sort on them. Is it possible to estimate the amount of time necessary for identifying where to put element A[j] in sub-array A[1... j–1] using a timer? Usually, 50% of the items included in A[1... j–1] are more than A[j], and 50% are less than A[j]. As a result, we would be inspecting around 50% of the sub-array A[1... j–1], and as a result, tj is approximately j=2. The running time of the average case is found to be a quadratic function of the amount of the input as the running time of the worst case is shown to be in the same way.

ACTIVITY 4.1:

Read latest case studies and research papers on data structures and algorithms in order to understand the real-world applications of data structures and algorithms.

When dealing with a given situation, the capability of average-case evaluation is controlled since it is not always evident what constitutes an "average" input. Most of the time, we want to suppose that almost all inputs of a particular size are equally probable. In actuality, such a supposition can be broken; yet, at times, we can utilize a *randomized algorithm*, which produces arbitrary selections to permit for probabilistic evaluation and to provide results in a predicted running time by using a randomized method.

4.6. SUMMARY

Data structures are used to organize and store data in a computer program, allowing for efficient retrieval and manipulation of the data. Common data structures include arrays, linked lists, stacks, queues, trees, and graphs. Algorithms on the other hand are step-by-step procedures used to solve a particular problem. Algorithms can be applied to data structures to perform operations such as searching, sorting, and traversing the data. Some common algorithms include binary search, bubble sort and quick sort. Choosing the right data structure and algorithm for a particular problem can greatly impact the efficiency and effectiveness of a program. It's important for computer scientists and programmers to have a strong understanding of these fundamental concepts in order to create efficient and effective software solutions.

REVIEW QUESTIONS

1. What is a data structure?
2. What are the common types of data structures?
3. Why is it important to choose the right data structure for a particular problem?
4. What is an algorithm and what are some common algorithms used in programming?
5. How can you implement a data structure or algorithm in a programming language?

MULTIPLE CHOICE QUESTIONS

1. Which of the following is a non-linear data structure?

a. Array
b. Linked list
c. Queue
d. Tree

2. Which of the following is not an algorithm?

a. Bubble sort
b. Quick sort
c. Binary tree
d. Linear search

3. What is the space complexity of an algorithm?

a. The amount of memory needed to store the input data
b. The amount of memory needed to store the output data
c. The amount of memory needed to store the program code
d. The amount of memory needed to execute the algorithm

4. Which of the following is not a common algorithm?

a. Array

b. Tree

c. Function

d. Graph

Answers to Multiple Choice Questions

1. (d); 2. (c); 3. (d); 4. (c)

REFERENCES

1. Abramowitz, M., & Stegun, I. A., (1965). *Handbook of Mathematical Functions with Formulas, graphs, and Mathematical Table* (Vol. 2172, pp. 1–23). New York: Dover.
2. Acar, U. A., (2009). Self-adjusting computation:(an overview). In: *Proceedings of the 2009 ACM SIGPLAN Workshop on Partial Evaluation and Program Manipulation* (pp. 1–6). ACM.
3. Ahuja, R. K., & Orlin, J. B., (1989). A fast and simple algorithm for the maximum flow problem. *Operations Research, 37*(5), 748–759.
4. Ahuja, R. K., Orlin, J. B., & Tarjan, R. E., (1989). Improved time bounds for the maximum flow problem. *SIAM Journal on Computing, 18*(5), 939–954.
5. Ajtai, M., Megiddo, N., & Waarts, O., (2001). Improved algorithms and analysis for secretary problems and generalizations. *SIAM Journal on Discrete Mathematics, 14*(1), 1–27.
6. Aki, S. G., (1989). *The Design and Analysis of Parallel Algorithms, 1*, 10.
7. Akra, M., & Bazzi, L., (1998). On the solution of linear recurrence equations. *Computational Optimization and Applications, 10*(2), 195–210.
8. Alon, N., (1990). Generating pseudo-random permutations and maximum flow algorithms. *Information Processing Letters, 35*(4), 201–204.
9. Amir, A., Aumann, Y., Benson, G., Levy, A., Lipsky, O., Porat, E., & Vishne, U., (2006). Pattern matching with address errors: Rearrangement distances. In: *Proceedings of the Seventeenth Annual ACM-SIAM Symposium on Discrete Algorithm* (Vol. 1, pp. 1221–1229). Society for Industrial and Applied Mathematics.
10. Amtoft, T., Consel, C., Danvy, O., & Malmkjær, K., (2002). The abstraction and instantiation of string-matching programs. In: *The Essence of Computation* (pp. 332–357). Springer, Berlin, Heidelberg.
11. Andersson, A. A., & Thorup, M., (2000). Tight (er) worst-case bounds on dynamic searching and priority queues. In: *Proceedings of the Thirty-Second Annual ACM Symposium on Theory of Computing* (Vol. 1, pp. 335–342). ACM.

12. Arge, L., (2001). External memory data structures. In: *European Symposium on Algorithms* (pp. 1–29). Springer, Berlin, Heidelberg.
13. Arora, S., & Lund, C., (1996). Hardness of approximations. In: *Approximation Algorithms for NP-Hard Problems* (pp. 399–446). PWS Publishing Co.
14. Arora, S., (1994). *Probabilistic Checking of Proofs and Hardness of Approximation Problems*. Doctoral dissertation, Princeton University, Department of Computer Science.
15. Arora, S., Lund, C., Motwani, R., Sudan, M., & Szegedy, M., (1998). Proof verification and the hardness of approximation problems. *Journal of the ACM (JACM), 45*(3), 501–555.
16. Aslam, J. A., (2001). *A Simple Bound on the Expected Height of a Randomly Built Binary Search Tree*, 1, 1-20.
17. Ausiello, G., Crescenzi, P., Gambosi, G., Kann, V., Marchetti-Spaccamela, A., & Protasi, M., (2012). *Complexity and Approximation: Combinatorial Optimization Problems and Their Approximability Properties*. Springer Science & Business Media.
18. Avidan, S., & Shamir, A., (2007). Seam carving for content-aware image resizing. In: *ACM Transactions on Graphics (TOG)* (Vol. 26, No. 3, p. 10). ACM.
19. Babaioff, M., Immorlica, N., Kempe, D., & Kleinberg, R., (2007). A knapsack secretary problem with applications. In: *Approximation, Randomization, and Combinatorial Optimization: Algorithms and Techniques* (pp. 16–28). Springer, Berlin, Heidelberg.
20. Bach, E., & Shallit, J. O., (1996). *Algorithmic Number Theory: Efficient Algorithms* (Vol. 1). MIT press.
21. Bach, E., (1990). Number-theoretic algorithms. *Annual Review of Computer Science, 4*(1), 119–172.
22. Bailey, D. H., Lee, K., & Simon, H. D., (1991). Using Strassen's algorithm to accelerate the solution of linear systems. *The Journal of Supercomputing, 4*(4), 357–371.
23. Bakker, M., Riezebos, J., & Teunter, R. H., (2012). Review of inventory systems with deterioration since 2001. *European Journal of Operational Research, 221*(2), 275–284.
24. Baswana, S., Hariharan, R., & Sen, S., (2002). Improved decremental algorithms for maintaining transitive closure and all-pairs shortest paths. In: *Proceedings of the 34th Annual ACM Symposium on Theory of Computing* (pp. 117–123). ACM.
25. Bateni, M., Hajiaghayi, M., & Zadimoghaddam, M., (2010). Submodular secretary problem and extensions. In: *Approximation, Randomization, and Combinatorial Optimization. Algorithms and Techniques* (pp. 39–52). Springer, Berlin, Heidelberg.
26. Bayer, R., (1972). Symmetric binary B-trees: Data structure and maintenance algorithms. *Acta Informatica, 1*(4), 290–306.
27. Beauchemin, P., Brassard, G., Crépeau, C., Goutier, C., & Pomerance, C., (1988). The generation of random numbers that are probably prime. *Journal of Cryptology, 1*(1), 53–64.

28. Bellare, M., & Sudan, M., (1994). Improved non-approximability results. In: *Proceedings of the Twenty-Sixth Annual ACM Symposium on Theory of Computing* (pp. 184–193). ACM.
29. Bender, M. A., Demaine, E. D., & Farach-Colton, M., (2000). Cache-oblivious B-trees. In: *Foundations of Computer Science, 2000; Proceedings. 41st Annual Symposium* (pp. 399–409). IEEE.
30. Ben-Or, M., (1983). Lower bounds for algebraic computation trees. In: *Proceedings of the Fifteenth Annual ACM Symposium on Theory of Computing* (pp. 80–86). ACM.
31. Bent, S. W., & John, J. W., (1985). Finding the median requires 2n comparisons. In: *Proceedings of the Seventeenth Annual ACM Symposium on Theory of Computing* (pp. 213–216). ACM.
32. Bentley, J. L., Haken, D., & Saxe, J. B., (1980). A general method for solving divide-and-conquer recurrences. *ACM SIGACT News, 12*(3), 36–44.
33. Berger, J., & Barkaoui, M., (2004). A parallel hybrid genetic algorithm for the vehicle routing problem with time windows. *Computers & Operations Research, 31*(12), 2037–2053.
34. Berry, M. V., & Howls, C. J., (2012). *Integrals with Coalescing Saddles, 36*, 775–793.
35. Bienstock, D., & McClosky, B., (2012). Tightening simple mixed-integer sets with guaranteed bounds. *Mathematical Programming, 133*(1), 337–363.
36. Bienstock, D., (2008). Approximate formulations for 0-1 knapsack sets. *Operations Research Letters, 36*(3), 317–320.
37. Blasgen, M. W., Casey, R. G., & Eswaran, K. P., (1977). An encoding method for multifield sorting and indexing. *Communications of the ACM, 20*(11), 874–878.
38. Blelloch, G. E., & Gibbons, P. B., (2004). Effectively sharing a cache among threads. In: *Proceedings of the 16th Annual ACM Symposium on Parallelism in Algorithms and Architectures* (pp. 235–244). ACM.
39. Blelloch, G. E., & Greiner, J., (1996). A provable time and space efficient implementation of NESL. In: *ACM SIGPLAN Notices* (Vol. 31, No. 6, pp. 213–225). ACM.
40. Blelloch, G. E., & Maggs, B. M., (1996). Parallel algorithms. *ACM Computing Surveys (CSUR), 28*(1), 51–54.
41. Blelloch, G. E., Hardwick, J. C., Sipelstein, J., Zagha, M., & Chatterjee, S., (1994). Implementation of a portable nested data-parallel language. *Journal of Parallel and Distributed Computing, 21*(1), 4–14.
42. Bloom, N., & VanReenen, J., (2002). Patents, real options and firm performance. *The Economic Journal, 112*(478).
43. Blumofe, R. D., & Leiserson, C. E., (1999). Scheduling multithreaded computations by work stealing. *Journal of the ACM (JACM), 46*(5), 720–748.
44. Bollerslev, T., Engle, R. F., & Nelson, D. B., (1994). ARCH models. *Handbook of Econometrics, 4*, 2959–3038.

45. Brassard, G., & Bratley, P., (1996). *Fundamentals of Algorithmics* (Vol. 33). Englewood Cliffs: Prentice Hall.
46. Brent, R. P., (1974). The parallel evaluation of general arithmetic expressions. *Journal of the ACM (JACM), 21*(2), 201–206.
47. Brodnik, A., Miltersen, P. B., & Munro, J. I., (1997). Trans-dichotomous algorithms without multiplication—Some upper and lower bounds. In: *Workshop on Algorithms and Data Structures* (pp. 426–439). Springer, Berlin, Heidelberg.
48. Buchbinder, N., Jain, K., & Singh, M., (2010). Secretary problems via linear programming. In: *International Conference on Integer Programming and Combinatorial Optimization* (pp. 163–176). Springer, Berlin, Heidelberg.
49. Buhler, J. P., Lenstra, H. W., & Pomerance, C., (1993). Factoring integers with the number field sieve. In: *The Development of the Number Field Sieve* (pp. 50–94). Springer, Berlin, Heidelberg.
50. Chan, T. H., (2000). HOMFLY polynomials of some generalized Hopf links. *Journal of Knot Theory and Its Ramifications, 9*(07), 865–883.
51. Chen, L. T., & Davis, L. S., (1990). A parallel algorithm for list ranking image curves in O (log N) time. In: *DARPA Image Understanding Workshop* (pp. 805–815).
52. Cheriyan, J., & Hagerup, T., (1989). A randomized maximum-flow algorithm. In: *Foundations of Computer Science, 1989, 30th Annual Symposium* (pp. 118–123). IEEE.
53. Cheriyan, J., & Hagerup, T., (1995). A randomized maximum-flow algorithm. *SIAM Journal on Computing, 24*(2), 203–226.
54. Cheriyan, J., Hagerup, T., & Mehlhorn, K., (1990). Can a maximum flow be computed in o (nm) time? In: *International Colloquium on Automata, Languages, and Programming* (pp. 235–248). Springer, Berlin, Heidelberg.
55. Cheriyan, J., Hagerup, T., & Mehlhorn, K., (1996). An o(n^3)-time maximum-flow algorithm. *SIAM Journal on Computing, 25*(6), 1144–1170.
56. Ciurea, E., & Ciupala, L., (2001). Algorithms for minimum flows. *Computer Science Journal of Moldova, 9*(3), 27.
57. Conforti, M., Wolsey, L. A., & Zambelli, G., (2010). Projecting an extended formulation for mixed-integer covers on bipartite graphs. *Mathematics of Operations Research, 35*(3), 603–623.
58. Courcoubetis, C., Vardi, M., Wolper, P., & Yannakakis, M., (1992). Memory-efficient algorithms for the verification of temporal properties. *Formal Methods in System Design, 1*(2, 3), 275–288.
59. D'Aristotile, A., Diaconis, P., & Newman, C. M., (2003). *Brownian Motion and the Classical Groups: Lecture Notes-Monograph Series*, 97–116.
60. Damgård, I., Landrock, P., & Pomerance, C., (1993). Average case error estimates for the strong probable prime test. *Mathematics of Computation, 61*(203), 177–194.

61. Dehling, H., & Philipp, W., (2002). Empirical process techniques for dependent data. In: *Empirical Process Techniques for Dependent Data* (pp. 3–113). Birkhäuser, Boston, MA.

62. Dengiz, B., Altiparmak, F., & Smith, A. E., (1997). Efficient optimization of all-terminal reliable networks, using an evolutionary approach. *IEEE Transactions on Reliability, 46*(1), 18–26.

63. Dickerson, M., Eppstein, D., Goodrich, M. T., & Meng, J. Y., (2003). Confluent drawings: Visualizing non-planar diagrams in a planar way. In: *International Symposium on Graph Drawing* (pp. 1–12). Springer, Berlin, Heidelberg.

64. Didier, F., (2009). *Efficient Erasure Decoding of Reed-Solomon Codes* (Vol. 1, pp. 1–22). arXiv preprint arXiv:0901.1886.

65. Drmota, M., & Szpankowski, W., (2013). A master theorem for discrete divide and conquer recurrences. *Journal of the ACM (JACM), 60*(3), 16.

66. Du, W., & Atallah, M. J., (2001). Protocols for secure remote database access with approximate matching. In: *E-Commerce Security and Privacy* (pp. 87–111). Springer, Boston, MA.

67. Duda, R. O., Hart, P. E., & Stork, D. G., (1973). *Pattern Classification* (Vol. 2). New York: Wiley.

68. Eppstein, D., Goodrich, M. T., & Sun, J. Z., (2005). The skip quadtree: A simple dynamic data structure for multidimensional data. In: *Proceedings of the 21st Annual Symposium on Computational Geometry* (pp. 296–305). ACM.

69. Eppstein, D., Goodrich, M. T., & Sun, J. Z., (2008). Skip quadtrees: Dynamic data structures for multidimensional point sets. *International Journal of Computational Geometry & Applications, 18*(1, 2), 131–160.

70. Faenza, Y., & Sanità, L., (2015). On the existence of compact ε-approximated formulations for knapsack in the original space. *Operations Research Letters, 43*(3), 339–342.

71. Festa, P., & Resende, M. G., (2002). GRASP: An annotated bibliography. In: *Essays and Surveys in Metaheuristics* (Vol. 1, pp. 325–367). Springer, Boston, MA.

72. Fourier, J. B. J., (1890). In: Darboux, G., (ed.), *From 1824, Republished as Second Extrait in Oeuvres de Fourier, Tome II* (pp. 38–42). Gauthier-Villars, Paris.

73. Fourier, J. B. J. (1973). *report in:" Analyse des travaux de l'Académie Royale des Sciences de l'Institut de France" 7 (1827) xlvii-lv. Partial English translation in: DA Kohler," translation of a Report by Fourier on his work on Linear Inequalities",* Opsearch, 10, 38-42

74. Fredman, M. L., & Willard, D. E., (1993). Surpassing the information theoretic bound with fusion trees. *Journal of Computer and System Sciences, 47*(3), 424–436.

75. Friedl, K., & Sudan, M., (1995). Some improvements to total degree tests. In: *Theory of Computing and Systems, 1995. Proceedings., Third Israel Symposium* (pp. 190–198). IEEE.

76. Frigo, M., Leiserson, C. E., & Randall, K. H., (1998). The implementation of the cilk-5 multithreaded language. *ACM Sigplan Notices, 33*(5), 212–223.
77. Fussenegger, F., & Gabow, H. N., (1979). A counting approach to lower bounds for selection problems. *Journal of the ACM (JACM), 26*(2), 227–238.
78. Glasser, K. S., & Austin, B. R. H., (1983). The d choice secretary problem. *Sequential Analysis, 2*(3), 177–199.
79. Goodrich, M. T., Atallah, M. J., & Tamassia, R., (2005). Indexing information for data forensics. In: *International Conference on Applied Cryptography and Network Security* (pp. 206–221). Springer, Berlin, Heidelberg.
80. Graefe, G., (2011). Modern B-tree techniques. *Foundations and Trends® in Databases, 3*(4), 203–402.
81. Hall, M., Frank, E., Holmes, G., Pfahringer, Badel'son-Vel'skii, G. M., & Landis, E. M., (1962). *Partial Differential Equations of Elliptic Type* (Vol. 1, pp. 1–22). Springer, Berlin.
82. Herr, D. G., (1980). On the history of the use of geometry in the general linear model. *The American Statistician, 34*(1), 43–47.
83. Icking, C., Klein, R., & Ottmann, T., (1987). Priority search trees in secondary memory. In: *International Workshop on Graph-Theoretic Concepts in Computer Science* (pp. 84–93). Springer, Berlin, Heidelberg.
84. Igarashi, Y., Sado, K., & Saga, K., (1987). Fast parallel sorts on a practical sized mesh-connected processor array. *IEICE Transactions (1976–1990), 70*(1), 56–64.
85. John, J. W., (1988). A new lower bound for the set-partitioning problem. *SIAM Journal on Computing, 17*(4), 640–647.
86. Kim, S. H., & Pomerance, C., (1989). The probability that a random probable prime is composite. *Mathematics of Computation, 53*(188), 721–741.
87. King, D. J., (1995). Functional binomial queues. In: *Functional Programming, Glasgow 1994* (Vol. 1, pp. 141–150). Springer, London.
88. Kirkpatrick, D. G., (1981). A unified lower bound for selection and set partitioning problems. *Journal of the ACM (JACM), 28*(1), 150–165.
89. Kwong, Y. S., & Wood, D., (1982). A new method for concurrency in B-trees. *IEEE Transactions on Software Engineering*, (3), 211–222.
90. Leighton, T., (1996). *Notes on Better Master Theorems for Divide-and-Conquer Recurrences*. Manuscript. Massachusetts Institute of Technology.
91. Maurer, S. B., (1985). The lessons of Williamstown. In: *New Directions in Two-Year College Mathematics* (Vol. 1, pp. 255–270). Springer, New York, NY.
92. Meijer, H., & Akl, S. G., (1987). Optimal computation of prefix sums on a binary tree of processors. *International Journal of Parallel Programming, 16*(2), 127–136.
93. Meijer, H., & Akl, S. G., (1988). Bit serial addition trees and their applications. *Computing, 40*(1), 9–17.

94. Monier, L., (1980). Evaluation and comparison of two efficient probabilistic primality testing algorithms. *Theoretical Computer Science, 12*(1), 97–108.
95. Morain, F., (1988). *Implementation of the Atkin-Goldwasser-Kilian Primality Testing Algorithm*. Doctoral dissertation, INRIA.
96. Munro, J. I., & Poblete, P. V., (1982). *A Lower Bound for Determining the Median*. Faculty of Mathematics, University of Waterloo.
97. Nelson, D. B., & Foster, D. P., (1992). *Filtering and Forecasting with Misspecified ARCH Models II: Making the Right Forecast with the Wrong Model, 67(2), 303-335.*
98. Nievergelt, J., (1974). Binary search trees and file organization. *ACM Computing Surveys (CSUR), 6*(3), 195–207.
99. Park, T. G., & Oldfield, J. V., (1993). Minimum spanning tree generation with content-addressable memory. *Electronics Letters, 29*(11), 1037–1039.
100. Phillips, S., & Westbrook, J., (1993). Online load balancing and network flow. In: *Proceedings of the Twenty-Fifth Annual ACM Symposium on Theory of Computing* (pp. 402–411). ACM.
101. Polishchuk, A., & Spielman, D. A., (1994). Nearly-linear size holographic proofs. In: *Proceedings of the Twenty-Sixth Annual ACM Symposium on Theory of Computing* (pp. 194–203). ACM.
102. Prechelt, L., (1993). *Measurements of MasPar MP-1216A Communication Operations*. Univ., Fak. für Informatik.
103. Price, G. B., (1973). Telescoping sums and the summation of sequences. *The Two-Year College Mathematics Journal, 4*(2), 16–29.
104. Ramadge, P. J., & Wonham, W. M., (1989). The control of discrete event systems. *Proceedings of the IEEE, 77*(1), 81–98.
105. Raman, R., (1996). Priority queues: Small, monotone and trans-dichotomous. In: *European Symposium on Algorithms* (pp. 121–137). Springer, Berlin, Heidelberg.
106. Regli, W. C., (1992). *A Survey of Automated Feature Recognition Techniques, 1*, 1–22.
107. Roura, S., (2001). Improved master theorems for divide-and-conquer recurrences. *Journal of the ACM (JACM), 48*(2), 170–205.
108. Sardelis, D. A., & Valahas, T. M., (1999). Decision making: A golden rule. *The American Mathematical Monthly, 106*(3), 215–226.
109. Schönhage, A., Paterson, M., & Pippenger, N., (1976). Finding the median. *Journal of Computer and System Sciences, 13*(2), 184–199.
110. Shen, Z., & Marston, C. M., (1995). A study of a dice problem. *Applied Mathematics and Computation, 73*(2, 3), 231–247.
111. Smith, R. S., (1986). Rolle over Lagrange—Another shot at the mean value theorem. *The College Mathematics Journal, 17*(5), 403–406.
112. Snyder, L., (1984). *Parallel Programming and the Poker Programming Environment*

(No. TR-84-04-02, pp. 1–30). Washington Univ Seattle Dept of Computer Science.

113. Stock, J. H., & Watson, M. W., (2001). Vector autoregressions. *Journal of Economic Perspectives, 15*(4), 101–115.
114. Sudan, M., (1992). *Efficient Checking of Polynomials and Proofs and the Hardness of Approximation Problems: Lecture Notes in Computer Science* (Vol. 1001).
115. Szymanski, T. G., & Van, W. C. J., (1983). Space efficient algorithms for VLSI artwork analysis. In: *Proceedings of the 20th Design Automation Conference* (pp. 734–739). IEEE Press.
116. Szymanski, T. G., (1975). *A Special Case of the Maximal Common Subsequence Problem*. Technical Report TR-170, Computer Science Laboratory, Princeton University.
117. Thorup, M., (1997). *Faster Deterministic Sorting and Priority Queues in Linear Space* (pp. 550–555). Max-Planck-Institut für Informatik.
118. Vanderbei, R. J., (1980). The optimal choice of a subset of a population. *Mathematics of Operations Research, 5*(4), 481–486.
119. Verma, R. M., (1994). A general method and a master theorem for divide-and-conquer recurrences with applications. *Journal of Algorithms, 16*(1), 67–79.
120. Verma, R. M., (1997). General techniques for analyzing recursive algorithms with applications. *SIAM Journal on Computing, 26*(2), 568–581.
121. Wallace, L., Keil, M., & Rai, A., (2004). Understanding software project risk: A cluster analysis. *Information & Management, 42*(1), 115–125.
122. Wang, Y., (2008). Topology control for wireless sensor networks. In: *Wireless Sensor Networks and Applications* (Vol. 1, pp. 113–147). Springer, Boston, MA.
123. Wilf, H. S., (1984). A bijection in the theory of derangements. *Mathematics Magazine, 57*(1), 37–40.
124. Williamson, J., (2002). Probability logic. In: *Studies in Logic and Practical Reasoning* (Vol. 1, pp. 397–424). Elsevier.
125. Wilson, J. G., (1991). Optimal choice and assignment of the best m of n randomly arriving items. *Stochastic Processes and Their Applications, 39*(2), 325–343.
126. Winograd, S., (1970). On the algebraic complexity of functions. In: *Actes du Congres International des Mathématiciens* (Vol. 3, pp. 283–288).
127. Wunderlich, M. C., (1983). A performance analysis of a simple prime-testing algorithm. *Mathematics of Computation, 40*(162), 709–714.
128. Xiaodong, W., & Qingxiang, F., (1996). A frame for general divide-and-conquer recurrences. *Information Processing Letters, 59*(1), 45–51.
129. Yap, C., (2011). A real elementary approach to the master recurrence and generalizations. In: *International Conference on Theory and Applications of Models of Computation* (pp. 14–26). Springer, Berlin, Heidelberg.
130. Zhu, X., & Wilhelm, W. E., (2006). Scheduling and lot sizing with sequence-dependent setup: A literature review. *IIE Transactions, 38*(11), 987–1007.

CHAPTER 5

FUNCTIONS

UNIT INTRODUCTION

A key element of the software design method known as modular programming is the division of a program's functionality into separate, interchangeable modules, each of which has all the components required to carry out just one particular aspect of the desired capability (Hanus, 1994).

The crucial aspect of any program is the ability to condense several separate code statements into a single, more manageable component that can be implemented elsewhere in the code. This was first written as separate software, all on its own. In addition, the words "macro," "sub-routine," "procedure," and "module" may be utilized. Because this is how most of the most common programming languages used today refer to them, developers will refer to them as functions. Functions are essential because they permit us to partition large, complicated programs into several smaller, more manageable pieces. The function is a more manageable portion of the overall program, which enables them to concentrate on what they want it to achieve and test it to ensure that it accomplishes what they want it to accomplish (Bickman, 1987).

Learning Objectives

Readers will have the chance to understand the following by the chapter's conclusion:

- Understand the fundamental concept of functions in programming;
- Learn about the categories of functions;
- Basic idea of hierarchy or structure chart in programming;
- Learn about the return statement and scope of functions;
- Understanding of the coding elegance in programming.

Key Terms

- Arguments
- Call by reference
- Call by value
- Categories
- Data type
- Functions
- Hierarchy
- Parameters
- Program
- Void

5.1. CATEGORIES OF FUNCTIONS

Normally, modules divided into two categories:

1. **Program Control-Straightforward Modules:** These for dividing the program up into sections and managing them. These characteristics are unique to the program that is currently under development. Although the names of some functions in different programs might be the same or even the same, the contents of those functions seldom share similarities (Chen et al., 2003).
2. **Task-Specific Components:** These are designed for use with a variety of different programs. These functions execute a particular task, which qualifies them for usage in some different programs. This is because those other programs also require the execution of the specific task in question. The phrase "building blocks" is a term that is employed on occasion to define particular task functions. They can use them with confidence since they have already been coded and tested, which allows them to write a huge application more quickly (Scott, 2000).

   Modules utilized by the primary application must be verified as existing before they can be used. There is a formal technique for, relying on the computer coding language:

- Define a module (i.e., the code that it will run);
- Invoke a module;
- Introduce a module (a description to a compiler is a prototype).

In a typical scenario, functions under Program Control do not share data; rather, they collaborate on using a shared area for variable storage. Customized Task modules are developed to facilitate data flow among the program component that is calling the function, the callback function, and the function that is being called. Because of their capability for data communication, they can create a specific task function that can be utilized in various applications. This ability allows them to do so. The fundamental idea behind data transmission inside and outside of a function is the same; however, the specific guidelines for doing so might be very different depending on the programming language used. The chunks of info passed along are called parameters. This is the origin of the term "parameter passing." The following are the four options for data communication (Carrier & Spafford, 2006):

Did you Know?

The concept of functions has been around in mathematics for centuries, but it was not until the 1950s that programming languages began to adopt them.

- No interaction in with no interaction out;
- Some interaction in with no interaction out;
- No communication in with some interaction out;
- Some interaction in with some interaction out.

5.1.1. Program Control Function

In many coding languages, the main program component is a specific module with the identification name main. The unusual or distinctive quality of the main module is that it serves as both the program's entry point and its customary exit point for code execution. It frequently appears as the first function declared in a program, following the sections used for involving other technical things, prototype declarations, the listing of worldwide constants and variables, and any other items the program will typically require. The main function's definition code is provided, but it isn't prototyped or frequently used like other modules in a program (Want et al., 1995).

5.1.2. Specific Task Function

Developers frequently need to carry out a particular task that could be used for other systems (Cytron et al., 1991).

The general structure of a module in a language with statically typed data, like Java, C++, or C#:

```
<return value data type> function identifier name(<data type> <identifier n
//lines of code; return <value>;
}
General layout of a function in a dynamically typed language such as JavaScript and Python:
function identifier name(<identifier name for input value>)
{
//statements of code;
return <value>;
}
def function identifier name(<identifier name for input value>):
//lines of code
```

```
return <value>
```

Functions in several coding languages have a set of brackets that are used to denote a collection of statements. To designate a code block, some languages employ indenting or begin and end statements. A function often contains multiple lines of code (Ramalingam & Wiedenbeck, 1998).

Depending on the language's coding norms, separate task functions will be defined before or after the main function.

A set of parentheses and the function's identifier name invoke a function. Any data that they are passing is put between parentheses. Following compilation and execution, the code in the main function is run. When the program reaches the calling of a particular task function, control is transferred to the function, where the function's lines of code are then run. After finishing the lines of code, it will go back to the location in the program from where it was called (in our case, the function main), where it will proceed to execute the remaining lines of code there (Albrecht & Gaffney, 1983).

5.2. PROGRAM LAYOUT

The majority of programs have several things before the functionality, such as:

i. Documentation: The majority of programs feature a remark section at the beginning with a range of comments relevant to the software.
ii. Import or include clauses used to admittance functions from a standard library (Shioji et al., 2012).
iii. Program is written in a particular language, like namespace reference or prototypes.
iv. When global, mandatory, or module-level constants and variables.

5.3. HIERARCHY OR STRUCTURE CHART

The link between the several modules is depicted on a hierarchy chart, which is also referred to as a structure chart. It got its name from the fact that it was traditionally used to illustrate the framework of a company. The President is at the top of the hierarchy, followed by the Vice Presidents, etc. It illustrates the connection between the various modules inside the overall structure of a computer program. There is no presentation of the program's logic in detail. It does, however, illustrate the organization of the functions that are used within the program by indicating which functions are calling on an inferior module. Those higher up are communicating with those on the level below them (Novick, 2004).

When a programmer wants to assist in documenting a program, they will develop hierarchy charts. They illustrate the overall arrangement of the modules utilized in a code (Van Merrienboer & Krammer, 1987) (Figure 5.1).

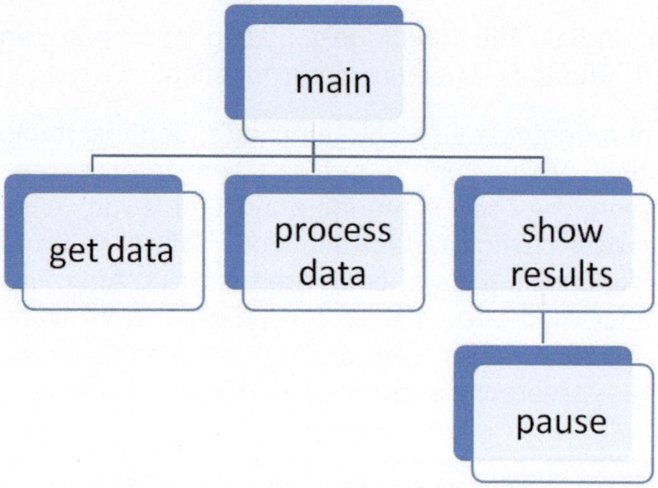

Figure 5.1. Illustration of structure chart for a program with five functions.

Source: Dave Braunschweig, Creative Commons License.

5.4. PARAMETERS AND ARGUMENTS

One of the bits of data supplied as input to a function is referred to by a parameter, a special sort of variable. These bits of information represent the values of the arguments that will be used to call or invoke the function. A function is typically defined with an ordered list of parameters so that each time it is called, the arguments are evaluated for that call, and the results can be assigned to the associated parameters (Baek & Chilimbi, 2010).

Remember that functional coding divides a program's functionality into different modules. Each function receives a unique set of input variables, or parameters, to distinguish the functionality of one module from another. When a module is called, the parameter values—or arguments. Think about the following code snippets function (Le Roy, 2017):

```
Function CalculateCelsius (Real Fahrenheit)

Declare Real celsius

Assign celsius = (Fahrenheit - 32) * 5 / 9

Return Real Celsius
```

The parameter is Fahrenheit, and the argument is 100 if the CalculateCelsius function is called, sending in the value 100, as in CalculateCelsius(100). The words arguments and parameters are frequently used synonymously. However, argument refers to the variable value (100%), whereas parameter refers to the variable identifier (Fahrenheit). Functions may have one or more parameters or none at all. Think about the following pseudocode for a function (Liu et al., 2016):

```
Function DisplayResult (Real Fahrenheit, Real Celsius)
Print Fahrenheit & "° Fahrenheit is " & celsius & "° Celsius"
End
```

The arguments or values for the Fahrenheit and Celsius parameters are 98.6 and 37.0, respectively, if the DisplayResult function is invoked while handing in those values, as in DisplayResults(98.6, 37.0). Take note of the positional passing of the arguments. Demanding DisplayResults(37.0, 98.6) would produce incorrect results because 37.0 would be the value for Fahrenheit, and 98.6 would be the value for Celsius (Charwat & Dvořák, 2012).

There are certain coding languages that support named parameters, including Python. Positions of parameters are not taken into account when calling modules with named parameters; just their given names, along with their values, are used. Arguments are distinguished by position when names are not used (Steensgaard-Madsen, 1981).

```
CalculateCelsius(98.6, 37.0)
CalculateCelsius(fahrenheit=98.6,celsius=37.0)
CalculateCelsius(celsius=37.0, fahrenheit=98.6)
```

5.5. CALL BY VALUE VS. CALL BY REFERENCE

When a function is called by value, each parameter serves as a new local variable inside the function that is assigned to the argument's value. When using call by reference, the called function's operations may impact the caller's supplied argument variable (Fateman & Toy, 2003).

5.5.1. Call by Value

The argument in the majority of modern programming languages is often a copy of the calling value, with parameters being supplied by value by default. Functions can modify parameter values without worrying about affecting the called function since arguments are isolated. Take a look at the following code snippets (Plotkin, 1975):

```
Function Main
Initialize Real Fahrenheit
Assign Fahrenheit = 100
Print "Main Fahrenheit = " & Fahrenheit
Invoke ChangeFahrenheit(Fahrenheit)
Print "Main Fahrenheit = " & Fahrenheit
End
Function ChangeFahrenheit (Real Fahrenheit)
Print "ChangeFahrenheit Fahrenheit = " & Fahrenheit
Assign Fahrenheit = 0
Print "ChangeFahrenheit Fahrenheit = " & Fahrenheit
End
```

- Output:

```
Main Fahrenheit = 100
ChangeFahrenheit fahrenheit = 100
ChangeFahrenheit fahrenheit = 0
Main Fahrenheit = 100
```

Remember

The idea of higher-order functions, or functions that takes other functions as inputs or outputs is a key concept in functional programming.

The value of the variable Fahrenheit is initially set to 100 by the Main function, which then displays the value before calling ChangeFahrenheit and supplying a duplicate of the displayed value as an argument.

The parameter is displayed initially, then the called function updates it and displays it once more. The execution is restarted by the function that was called, and the value of the beginning variable is displayed by the main program.

Since the argument Fahrenheit and the field containing Fahrenheit in the function that calls it to refer to different addresses, the called function cannot change the value of the variable in the calling function when call by value is used (Hempel et al., 2019).

5.5.2. Call by Reference

When a coding employs or enables a call by reference, an argument in the called function and a variable in the function that calls it both refer to the same memory address. The invoked module can modify the value of the calling function's variable. The output from the identical code sample as before would change to (Plotkin, 1975):

```
Main Fahrenheit = 100

ChangeFahrenheit Fahrenheit = 100
ChangeFahrenheit Fahrenheit = 0

Main Fahrenheit = 0
```

In programming languages that enable both calls by value and calls by reference, the parameter passing mode is denoted by a word or symbol (Gries & Levin, 1980) (Table 5.1).

Table 5.1. Keywords or Symbols Used by Programming Languages to Indicate which Parameter Passing Method is Used

Language	Call By Value	Call by Reference
C#	refer	Use ref parameter in calling and called functions.
Java	refer	Put on to objects and arrays.
Python	refer	Put on mutable objects and arrays (lists).
C++	refer	Use and Parameter in the called function.
JavaScript	refer	Put on to objects and arrays.

Source: Abass Alamnehe, Creative Commons License.

5.6. RETURN STATEMENT

A return statement forces the code to exit the current function and continue where the function was called in the following line of code. Many programming languages allow functions to postulate a return value that will be sent to the program that called the function via return statements (Prandini & Ramilli, 2012).

When a module is called, the return statement ends the module and goes back to the calling statement. A single value can be optionally returned to the caller function in the majority of computer languages. Take a look at the following code snippets (Li et al., 2020):

```
Function Main

Assign Fahrenheit = GetFahrenheit()
```

```
End
Function/Module GetFahrenheit
Initialize Real Fahrenheit
Print "Enter Fahrenheit temperature:"
Input Fahrenheit
Return Real Fahrenheit
```

The GetFahrenheit module is called in English by the Main function without any parameters being passed. The main function assigns the user's input to the variable Fahrenheit after receiving it from the GetFahrenheit function, which also returns the user's input. The Main function in this example has no return value (Bothwell & Timmerman, 2020).

Keep in mind that modules are autonomous and that they each need to declare their variables. Although Fahrenheit is variable in both functions, they are different. Each variable alludes to a distinct memory location. Return values are also passed by position rather than name, just as parameters are by default instead of by name. The identical outcomes would be produced with the following code (Adelson, 1981).

```
Function Main
Assign Fahrenheit = GetTemperature()…
End
Module GetTemperature
Initialize Real temperature
Print "Enter Fahrenheit temperature:"
Input temperature
Return Real temperature
```

The majority of computer languages let a function's return value be either 0 or 1. Some ancient programming languages do not offer return values. Instead of being called functions in such languages, code modules are frequently called subroutines. Although this book will only use single or no return values, some programming languages allow several return values in a single return statement (Chaki et al., 2004).

5.7. VOID DATA TYPE

The module's output that returns correctly but does not give it call a result value is represented by the void data type, which is comparable to the null data type previously mentioned.

Both values and operations are absent from the void data type. A data type that symbolizes the absence of a data type (Reuter et al., 2007) (Table 5.2).

Table 5.2. Reserve Words for Void Data Types in Different Programming Languages

Language	Reserved Word
C++	void
Swift	void
C#	void
Java	void
Python	N/A
JavaScript	void

Source: Joyce Farell, Creative Commons License.

To describe the absence of a return value, which indicates that none is being returned, many computer languages require a data type. When defining and prototyping functions, the void data type is typically used to denote that either not nothing is being passed in or nothing is being returned (Tung et al., 2022).

5.8. SCOPE

The area in a computer program in which an obligatory is valid—that is, the area in which a name can be used to refer to an entity such as a variable—is referred to as the binding. The domain of an identifier name is this area. One phrase that might be utilized when referring to such a region is "scope block." In certain other parts of the software, the phrase may refer to an entirely other entity or it may not refer to anything at all (Englund, 1990).

The term "scope" refers to the portion of the program in which a component bearing an identifying name can be found to be recognized. They will make use of a variable during our conversation; the scope of the variable is determined by where in the program it is defined.

A variable is said to be "outside of a function" when its scope extends beyond the confines of a single function. During the process of compiling the program, the space for the variable's storage is generated as part of the object code that is stored in the data portion of the program. The object code contains several components, including a chunk of machine code, a data region, and instructions for linker resolution. Due to the fact that it has a global scope, the variable can be accessed by all of the functions in its code. In the same vein, they will not delve into that justification exactly at this moment (Clapes et al., 1986). It is also possible to make it accessible to functions within other object modules, which will result in the code of those modules being connected to it. At this juncture, it is essential to have a good understanding of a phrase shift. Despite the fact that the variable has global scope, it is actually only accessible from the point at which it is defined all the way up until the end of the source code for the program. As a consequence of this, the vast majority of global variables are located quite close to the beginning of the source code, prior to the beginning of any functions. By doing so, they will have access to each and every function (Bostock, 2009).

Remember

In some programming languages, such as JavaScript, functions can be used to create closures, which are a powerful technique for encapsulating data and behavior.

When a variable is defined "inside of a function," local scope occurs. When a program is being compiled, the compiler generates machine instructions that tell the computer to create storage locations on a portion of memory known as the stack. Until the function finishes its task and returns to its calling function, these memory locations are accessible. When a function terminates, items are inserted into the stack and exploded off of the stack, respectively, in assembly language. Even though the variable has a regional scope, it only exists from the function's beginning to its end. When data objects are passed as parameters into a function, they become local variables. To ensure they are accessible throughout the execution of the function's code, any additional variables or constants required by the function are often located toward the beginning of the definition (Wharton, 1984).

The concept of scope is crucial for modularization. Variables and constants may be used in program control functions with global scope, which places them near the program's top before any functions. Only local scope variables are used by specific task functions, which transfer data into them as needed via parameter passing and create local variables and constants as necessary. Again, parameter passing is used to transfer any info that has to be sent back to the caller module. This closed communications model creates a crucial antecedent idea for encapsulation, employed in OOP, by passing all data into and out of a function (Jordan, 1989).

5.9. PROGRAMMING STYLE

A collection of standards or rules used while creating the code for a computer is known as coding elegance. Developers that adhere to a specific coding style are better able to read, comprehend, and prevent the introduction of errors in source code (Oman et al., 1988).

Making software applications simple to maintain is a goal shared by the programming community. The focus of the desire is money. Said a well-written program is less expensive to maintain. Making source code listings as readable and clear as feasible is crucial to software maintenance. In light of it, they shall think about the succeeding (Oman & Cook, 1989):

- Documentation;
- Vertical alignment;
- Comments;
- Indentation;
- Meaningful identifier names and more consistently typed;
- Use of typedef appropriately.

The code can be compiled without the aforementioned components. Technically speaking, the compiler doesn't read source code like people do. But that is precisely the goal—to make the code easy for people to read. There is a difference between what is technically viable and what is acceptable (Oman & Cook, 1990).

Check the style guides for the programming language they have chosen to use to learn the standards and best practices for each of these items. Here are some general suggestions to think about (Ala-Mutka et al., 2004).

5.9.1. Documentation

The program's documentation is often added at the top using multiple comment lines. Depending on the needs or expectations of the business paying its workers or independent contractors to produce the code, the quantity of information would change (Yngve & Sammet, 1963).

5.9.2. Vertical Alignment

This is visible in the documentation section. The components are all arranged vertically within the same column. When variables are defined, this vertical alignment happens once more. Many textbooks place multiple items on one line when declaring variables or constants, like this: length, width, and height float (Fwa, 1989).

Regardless of how frequent this is in textbooks; it is typically not acceptable by the standards employed by the majority of businesses. Each item should be declared on a separate line, like in this (Green & Ledgard, 2011):

float length; float width; float height;

It is easier for humans to read when using one item per line. They can browse the list vertically more quickly than they can search horizontally, making it easier to find an identifying name. Some programmers provide an alphabetical list of them.

The lines of code that make up functions are normally indented two or four spaces from the left and are also vertically oriented. The indentation aids in visually highlighting the block (Oman & Cook, 1991).

5.9.3. Comments

Expert opinions on whether and when comments should be included in source code differ. Some claim that because the code should be straightforward or self-documenting, it ought to be composed with few comments. Others contend that comments should be plentiful in code, making up more than half of the pseudo-whitespace characters in the source code (Garvey, 1986).

The claim that comments are neither helpful nor harmful by themselves and that what is important is that they are accurate and kept in synchronization with the source code and that they should be omitted if they are unnecessary, excessive, difficult to maintain, or otherwise unhelpful, lies in the middle of these two points of view (Goldstein, 1994).

5.9.4. Indentation

For languages that use curly braces, there are two common indentation styles:

```
function(parameters) {

// code

}
```

```
function(parameters)

{

// code

}
```

It's crucial for preserving vertical alignment between the opening curly brace and the beginning of the code block in both scenarios (Miara et al., 1983).

Coding blocks are indented in two to four spaces, depending on the style. To avoid using tab characters for indents, care should be taken to make sure that the IDE or editor for code places spaces instead.

5.9.5. Meaningful Identifier Names Consistently Typed

As the name suggests, "identifier names" should make it abundantly apparent who (or what) they refer to. It might only have personal significance to them that they refer to their spouse as "Snooky." To properly identify the person they are referring to, others may need to see the entire name (Jane Mary Smith). The same idea holds for coding. Useful names should be given to variables, constants, functions, and other identifiers. Additionally, since the program uses those names, they should be typed consistently in both upper- and lowercase. If they define a variable like "Pig," don't type "pig" later in their program (Patra & Pradel, 2022).

Use noun or adjective-noun combinations for constant and variable identifiers and verb-noun combinations for function identifiers in procedural programs (as opposed to object-oriented programming (OOP)). It is typically best to break a function name into two independent functions if it requires two verbs or two nouns to express the function completely (Butler et al., 2011).

5.10. STANDARD LIBRARIES

Numerous common or standard functions are ready to be utilized in any program and whose definitions have already been created. They are collectively referred to as a standard library and are arranged into a collection of functions (consider them as many books). Numerous functions are arranged into various libraries. For instance, numerous arithmetic functions are available and have been developed (and stored in libraries) for the majority of computer languages. Programmers created these functions and tested them to ensure they operated as intended. The functions were typically inspected by numerous people to double- and triple-check that they performed as expected. The benefit is that they can use these functions knowing they will function correctly in our programs, saving us time and money (Taft, 1997).

Functions utilized by the main program must be verified as existing before they can be used. There is a formal technique, depending on the programming language:

- Define a function;

- Declare a function (a prototype is a declaration to a compiler);
- Call a function.

When they create functions in our program, they usually see them in the following order in our source code listing:

- Declare the function (prototype);
- Call the function;
- Define the function.

When they employ functions developed by others and collected into a library, they incorporate a header file into our program that houses the function prototypes. They appear in our source code listing in the same order that they create functions:

- Declaring the function (the included file contains a prototype);
- Call the function (passing values as parameters);
- Define the function (the linker software either delivers the actual object code from a Standard Library object area or defines the function in the header file).

Most of the time, a user can examine a prototype and determine precisely how an argument passing into and out of a function will work when the function is called. Let's examine a math illustration of absolute value (Table 5.3).

Table 5.3. Representation of Standard Libraries in Different Programming Languages

Language	Example
C++	#include<cmath> std::abs(number);
Swift	abs(number)
C#	Math.Abs(number);
Java	Java.lang.Math.abs(number)
JavaScript	Math.abs(number);
Python	abs(number)

Source: Zoe Wake, Creative Commons License.

The function's inventors chose to call it abs rather than "absolute" to avoid having a big function name. Although this could go against the identifier naming principle that names should be meaningful, identifier names for standard libraries are frequently abbreviated to names that are clear to all users. The line of code to invoke this function would be if I had two integer variables named apple and banana and were interested in saving the absolute value of banana into apple:

```
apple = abs(banana);
```

Let's express it in English: assign the function's return value to the variable apple and provide it the value that is stored in the variable banana as an absolute. Therefore, if they are familiar with the prototype, they can typically call the function correctly and use its return value (if it has one) without ever having to view the definition of the code (i.e., the source code that instructs the function how to obtain the answer; written by someone else; included in the header file; compiled and placed into a component library; and connected during the compilation and linking process in the IDE (Taft et al., 2007).

ACTIVITY 5.1:

Write a function that takes in two numbers as parameters and returns their sum. Then, have them call the function and print the result to the console.

5.11. SUMMARY

In programming, a function is a block of code that performs a specific task and can be called or invoked from other parts of a program. Functions are a fundamental concept in programming and are used to encapsulate reusable pieces of code that perform a specific task. Function typically takes input values and return a result. They are used to break down a program into smaller, more manageable pieces, and to make code more modular and easier to understand and maintain. Functions can be defined in many programming languages, including, C, C++, Java, Python, and JavaScript, among others. They can be written in many styles, such as procedural, object-oriented, and functional programming.

REVIEW QUESTIONS

1. What is a function in programming and why is it important?
2. How are functions called and executed in different programming languages?
3. How can function be used to improve the performance and efficiency of a program?
4. What is the difference between a function and a method in programming?
5. Can functions be nested inside of other functions, and if so, what are the benefits and drawbacks of this approach?

MULTIPLE CHOICE QUESTIONS

1. What is an argument in a function?

a. A keyword used to declare a variable
b. A value that is passed into the function when it is called
c. A value that is returned by the function
d. A type of loop

2. What is return value in a function?

a. A value that is passed into the function when it is called
b. A value that is returned by the function
c. A value that is used to declare a variable
d. A type of loop

3. What is the purpose of function?

a. To create variables
b. To encapsulate functionality that can be reused throughout a program
c. To write comments in code
d. To create loops

4. Which keyword is used to define a function in Python?

a. Def

b. Function

c. Define

d. Fun

Answers to Multiple Choice Questions

1. (b); 2. (b); 3. (b); 4. (a)

REFERENCES

1. Adelson, B., (1981). Problem solving and the development of abstract categories in programming languages. *Memory & Cognition, 9*(4), 422–433.
2. Ala-Mutka, K., Uimonen, T., & Jarvinen, H. M., (2004). Supporting students in C++ programming courses with automatic program style assessment. *Journal of Information Technology Education: Research, 3*(1), 245–262.
3. Albrecht, A. J., & Gaffney, J. E., (1983). Software function, source lines of code, and development effort prediction: A software science validation. *IEEE Transactions on Software Engineering*, (6), 639–648.
4. Baek, W., & Chilimbi, T. M., (2010). Green: A framework for supporting energy-conscious programming using controlled approximation. In: *Proceedings of the 31st ACM SIGPLAN Conference on Programming Language Design and Implementation* 10, pp. 198–209.
5. Bickman, L., (1987). The functions of program theory. *New Directions for Program Evaluation, 1987*(33), 5–18.
6. Bostock, M., (2009). The scope of computer control within technology. *Design & Technology Teaching, 26*(3).
7. Bothwell, S., & Timmerman, K., (2020). The return statement: Establishing a continuous assessment database system for consistent program feedback. In: *Proceedings of the 51st ACM Technical Symposium on Computer Science Education,* p. 905–911.
8. Butler, S., Wermelinger, M., Yu, Y., & Sharp, H., (2011). Improving the tokenization of identifier names. In: *ECOOP 2011–Object-Oriented Programming: 25th European Conference, Lancaster, Uk, July 25–29, 2011 Proceedings* 25, pp. 130–154.
9. Carrier, B. D., & Spafford, E. H., (2006). Categories of digital investigation analysis techniques based on the computer history model. *Digital Investigation, 3*, 121–130.
10. Chaki, S., Clarke, E. M., Groce, A., Jha, S., & Veith, H., (2004). Modular verification of software components in C. *IEEE Transactions on Software Engineering, 30*(6), 388–402.

11. Charwat, G., & Dvořák, W., (2012). dynPARTIX 2.0-dynamic programming argumentation reasoning tool. In: *Computational Models of Argument* 11, pp. 507, 508. IOS Press.
12. Chen, J., Prodic, A., Erickson, R. W., & Maksimovic, D., (2003). Predictive digital current programmed control. *IEEE Transactions on Power Electronics, 18*(1), 411–419.
13. Clapes, A. L., Lynch, P., & Steinberg, M. R., (1986). Silicon epics and binary bards: Determining the proper scope of copyright protection for computer programs. *UCLA L. Rev., 34*, 1493.
14. Cytron, R., Ferrante, J., Rosen, B. K., Wegman, M. N., & Zadeck, F. K., (1991). Efficiently computing static single assignment form and the control dependence graph. *ACM Transactions on Programming Languages and Systems (TOPLAS), 13*(4), 451–490.
15. Englund, S. R., (1990). Idea, process, or protected expression?: Determining the scope of copyright protection of the structure of computer programs. *Michigan Law Review, 88*(4), 866–909.
16. Fateman, R. J., & Toy, R., (2003). Converting call-by-reference to call-by-value: Fortran and lisp coexisting. In: *Proceedings of the 2003 International Symposium on Symbolic and Algebraic Computation,* pp. 95–102.
17. Fwa, T. F., (1989). Highway vertical alignment analysis by dynamic programming. *Transportation Research Record, 1239*(1–9), 2, 3.
18. Garvey, R. G., (1986). Computer comments. *Powder Diffr, 1*, 114–118.
19. Goldstein, P., (1994). Comments on "a manifesto concerning the legal protection of computer programs." *Columbia Law Review, 94*(8), 2573–2578.
20. Green, R., & Ledgard, H., (2011). Coding guidelines: Finding the art in the science. *Communications of the ACM, 54*(12), 57–63.
21. Gries, D., & Levin, G., (1980). Assignment and procedure call proof rules. *ACM Transactions on Programming Languages and Systems (TOPLAS),* 2(4), 564–579.
22. Hanus, M., (1994). The integration of functions into logic programming: From theory to practice. *The Journal of Logic Programming, 19*, 583–628.
23. Hempel, B., Lubin, J., & Chugh, R., (2019). Sketch-n-sketch: Output-directed programming for SVG. In: *Proceedings of the 32nd Annual ACM Symposium on User Interface Software and Technology* (Vol. 1, pp. 281–292).
24. Jordan, R. A., (1989). On the scope of protection for computer programs under copyright. *AIPLA QJ, 17*, 199.
25. Le Roy, R. J., (2017). LEVEL: A computer program for solving the radial Schrödinger equation for bound and quasibound levels. *Journal of Quantitative Spectroscopy and Radiative Transfer, 186*, 167–178.
26. Li, G., Liu, H., Jin, J., & Umer, Q., (2020). Deep learning based identification of suspicious return statements. In: *2020 IEEE 27th International Conference on Software Analysis, Evolution and Reengineering, (SANER)* (Vol. 4, pp. 480–491).

27. Liu, H., Liu, Q., Staicu, C. A., Pradel, M., & Luo, Y., (2016). Nomen est omen: Exploring and exploiting similarities between argument and parameter names. In: *Proceedings of the 38th International Conference on Software Engineering* 1, pp. 1063–1073.

28. Miara, R. J., Musselman, J. A., Navarro, J. A., & Shneiderman, B., (1983). Program indentation and comprehensibility. *Communications of the ACM, 26*(11), 861–867.

29. Novick, L. R., (2004). Diagram literacy in preservice math teachers, computer science majors, and typical undergraduates: The case of matrices, networks, and hierarchies. *Mathematical Thinking and Learning, 6*(3), 307–342.

30. Oman, P. W., & Cook, C. R., (1988). A paradigm for programming style research. *ACM Sigplan Notices, 23*(12), 69–78.

31. Oman, P. W., & Cook, C. R., (1989). Programming style authorship analysis. In: *Proceedings of the 17th Conference on ACM Annual Computer Science Conference* 1, pp. 320–326.

32. Oman, P. W., & Cook, C. R., (1990). A taxonomy for programming style. In: *Proceedings of the 1990 ACM Annual Conference on Cooperation* 7(2), pp. 244–250.

33. Oman, P. W., & Cook, C. R., (1991). A programming style taxonomy. *Journal of Systems and Software, 15*(3), 287–301.

34. Patra, J., & Pradel, M., (2022). Nalin: Learning from runtime behavior to find name-value inconsistencies in Jupyter notebooks. In: *Proceedings of the 44th International Conference on Software Engineering* 1, pp. 1469–1481.

35. Plotkin, G. D., (1975). Call-by-name, call-by-value and the λ-calculus. *Theoretical Computer Science, 1*(2), 125–159.

36. Prandini, M., & Ramilli, M., (2012). Return-oriented programming. *IEEE Security & Privacy, 10*(6), 84–87.

37. Ramalingam, V., & Wiedenbeck, S., (1998). Development and validation of scores on a computer programming self-efficacy scale and group analyses of novice programmer self-efficacy. *Journal of Educational Computing Research, 19*(4), 367–381.

38. Reuter, H. I., Nelson, A., & Jarvis, A., (2007). An evaluation of void-filling interpolation methods for SRTM data. *International Journal of Geographical Information Science, 21*(9), 983–1008.

39. Scott, P. J., (2000). Some aspects of categories in computer science. In: *Handbook of Algebra* (Vol. 2, pp. 3–77). North-Holland.

40. Shioji, E., Kawakoya, Y., Iwamura, M., & Hariu, T., (2012). Code shredding: Byte-granular randomization of program layout for detecting code-reuse attacks. In: *Proceedings of the 28th Annual Computer Security Applications Conference* (Vol. 12(2), pp. 309–318).

41. Steensgaard-Madsen, J., (1981). Modular programming with Pascal. *Software: Practice and Experience, 11*(12), 1331–1337.

42. Taft, S. T., Duff, R. A., Brukardt, R. L., Ploedereder, E., & Leroy, P., (2007). *Ada*

2005 Reference Manual. Language and Standard Libraries: International Standard ISO/IEC 8652/1995 (E) with Technical Corrigendum 1 and Amendment, 1 (Vol. 4348).

43. Taft, T. S., (1997). *Ada 95 Reference Manual. Language and Standard Libraries: International Standard ISO/IEC 8652: 1995,* (Vol. 8652, pp. 37–60).
44. Tung, L. N., Tran, H. V., Le, K. N., & Hung, P. N., (2022). An automated test data generation method for void pointers and function pointers in C/C++ libraries and embedded projects. *Information and Software Technology, 145*, 106821.
45. Van, M. J. J., & Krammer, H. P., (1987). Instructional strategies and tactics for the design of introductory computer programming courses in high school. *Instructional Science, 16*(3), 251–285.
46. Want, R., Schilit, B. N., Adams, N. I., Gold, R., Petersen, K., Goldberg, D., & Weiser, M., (1995). An overview of the PARCTAB ubiquitous computing experiment. *IEEE Personal Communications, 2*(6), 28–43.
47. Weinberg, G. M., & Schulman, E. L., (1974). Goals and performance in computer programming. *Human Factors, 16*(1), 70–77.
48. Wharton, L., (1984). Use and expression: The scope of copyright protection for computer programs. *Computer/LJ, 5*, 433.
49. Yngve, V. H., & Sammet, J. E., (1963). Toward better documentation of programming languages: Introduction. *Communications of the ACM, 6*(3), 76.

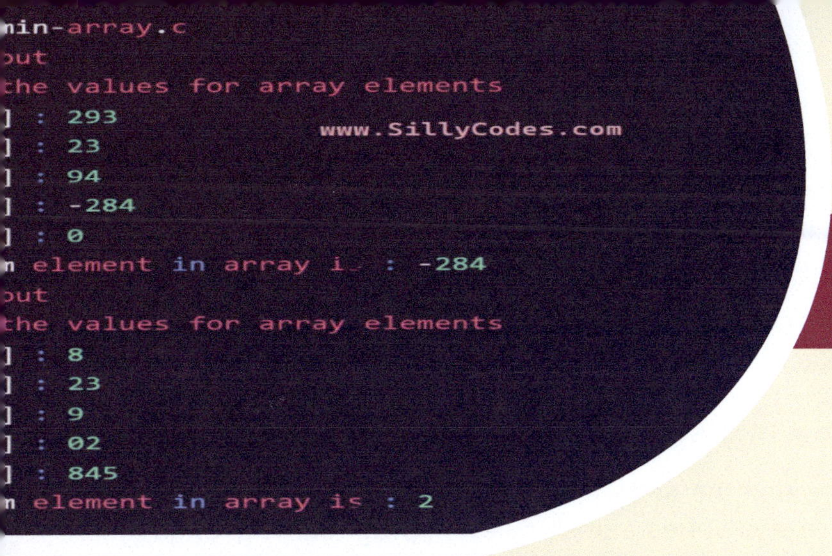

CHAPTER 6

ARRAYS

UNIT INTRODUCTION

An array is a fundamental data structure consisting of a collection of elements, including variables or values. A unique array index or key identifies each element within the array (Harris et al., 2020).

The variability of the identification or overlap of array types with other data types that indicate value collections, such as lists and strings, is contingent upon the specific programming language. Array data structures are commonly utilized to implement array types. Nevertheless, these could be executed in specific scenarios via alternative techniques such as linked lists, hash tables, or search trees. The list is a pre-defined array data structure in the Python programming language (Nieplocha et al., 1996).

Arrays can possess multiple axes, surpassing the constraint of a solitary axis. Each axis denotes a unique dimension. A list is a term commonly used to refer to a one-dimensional array. The term "table" is commonly used to refer to a two-dimensional array resembling spreadsheet software like Microsoft Excel. The requirement to arrange information into arrays comprising numerous dimensions is frequently encountered in real-world situations. The three dimensions attributed to theater tickets are section, seat, and row. The employment of vertical visualization is a prevalent practice for arrays that possess a singular dimension (Bikshandi et al., 2006).

Programmers commonly recognize a particular category of array known as a string. Strings are a type of one-dimensional array that consists of characters. In contrast to other arrays with a single dimension, strings are commonly conceptualized as a linear sequence of characters rather than a vertical arrangement (Nieplocha et al., 2006).

The individual values contained within the array are commonly referred to as members or elements. The implementation of arrays varies across different programming languages. Using a singular identifier name for an array necessitates using operators to retrieve or manipulate individual array elements. The index operator is the operator typically linked with referencing array members. It is of utmost significance to acquire the skill of defining an array and initializing its members (Skolnik et al., 1964).

Learning Objectives

After the chapter, students will be able to understand the following:

- Basic concept of arrays in programming;
- Understanding the utilization of index notation;
- Learn about displaying array members in programming;
- Fundamental idea of arrays and functions in programming;
- Understanding about searching, sorting, and multidimensional arrays.

Key Terms

- Array
- C++
- Capacity
- Declare
- Dimension
- Functions
- Index
- Java
- Multidimensional arrays
- Python
- Sorting arrays

6.1. ARRAY

An array is a structured grouping of homogeneous data elements, identified by a singular name, which is arranged successively. Python lists exhibit similarities to arrays in other programming languages. However, they are not limited to a singular data type (Nieplocha et al., 1994) (Table 6.1).

Table 6.1. Representation of Array in Different Programming Languages

Language	Example
C++	int numbers[] = {10, 20, 30, 40, 50};
C#	int[] numbers = {10, 20, 30, 40, 50};
Java	int[] numbers = {10, 20, 30, 40, 50};
Java Script	var numbers = [10, 20, 30, 40, 50];
Python	numbers = [10, 20, 30, 40, 50]
Swift	var numbers: [Int] = [10, 20, 30, 40, 50]

Source: Kenneth Leroy, Creative Commons License.

Did you Know?

The concept of arrays dates back to the early days of computer programming and was first introduced by Grace Hopper in the 1950s.

This is the definition of storage capacity. The array with five integer members is created using square brackets [] and assigned the "numbers" identifier name. The block assignment utilizing braces serves to initialize the values initially assigned to the array's members. The utilization of a sequence or comma operator should be observed. A comparable approach could have been employed as well, such as (Rose et al., 1993) in Table 6.2.

Table 6.2. Representation of Defining Storage Space for Arrays

Language	Examples	The Initial Values
C++	int numbers[5];	undefined
C#	int[] numbers = new int[5];	0
Java	int[] numbers = new int[5];	0
JavaScript	var numbers = Array(5);	undefined
Python	numbers = [None] * 5	None

Source: Dave Braunschweig, Creative Commons License.

The code above snippet would have allocated memory for a collection of five integers, denoted by the identifier "numbers." However, the initial values of these integers would have been undetermined or assigned based on the specific initialization protocol of the given programming language. Values can be assigned later in the program by omitting semicolons in Python, as demonstrated below (Bulutoglu & Margot, 2008):

```
numbers = [10, 20, 30, 40, 50]

initial_value = numbers[0]
```

In this case, the initial_value would be equal to 10 (Figure 6.1).

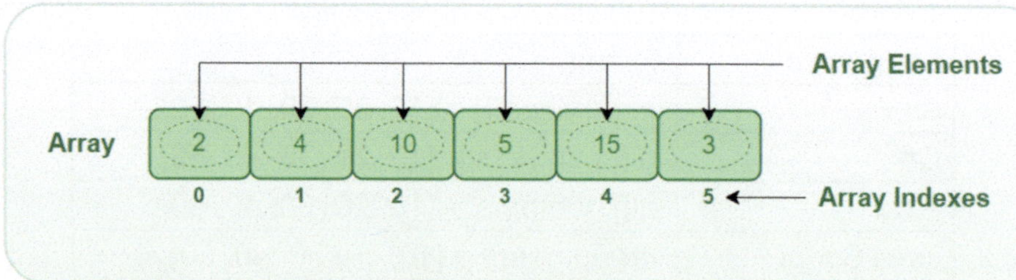

Figure 6.1. Illustration of an array in programming.

Source: Geeks for Geeks, Creative Commons License.

6.2. INDEX NOTATION

The specification of array elements is accomplished through the utilization of index notation. Square brackets represent the array index operator employed by most contemporary programming languages [ ]. The array index operator in older programming languages, namely COBOL, FORTRAN, and BASIC, is frequently represented by parentheses ( ) (Egi, 2017) (Table 6.3).

Table 6.3. Example of Index Notation in Different Programming Languages

Language	Example
C++	int numbers[] = {10, 20, 30, 40, 50}; int first_element = numbers[0];
C#	int[] numbers = {10, 20, 30, 40, 50}; int first_element = numbers[0];
Java	int[] numbers = {10, 20, 30, 40, 50}; int first_element = numbers[0];

JavaScript	var numbers = [10, 20, 30, 40, 50];
	
	let first_element = numbers[0];

Python	numbers = [10, 20, 30, 40, 50] first_element = numbers[0]
Swift	var numbers: [Int] = [10, 20, 30, 40, 50] var first_element = numbers[0]

Source: Devin Cook, Creative Commons License.

Comprehending the fundamental syntax of index notation in diverse programming languages is imperative for optimizing programming efficiency. While there may be variations in syntax and nuances across different languages, the fundamental principle of index notation remains uniform (Egi, 2018). The programming languages, namely C++, C#, Java, JavaScript, Python, and Swift, utilize a syntax whereby arrays or lists are instantiated through brackets to enclose their constituent elements. The utilization of index notation is employed to retrieve specific elements within said data structures by indicating the index of the desired element enclosed within square brackets. Indices in every language commence at 0 for the initial element, increase by 1 for each consecutive element, and persist until the final element is attained. The consistent utilization of index notation across various programming languages enables developers to seamlessly transition between languages and proficiently manipulate data stored in arrays or lists (Castellvi et al., 1995).

Did you Know?

Arrays are widely used in video game programming, as they provide a convenient way to represent game objects and data structures.

The utilization of index notation is a crucial concept in programming, as it enables developers to retrieve and modify data stored in arrays or lists, regardless of the programming language being used. Notwithstanding slight variations in syntax, the fundamental principle remains unchanged. In programming languages such as C++ and C#, arrays are declared by specifying the type followed by square brackets, as exemplified by the declaration of int[] numbers. Conversely, in Python, lists are instantiated by assigning an empty set of brackets to a variable, as demonstrated by the statement numbers = [] (Iverson, 1963).

The index notation is utilized to retrieve specific elements within these data structures, whereby the desired index is enclosed in square brackets, as exemplified by the expression numbers[0]. The indices utilized in this context adhere to a zero-based system. The initial element is assigned an index of 0, and each subsequent element is assigned an index incremented by 1 (Iverson, 1962). Using index notation is crucial for developers to switch between programming languages smoothly and proficiently execute fundamental operations on arrays or lists, including iteration, insertion, deletion, and searching, across various applications (Figure 6.2).

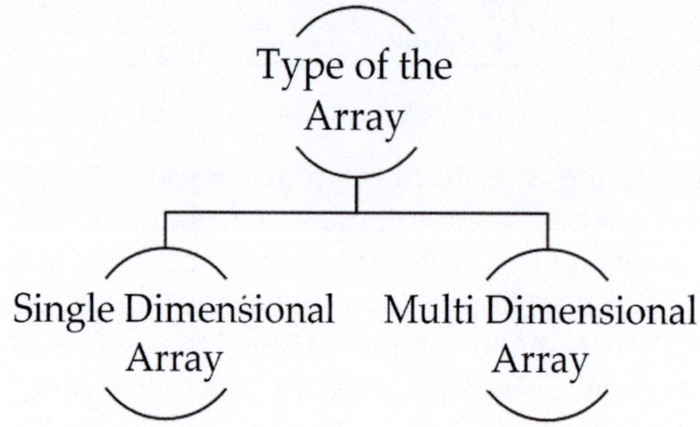

Figure 6.2. Representation of different types of arrays.

Source: Sairam Panigrahi, Creative Commons License.

6.3. DISPLAYING ARRAY MEMBERS

To display all components of an array, it is imperative to iterate through each element using a for loop and generate the element utilizing indices notation and the loop control variable (Pickett & Grinstein, 1988).

This study examines an integer array labeled "ages" with five distinct values, specifically 49, 48, 26, 19, and 16. The proposed solution can be articulated in pseudocode:

```
Declare Integer Array ages[5]
Assign ages = [49, 48, 26, 19, 16]
```

To display all elements of the array in order, it might be written as:

```
Output ages[0]
Output ages[1]
Output ages[2]
Output ages[3]
Output ages[4]
```

While this methodology may be appropriate for arrays with restricted dimensions, it could be more efficient and rapidly become unwieldy for arrays of greater magnitude. The software development principle that advocates against code repetition is widely known as "don't repeat yourself" (DRY). WET solutions are frequently used to refer to cases where the DRY principle is not followed. The initialism WET is commonly understood to have multiple interpretations, including "write everything twice," "we enjoy typing," or "waste everyone's time" (Pardoe et al., 1997).

Implementing a for loop to traverse every element of an array while utilizing the loop control variable as the array index can effectively mitigate redundancy. Kindly consider the subsequent pseudocode:

```
Declare Integer Array ages[5]
Declare Integer index
Assign ages = [49, 48, 26, 19, 16]
For index = 0 to 4
Output ages[index]
End
```

The methodology above demonstrates enhanced programming efficiency, resulting in a decreased program size. Nevertheless, there exists a further opportunity for improvement. Most programming languages provide an intrinsic mechanism for determining the dimensions of an array. It is recommended to establish loop control based on the dimensions of an array instead of relying on a fixed value to reduce the probability of errors and the frequency of necessary maintenance (Brereton, 1994).

```
Declare Integer Array ages[5]
Declare Integer index
Assign ages = [49, 48, 26, 19, 16]
For index = 0 to Size(ages) - 1
Output ages[index]
End
```

This methodology facilitates flexible programming. This specific format for the "for" loop enables adjustments to the declaration of the array by adding or removing elements without requiring modifications to the code (Astrachan & Rodger, 1998).

Remember

The speed and efficiency of array operations are a critical factor in the performance of many types of software, including scientific simulations, financial modeling, and machine learning algorithms.

6.4. ARRAYS AND FUNCTIONS

Modular programming involves creating and utilizing task-specific functions for array processing, often involving their reuse. Typically, array processing functions receive the array and any requisite data to execute the array processing operation for the specific task (Harris et al., 2020).

It is noteworthy that in the majority of contemporary programming languages, arrays are transmitted by reference.

Array processing functions must exercise caution to avoid unintended modifications to the array. Arrays represent a crucial and intricate data structure that finds application in virtually all programming paradigms. The focus remains on utilizing basic one-dimensional arrays, commonly called lists. Programmers typically create a set of user-defined task-specific functions that can be employed with an array for standard processing. Typically, these functions are provided with the array and the count of its elements. Certain functions may additionally transmit additional data elements necessary to accomplish the specific task assigned to that function (Nieplocha et al., 2006).

The present module pertains to the exhibition of the elements of an array on the monitor by invoking a specialized array function for the purpose.

- Pseudocode:

```
Function Main

Declare Integer Array ages[5]

Assign ages = [49, 48, 26, 19, 16]

Call DisplayArray(ages)

End

Function DisplayArray (Integer Array array)

Declare Integer index

For index = 0 to Size(array) - 1

Output array[index]

End

End
```

- Output:

```
49

48
```

```
26

19

16
```

6.5. MATH STATISTICS WITH ARRAYS

Statistics is a mathematical discipline that encompasses the processes of gathering, arranging, scrutinizing, comprehending, and exhibiting data. Frequently employed statistical techniques encompass mean, average, and standard deviation measures (Diaconis & Gangolli, 1995).

Arrays are a significant and intricate data structure utilized in virtually all programming. Our focus remains on utilizing basic one-dimensional arrays, also called lists. Programmers commonly create a set of user-defined task-specific functions that can be used with an array for typical processing. Typically, these functions receive the array and the number of elements contained within the array. Certain functions may also transmit additional data elements necessary to accomplish the specific task assigned to said functions (Van Der Walt et al., 2011).

The present module pertains to computing the sum of the elements contained within an array of integers. The act of computing the aggregate of numerical values is called summation in academic discourse, derived from the Latin term "summa," occasionally abbreviated as "sum." The function named "sum" calculates the total value of the array that is provided as an argument. Mathematical functions commonly linked with statistics, such as mean, count, minimum, maximum, and standard deviation, are frequently formulated to manipulate arrays (Brent & Luk, 1985).

- Pseudocode:

```
Function Main

Declare Integer Array ages[5]

Declare Integer total

Assign ages = [49, 48, 26, 19, 16]

Assign total = sum(ages)

Output "Total age is: " & total

End

Function sum (Integer Array array)
```

```
Declare Integer total
Declare Integer index
Assign total = 0
For index = 0 to Size(array) - 1
Assign total = total + array[index]
End
Return Integer total
```

- Output:

```
Total age is: 158
```

6.6. SEARCHING ARRAYS

A linear or sequential search is a technique to locate a specific value within a given list. The algorithm examines each element in the given list to determine if it matches the target value. This process continues until either a match is identified or all elements in the list have been exhaustively searched (Hoang, 1993).

Locating a particular element within an array involves searching until the desired element is located. The existence of the member is a potentiality that the programmer must account for within the algorithmic logic.

The algorithm of linear search is considered to be elementary. The method, also known as sequential search, involves iterating through an array using a loop, beginning with the initial element. The algorithm evaluates each element concerning the search value and terminates upon encountering either a match or the conclusion of the array. If the sought-after value is absent from the array, the algorithm will continue searching until the conclusion of the array (Cohen et al., 2005).

The array can be subject to two distinct linear searches, one for the maximum value and the other for the minimum value. The terms "maximum" and "minimum" are commonly abbreviated as "max" and "min," respectively. It should be noted that the maximum and minimum functions presented here are predicated on the condition that the size of the array >= 1 (Wang & Jiao, 2020).

- Pseudocode:

```
Function Main
Declare Integer Array ages[5]
```

```
Declare Integer maximum
Declare Integer minimum
Assign ages = [49, 48, 26, 19, 16]
Assign maximum = max(ages)
Assign minimum = min(ages)

Output "Maximum age is: " & maximum
Output "Minimum age is: " & minimum
End
Function max (Integer Array array)
Declare Integer maximum
Declare Integer index
Assign maximum = array[0]
For index = 1 to Size(array) - 1
If maximum < array[index]
Assign maximum = array[index]
End
End
Return Integer maximum
Function min (Integer Array array)
Declare Integer minimum
Declare Integer index
Assign minimum = array[0]
For index = 1 to Size(array) - 1
If minimum > array[index]
Assign minimum = array[index]
End
```

```
End

Return Integer minimum
```

- Output:

```
The maximum age is: 49

The minimum age is: 16
```

6.7. SORTING ARRAYS

A sorting algorithm is a computational procedure that arranges the elements of a given list in a specific order. The two most commonly utilized orders are numerical order and lexicographical order. Most contemporary programming languages incorporate preexisting or standardized library functions that facilitate the sorting of arrays (Knuth, 1973).

Sorting refers to the systematic arrangement of data based on their respective values. The subsequent illustrations exhibit conventional library and inherent array sorting techniques for diverse programming languages (Thompson & Kung, 1977) (Table 6.4).

Table 6.4. Standard Library and Built-In Array Sorting Methods for Different Programming Languages

Language	Sort Example
C++	#include <algorithm> sort(array, array + sizeof(array) / sizeof(int));
C#	System.Array.Sort(array)
Java	import java.util.Arrays; Arrays.sort(array);
JavaScript	array.sort();
Python	array.sort()
Swift	array.sort()

Source: Zoe Wake, Creative Commons License.

6.8. PARALLEL ARRAYS

The utilization of multiple arrays for presenting a singular array of records is a manifestation of an implicit data structure known as a group of parallel arrays. Each field of the record is associated with a distinct, uniform data array that shares an identical number of elements. Objects situated at identical indices in each array are inherently regarded as the fields of a solitary record (Keller et al., 2010).

A data structure is a method of organizing and storing data that facilitates efficient modification and access. In precise terms, a data structure refers to a set of data elements, their interrelationships, and the associated operations or functions that can be performed on the data. The available choices for data structures encompass arrays, linked lists, records, and classes (Kristensen et al., 2016). Parallel arrays are a data structure that utilizes multiple arrays to represent a set of data, where each index of the corresponding arrays corresponds to a matching field for a specific record. In the scenario where two arrays are present, namely one for names and the other for ages, the elements located at names[2] and ages[2] would correspondingly denote the name and age of the third individual (Deitz et al., 2003).

- Pseudocode:

```
Function Main

Declare String Array names[5]

Declare Integer Array ages[5]

Assign names = ["Lisa," "Michael," "Ashley," "Jacob,"
"Emily"]

Assign ages = [49, 48, 26, 19, 16]

DisplayArrays(names, ages)

End

Function DisplayArrays (String Array names, Integer
Array ages)

Declare Integer index

For index = 0 to Size(array) - 1

Output names[index] & " is " & ages[index] & " years
old"

End

End
```

- Output:

```
Lisa is 49 years old

Michael is 48 years old
```

```
Ashley is 26 years old
Jacob is 19 years old
Emily is 16 years old
```

6.9. MULTIDIMENSIONAL ARRAYS

An array's term dimension or dimensional refers to the number of indices required to identify a specific element within the array. It is possible to store a table, also known as a two-dimensional array, as a single-dimensional array consisting of one-dimensional arrays representing rows of columns. This can be accessed using double indexing, denoted as array[row][column] in standard notation (Moreira et al., 2003). An array is a structured grouping of homogeneous data elements that share a common identifier and are arranged sequentially. The array data type is classified under the "Complex" category or group of data types. Arrays can possess multiple axes, exceeding the limit of a single axis. Each axis represents a distinct dimension. A one-dimensional array is commonly referred to as a list. A two-dimensional array is often referred to as a table, akin to a spreadsheet such as Excel, which also functions as a two-dimensional array. In practical scenarios, it is common to encounter situations where data needs to be structured into arrays with multiple dimensions. Theatrical admission may be three-dimensional, incorporating section, row, and seat variables (de Carvalho Junior & Rezende, 2016) (Figure 6.3).

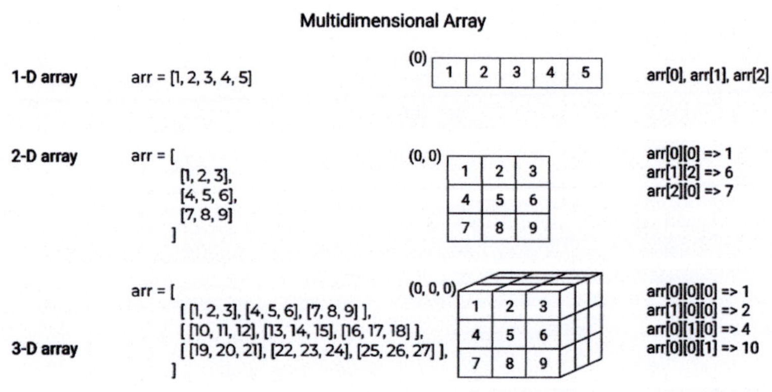

Figure 6.3. Image of the multidimensional arrays in java script language.

Source: Tutorials Tonight, Creative Commons License.

The individual values within the array are commonly called its members or elements. Multidimensional arrays are structured with square brackets for each dimension or axis of the array. An array variable with two dimensions can be defined using two sets of square brackets, while accessing its members would require using two sets of square brackets as index operators. The implementation of arrays varies across programming languages. The maximum number of dimensions permitted in an array is contingent upon the programming language in use and is further restricted by the amount of memory accessible (Moreira et al., 2003).

- Pseudocode:

```
Function Main
Declare String Array game[3][3]
Assign game = [ ["X," "O," "X"], ["O," "O," "O"], ["X," "O," "X"] ]
DisplayGame(game)
Function DisplayGame (String Array game)
Declare Integer row
Declare Integer column
Output "Tic-Tac-Toe" For row = 0 to 2
For column = 0 to 2
Output game[row][column]
If column < 2 Then
Output " | "
End
End
```

- Output:

```
Tic-Tac-Toe
X | O | X
O | O | O
X | O | X
```

6.10. DYNAMIC ARRAYS

The dynamic array is a list-based data structure that permits adding or removing elements and enables random access. Numerous contemporary programming languages come equipped with standard libraries. Dynamic arrays are a type of data structure that surpasses the limitation of static arrays. Unlike static arrays requiring a predetermined capacity to be specified during allocation, dynamic arrays can adjust their size as needed (Parmar & Kumbharana, 2015).

One constraint of the static arrays that have been discussed is that their size is established during the array's creation and/ or allocation. Dynamic arrays enable the addition and removal of elements during program execution. Most contemporary programming languages incorporate inherent or standardized library functions to generate and handle dynamic arrays (Breen et al., 1992) (Table 6.5).

ACTIVITY 6.1:

Write a program that declares an integer array of size 5, initializes it with some values, and prints the values to the console.

Table 6.5. Library Functions for Managing Dynamic Arrays in Different Programming Languages

Language	Class	Add	Remove
C++	#include <list> std::list	Insert	erase
C#	System. Collections. Generic.List	Add	Remove
Java	java.util.ArrayList	Add	remove
JavaScript	Array	push, splice	pop, splice
Python	List	append	remove
Swift	Array	append	remove

Source: Devin Cook, Creative Commons License.

6.11. SUMMARY

In programming, an array is a data structure that stores a collection of elements, such as numbers or strings, in contiguous memory locations. Each element in the array is identified by its index, which is an integer value that represents its position in the array. Arrays are commonly used in programming because they provide a convenient way to store and manipulate large amounts of data. Arrays can be declared with a fixed size, which means that the number of elements in the array is determined at compile time and cannot be changed during program execution. Alternatively, dynamic arrays can be used, which allow the size of the array to be changed at runtime. Programmers can access and manipulate array elements using various methods, such as loops, pointer arithmetic, and built-in-array functions.

REVIEW QUESTIONS

1. What is an array in programming?
2. What is the purpose of using arrays in programming?
3. How do you declare an array in a programming language?
4. How do you access and manipulate array elements in a programming language?
5. What is the difference between a fixed-size array and a dynamic array?
6. How do you avoid errors when working with arrays?

MULTIPLE CHOICE QUESTIONS

1. What is an array?

a. A collection of variables
b. A collection of functions
c. A collection of objects
d. A collection of data elements

2. What is the index of the first element in an array?

a. 0
b. 1
c. –1
d. None of the above

3. How do you declare an array in most programming languages?

a. Array[]
b. Int[]
c. Array()

d. None of the above

4. How do you access an element in an array with index i?

a. Array(i)

b. Array[i]

c. Array{i}

d. Array<i>

5. How do you add an element to the end of an array?

a. Use the push() method

b. Use the pop() method

c. Use the shift() method

d. Use the unshift() method

Answers to Multiple Choice Questions

1. (d); 2. (a); 3. (b); 4. (b); 5. (a)

REFERENCES

1. Arora, N., Bhasin, G., & Sharma, N., (2014). Two way linear search algorithm. *International Journal of Computer Applications, 107*(21).
2. Astrachan, O., & Rodger, S. H., (1998). Animation, visualization, and interaction in CS 1 assignments. *ACM SIGCSE Bulletin, 30*(1), 317–321.
3. Bikshandi, G., Guo, J., Hoeflinger, D., Almasi, G., Fraguela, B. B., Garzarán, M. J., & VonPraun, C., (2006). Programming for parallelism and locality with hierarchically tiled arrays. In: *Proceedings of the Eleventh ACM SIGPLAN Symposium on Principles and Practice of Parallel Programming*, pp. 48–57.
4. Breen, E. J., Joss, G. H., & Williams, K. L., (1992). Dynamic arrays for fast, efficient, data manipulation during image analysis: A new software tool for exploratory data analysis. *Computer Methods and Programs in Biomedicine, 37*(2), 85–92.
5. Brent, R. P., & Luk, F. T., (1985). The solution of singular-value and symmetric eigenvalue problems on multiprocessor arrays. *SIAM Journal on Scientific and Statistical Computing, 6*(1), 69–84.
6. Brereton, R. G., (1994). Tutorial review. Object-oriented programming on personal computers. *Analyst, 119*(10), 2149–2160.
7. Bulutoglu, D. A., & Margot, F., (2008). Classification of orthogonal arrays by integer programming. *Journal of Statistical Planning and Inference, 138*(3), 654–666.
8. Castellvi, P., Jaén, X., & Llanta, E., (1995). Symbolic tensor calculus using index notation. *Computers in Physics, 9*(3), 335–340.

9. Chow, P., Seo, S. O., Rose, J., Chung, K., Páez-Monzón, G., & Rahardja, I., (1999). The design of a SRAM-based field-programmable gate array-Part II: Circuit design and layout. *IEEE Transactions on Very Large Scale Integration (VLSI) Systems, 7*(3), 321–330.
10. Cohen, A., Sigler, M., Girbal, S., Temam, O., Parello, D., & Vasilache, N., (2005). Facilitating the search for compositions of program transformations. In: *Proceedings of the 19th Annual International Conference on Supercomputing* (pp. 151–160).
11. De Carvalho, Jr. F. H., & Rezende, C. A., (2016). Performance evaluation of virtual execution environments for intensive computing on usual representations of multidimensional arrays. *Science of Computer Programming, 132*, 29–49.
12. Deitz, S. J., Chamberlain, B. L., Choi, S. E., & Snyder, L., (2003). The design and implementation of a parallel array operator for the arbitrary remapping of data. *ACM SIGPLAN Notices, 38*(10), 155–166.
13. Diaconis, P., & Gangolli, A., (1995). Springer New York. *Rectangular Arrays with Fixed Margins* 11(3), pp. 15–41.
14. Egi, S., (2017). *Scalar and Tensor Parameters for Importing Tensor Index Notation, Including Einstein Summation Notation*. arXiv preprint arXiv,1(1702.6343).
15. Egi, S., (2018). *Symbolical Index Reduction and Completion Rules for Importing Tensor Index Notation Into Programming Languages*. arXiv preprint arXiv, 1(1804.3140).
16. Harris, C. R., Millman, K. J., Van, D. W. S. J., Gommers, R., Virtanen, P., Cournapeau, D., & Oliphant, T. E., (2020). Array programming with NumPy. *Nature, 585*(7825), 357–362.
17. Hoang, D. T., (1993). Searching genetic databases on splash 2. In: *[1993] Proceedings IEEE Workshop on FPGAs for Custom Computing Machines* 1, pp. 185–191.
18. Hobson, R. F., Hoskin, J. D., Simmons, J. L., & Spilsbury, R. W., (1992). SAM-I: A prototype machine for dynamic, array-oriented programming languages. *IEE Proceedings E-Computers and Digital Techniques, 139*(4), 335–347.
19. Iverson, K. E., (1962). A programming language. In: *Proceedings of the May 1–3, 1962, Spring Joint Computer Conference* (Vol. 1, pp. 345–351).
20. Iverson, K. E., (1963). Programming notation in systems design. *IBM Systems Journal, 2*(2), 117–128.
21. Kaviani, A., & Brown, S., (1999). The hybrid field-programmable architecture. *IEEE Design & Test of Computers, 16*(2), 74–83.
22. Keller, G., Chakravarty, M. M., Leshchinskiy, R., Peyton, J. S., & Lippmeier, B., (2010). Regular, shape-polymorphic, parallel arrays in Haskell. *ACM Sigplan Notices, 45*(9), 261–272.
23. Knuth, D. E., (1973). *The Art of Computer Programming, Searching and Sorting* (No. 3, pp. 543–583). Reading MA: Addison-Wisley.
24. Korel, B., & Laski, J., (1988). Dynamic program slicing. *Information Processing Letters, 29*(3), 155–163.

25. Kristensen, M. R., Lund, S. A., Blum, T., & Avery, J., (2016). Fusion of parallel array operations. In: *Proceedings of the 2016 International Conference on Parallel Architectures and Compilation* 1, pp. 71–85.
26. Moreira, J. E., Midkiff, S. P., & Gupta, M., (2003). Supporting multidimensional arrays in Java. concurrency and computation. *Practice and Experience, 15*(3–5), 317–340.
27. Nieplocha, J., Harrison, R. J., & Littlefield, R. J., (1994). Global arrays: A portable "shared-memory" programming model for distributed memory computers. In: *Supercomputing'94: Proceedings of the 1994 ACM/IEEE Conference on Supercomputing* 1, pp. 340–349. IEEE.
28. Nieplocha, J., Harrison, R. J., & Littlefield, R. J., (1996). Global arrays: A nonuniform memory access programming model for high-performance computers. *The Journal of Supercomputing, 10*, 169–189.
29. Nieplocha, J., Palmer, B., Tipparaju, V., Krishnan, M., Trease, H., & Apra, E., (2006). Advances, applications, and performance of the global arrays shared memory programming toolkit. *The International Journal of High-Performance Computing Applications, 20*(2), 203–231.
30. Pardoe, J., King, M., Pardoe, J., & King, M., (1997). Arrays of objects. *Object Oriented Programming Using C++ An Introduction, 1*, 124–131.
31. Parmar, V. P., & Kumbharana, C. K., (2015). Comparing linear search and binary search algorithms to search an element from a linear list implemented through static array, dynamic array, and linked list. *International Journal of Computer Applications, 121*(3).
32. Pickett, R. M., & Grinstein, G. G., (1988). Iconographic displays for visualizing multidimensional data. In: *Proceedings of the 1988 IEEE Conference on Systems, Man, and Cybernetics* (Vol. 514, p. 519).
33. Rose, J., El Gamal, A., & Sangiovanni-Vincentelli, A., (1993). Architecture of field-programmable gate arrays. *Proceedings of the IEEE, 81*(7), 1013–1029.
34. Rose, J., Francis, R. J., Lewis, D., & Chow, P., (1990). Architecture of field-programmable gate arrays: The effect of logic block functionality on area efficiency. *IEEE Journal of Solid-State Circuits, 25*(5), 1217–1225.
35. Sangiovanni-Vincentelli, A., El Gamal, A., & Rose, J., (1993). Synthesis method for field programmable gate arrays. *Proceedings of the IEEE, 81*(7), 1057–1083.
36. Skolnik, M., Nemhauser, G., & Sherman, J., (1964). Dynamic programming applied to unequally spaced arrays. *IEEE Transactions on Antennas and Propagation, 12*(1), 35–43.
37. Thompson, C. D., & Kung, H. T., (1977). Sorting on a mesh-connected parallel computer. *Communications of the ACM, 20*(4), 263–271.
38. Van, D. W. S., Colbert, S. C., & Varoquaux, G., (2011). The NumPy array: A structure for efficient numerical computation. *Computing in Science & Engineering, 13*(2), 22–30.

39. Wang, R. Q., & Jiao, Y. C., (2020). Synthesis of sparse linear arrays with reduced excitation control numbers using a hybrid cuckoo search algorithm with convex programming. *IEEE Antennas and Wireless Propagation Letters, 19*(3), 428–432.

40. Wirth, N., (1976). Comment on a note on dynamic arrays in Pascal. *ACM SIGPLAN Notices, 11*(1), 37, 38.

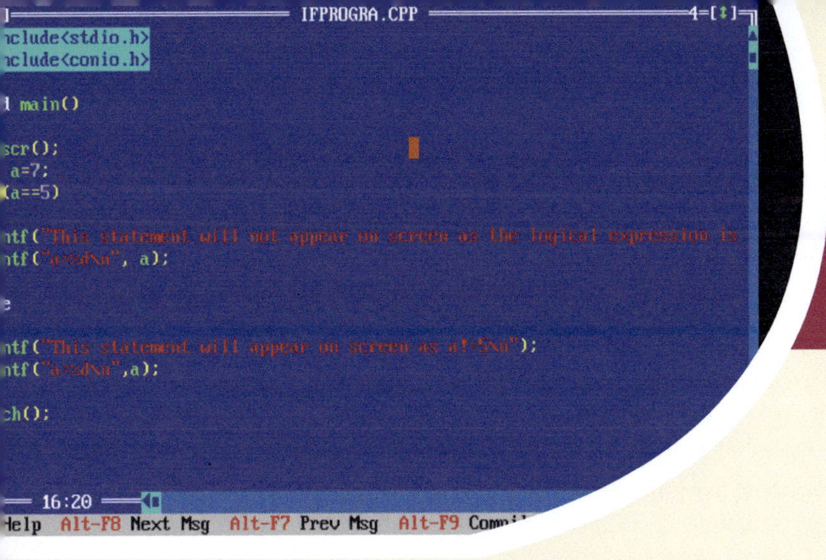

CHAPTER 7

CONTROL STRUCTURES

UNIT INTRODUCTION

Structured programming is a coding methodology that emphasizes utilizing selection constructs, such as if/then/else, and repetition constructs, such as while and for, in addition to block structures and subroutines. The methodology being discussed presents a juxtaposition between rudimentary assessments and leaps, such as the employment of the go-to statement, which has the potential to generate intricate and arduous-to-sustain code, colloquially referred to as "spaghetti code." The observation of enhancing a computer program's quality, clarity, and development time is noted (Riccardi, 1981).

The capacity to modify a program to execute distinct lines of code or to execute distinct lines of code, or to repeat particular lines of code multiple times is considered a crucial programming concept. Control structures refer to the mechanisms that enable us to manage the flow of execution. Flowcharting refers to delineating the anticipated course(s) of execution for a program. There exist three primary categories of control structures (Spector, 1996):

- **Sequence:** The content is lacking in interest or excitement. It is recommended to adhere to each instruction sequentially. It is recommended to adhere to the specified order or prescribed sequence. This is the typical appearance of a line of code.
- **Selection:** One may choose one or multiple flows from a given list of options.

A method of inquiry is employed to arrive at a determination. The execution of specific lines of code is contingent upon the response received, or in other words, the path taken (Al-Gherwi et al., 2010).

- **Iteration:** The programming concept known as iteration facilitates the execution or repetition of a particular set of code, which may consist of one or more lines, for multiple instances. The program can manifest three distinct behaviors: it may remain unexecuted, execute a fixed number of times, or execute continuously until a specific condition is met. The iterative process, commonly called looping, is distinguished by the flowchart that illustrates the return of the flow to repeat the task (Young et al., 1995) (Figure 7.1).

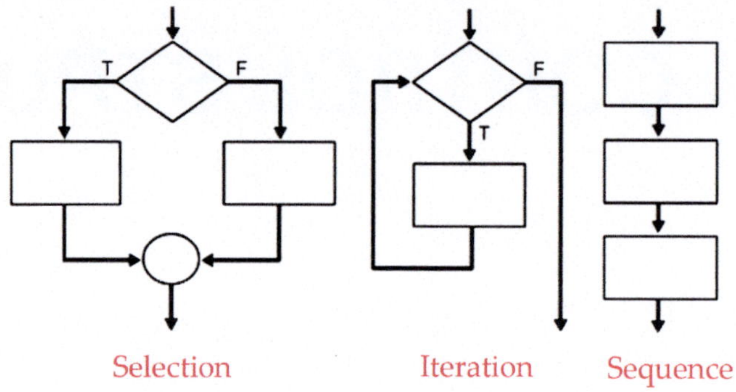

Figure 7.1. Categories of control structures in programming.

Source: Net-Information's, Creative Commons License.

The fourth category concerns unstructured code:

1. **Branching:** An unstandardized arrangement that enables the transfer of program execution to a distinct segment. The employment of this particular categorization is infrequent within the framework of modular programming.

Control structures are a prevalent characteristic in programming languages operating at a high level. Notably, the three fundamental categories of control structures, sequence, selection, and iteration, are universally present in all programming languages. Most programming constructs utilize the if-then-else framework, which falls under the conditional category, and the complete structure, which falls under the iterative category. Linguistic variations typically arise from two fundamental structures (Messac, 1998).

The origins of structured programming can be attributed to the latter half of the 1960s when Edsger Dijkstra published the topic. The person proposed a methodology of programming logic design that involves minimizing the use of control structures in the branching category, referred to as a "go to less" approach. The topic was subjected to discourse and examination lasting approximately two decades. Based on the available evidence, it can be deduced that by the end of the 20th century, most computer scientists had reached a consensus regarding the importance of pursuing the acquisition and implementation of structured programming principles (Syahidi & Asyikin, 2018).

Learning Objectives

Upon completion of the chapter, students will possess the ability to comprehend the subsequent concepts:

- The fundamental principles of control structures in programming;
- Acquiring knowledge about if/else and case-control structures are recommended;
- The comprehension of relational operators;
- The fundamental concept of iteration control structures, also known as loops, is to repeatedly execute a code block until a certain condition is met;
- One can acquire knowledge regarding branching statements in the field of programming.

Key Terms

- Branching
- Break
- Case-control
- Conditional statements
- Continue
- Exit
- Goto
- If/else
- Iteration
- Loop structures
- Operators
- Sequence

7.1. SELECTION CONTROL STRUCTURES

Conditional statements are a fundamental aspect of programming languages within selection control structures. They enable the execution of distinct computations or actions based on evaluating a Boolean condition specified by the programmer (Narraway & Perkins, 1994).

The fundamental characteristic of a system for selection control is its ability to choose among multiple alternative paths. Those, as mentioned earlier, can be classified as either binary selection or non-binary selection. A query that employs Boolean principles typically governs the selection of a particular route. The paths emanating from a structure for controlling selection converge at the termination of the control structure before proceeding with the subsequent lines of code within a program (Kookos & Perkins, 2002) (Figure 7.2).

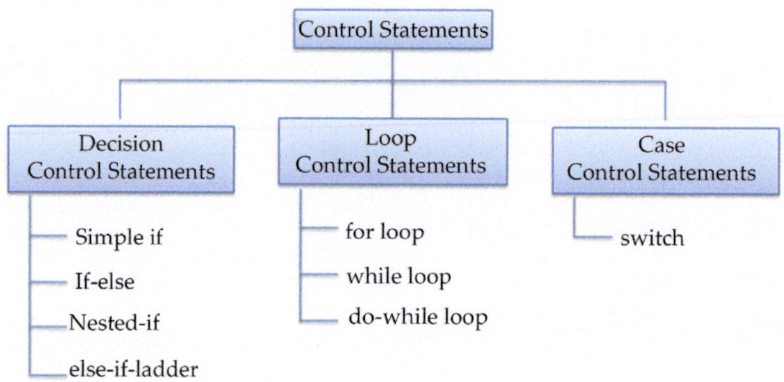

Figure 7.2. Types of control statements in programming.

Source: Soft Schools, Creative Commons License.

7.1.1. If Then Else Control Structure

A two-way choice is made using the if-then-else control structure.

```
temperature = 25
if temperature > 30:
print("It's hot outside.")
else:
print("It's not too hot outside.")
```

The reserved words for C# and C++, Java, JavaScript, Swift, and Python are If, else (Al-Gherwi et al., 2010).

7.1.2. Case-Control Structure

The case-control structure is a programming paradigm that facilitates the implementation of multi-way selection. Within the realm of programming, case-control structures entail the comparison of a designated value with constants that have been predetermined, thereby executing a particular action contingent upon the initial expression that corresponds (Raftery et al., 2012).

```
score = 85
if score >= 90:
print("You got an A!")
elif score >= 80 and score < 90:
print("You got a B.")
elif score >= 70 and score < 80:
print("You got a C.")
elif score >= 60 and score < 70:
print("You got a D.")
else:
print("You failed the class.")
End
```

In this case, the reserved words for C# and C++, Java, JavaScript, and Swift are "Switch, case, break, default." Python does not support the case-control structure. Although alternative solutions exist, they are outside the purview of this publication (Hewitt, 1977).

7.2. IF THEN ELSE

The if-then-else construct, also known as if-then, is a binary selection structure prevalent in numerous programming languages. While the syntax may differ across various programming languages, the fundamental structure typically exhibits the following form (Meyer & Masterson, 2000):

```
If (boolean condition)
Then (consequent)
Else
(alternative) End If
```

The present discourse aims to introduce the control structure of the selected category, a ubiquitous feature in high-level programming languages. The programming construct commonly called the "if-then-else" structure is a conditional statement used to execute specific code blocks based on evaluating a given condition. Formulating a query that can be answered with a binary response regulates the conditional statement of if-then-else (Burnett & Baker, 1994).

```
if the answer to the question is true
then do this
else because it is false
do this
```

The test expression, commonly called the question, is typically a Boolean expression in most programming languages. The Boolean data type comprises a binary set of two distinct values: true and false. Improving further (Ahmad, 1999):

```
if an expression is true
then do this
else because it is false
do this
```

Did you Know?

Early programming languages like COBOL and FORTRAN were developed. introduced control mechanisms.

Certain programming languages incorporate reserved keywords such as "if," "then," and "else." The use of "then" is often omitted. Moreover, the instruction "do this" can be associated with binary values of 1 and 0. One may perceive it as:

```
if an expression is true
action true
else
action false
```

Four control structures say the same thing. Modern English rarely uses otherwise. But consider this mother-child conversation (Hils, 1992).

```
"Mommy, can I play outside?"
```

The mother replies, "If your bed is washed, you may, or else you may stand on the porch for one hour as a penalty for asking me even when you saw your bed was not washed."

Notably, all the necessary elements have been included for identifying the action or flow the child will undertake. Given that the inquiry about the cleanliness of one's room is dichotomous, with only two possible responses, i.e., affirmative or negative, the corresponding actions are mutually exclusive. The child has two options: engage in outdoor physical activity or remain seated for five minutes (Schaefer, 2011).

7.3. NESTED IF THEN ELSE

Multi-way selection can be achieved by nesting two-way selection structures within other two-way selection structures.

The present discourse aims to introduce the notion of nested control structures. The concept of nesting involves the placement of one item within another. Consider (Ni et al., 2007):

```
num = 10

if num > 0:

if num % 2 == 0:

print("num is positive and even")

else:

print("num is positive and odd")

else:

print("num is zero or negative")

End
```

In this instance, the program initially assigns the numerical value of 10 to the variable denoted as "num." Subsequently, a nested conditional statement is employed to verify whether the numerical value of "num" is superior to zero and whether it is categorized as an even or odd integer (Henriksen et al., 2017).

If the value of "num" is larger than zero, the program executes the code within the initial "if" block. Within the specified code block, an evaluation is performed to determine if the value of "num" is classified as even or odd, utilizing the subsequent conditional statement. If the value of "num" is determined to be even, the program will proceed to execute the code contained within the nested "if" block, which entails the output of the string "num is positive and even." If the value of 'num' is determined to be an odd integer, the program will execute the code within the nested 'else' block, designed to output the string "num is positive and odd" (Batrinu et al., 2004).

If the value of num fails to exceed 0, the initial conditional statement is bypassed, and the subsequent alternative statement is executed. This alternative statement entails the output of the textual representation "num is zero or negative." Given that the value of num is 10, which satisfies the conditions of being both positive and even, the program will output the string "num is positive and even" (Ding et al., 2020).

7.4. RELATIONAL OPERATORS

A relational operator is a programming language construct or operator that examines or defines a relationship between two entities. The concepts mentioned earlier encompass numerical equivalence, as exemplified by the equation 5 = 5, and numerical inequalities, as demonstrated by the inequality 4 ≥ 3.1 (White & Cohen, 1980).

Relational operators are commonly employed to create a test expression that controls the execution of a program. This particular type of linguistic construction is frequently referred to as a Boolean expression, owing to its capacity to produce a Boolean result or output when assessed. Six commonly used relational operators produce a Boolean result by evaluating and indicating the connection between two operands. Implicit promotion is employed to convert operands with dissimilar data types into homogeneous data type (Woodward, 1991).

The terminology and/or notations employed for operators may vary among diverse programming languages. Most programming languages utilize relational operators that resemble the following (Table 7.1):

Table 7.1. Representation of Relational Operators and Their Meanings

Operator	Meaning
<	Less than
>	Greater
<=	Less than or equal to
>=	Greater than or equal to
==	Equal to
!= or <>	Not equal to

Source: Devin Cook, Creative Commons License.

- Examples:

```
7 < 12
7 > 21
7 <= 9
7 >= 16
```

```
7 == 5
7 != 5
7 !< 18
7 <> 18
```

7.5. ASSIGNMENT VS. EQUALITY

The assignment process entails modifying the present value stored in a specified memory location that a variable identifier has identified. The notion of equality refers to a binary operator that assesses or establishes the relationship between two separate entities (Early et al., 2018).

Most control structures depend on a test expression that executes either selection, as demonstrated by the if-then-else statement, or iteration, as observed in the while, do-while, or for loops, based on the truth or falsity of the expression. Therefore, the Boolean expression that governs the structure is frequently discussed in academic discourse. When implemented in diverse programming languages, the expression above must conform to strict standards and exhibit Boolean behavior.

In several programming languages, employing each data type as a Boolean expression is feasible. The principle that ascribes a Boolean value to each data type is founded on the concept that the values of zero and null denote false, while all non-zero values signify true. In certain linguistic contexts, there exists a potential for heightened ambiguity surrounding the equals symbol (=) as an operator that deviates from the established mathematical interpretation of equality, which has been widely adopted. In programming, it is common for the equals symbol to denote the assignment operator. In mathematics, the relational operator of equality is commonly represented by a pair of equal symbols (Alpern et al., 1988).

```
If (dog = 'y')
Output "Dogs are nice."
Else
Output "Dogs are harmful."
```

The control structure's test expression will invariably evaluate to true, as the expression in question is an assignment rather than the relational operator of ==. The code assigns the value 'y' to the variable 'dog' and subsequently evaluates the value of 'dog' to determine its truthiness, which is true since it is not equal to zero. The statement will consistently hold, and the alternative code branch will not be executed. The intended outcome of the programmer was not achieved. The accurate syntax is (Bowman et al., 2020):

```
If (dog == 'y')
Output "Dogs are nice."
Else
Output "Dogs are harmful."
```

This instance serves as a reminder to exercise caution when formulating test expressions to ensure they are genuinely interrogative, frequently entailing relational operators. Certain programming languages may issue a warning or an error message if an assignment is employed within a Boolean expression, whereas others may not. Avoid using the assignment operator to test equality (Rubin, 2013).

7.6. ITERATION CONTROL STRUCTURES

Iteration control structures involve the execution of a statement or block until a specific condition is met or until operations have been performed on each element of a collection. Typically, this is conveyed using specific terms such as "or" and "do.until."

The fundamental characteristic of an iteration control structure is its ability to execute a set of code repeatedly. The circular pattern that results from flowcharting a visual representation of iteration is commonly linked to iteration control structures, hence the term "loop." Iterative processes can be implemented using pre-test, post-test, and count-controlled loops. A Boolean-based inquiry typically determines the frequency of loop execution (Young et al., 1995).

7.6.1. Iteration (Repetition) Control Structures

- Pseudocode: While

```
sum = 0
count = 1
while count <= 10:
sum = sum + count
Increment count
End
```

- Pseudocode: Do while

```
guess = 0
```

```
answer = 42
Do
Display "Guess the number (between 1 and 100): "
Get user input for guess
While guess != answer
Display "Congratulations, you guessed the number!"
```

- Pseudocode: Repeat Until

```
Count assigned five Repeat.
Display "Blast off is soon!"
Decrement count
Until count < one
```

- Pseudocode: For

```
For x starts at 0, x < 5, increment x
Display "Are we having fun?"
End
```

Did you Know?

Control structures are a useful tool for developing interactive software applications, including but not limited to games, simulations, and chatbots.

7.7. BRANCHING STATEMENTS

A branch is a type of instruction in a computer program that can alter the standard practice of executing instructions in sequential order.

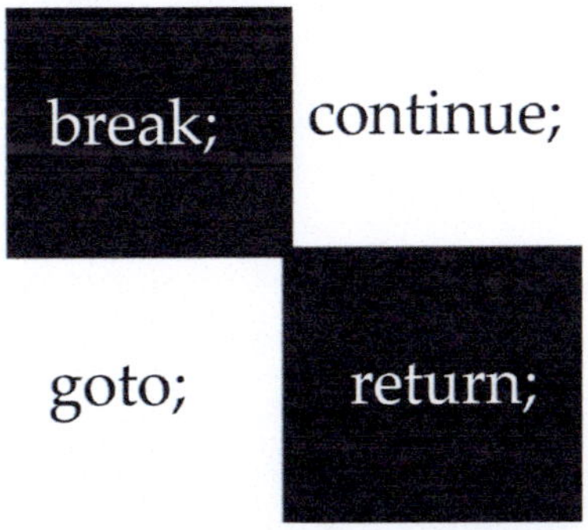

Source: Nishirika, Creative Commons License.

Figure 7.3. Illustration of unconditional branching statements in programming.

By initiating a branch instruction, a computer can commence the execution of a distinct instruction sequence, thereby deviating from its default behavior. Frequently utilized conditional statements encompass break and continue, return, and goto (Seidman, 1989) (Figure 7.3).

7.7.1. Break

The break statement serves a dual purpose, functioning as a case structure when used with a switch statement or as a means of terminating a loop when employed within a looping construct. The scenario, as mentioned earlier, suggests that the loop will iterate 8 times; however, the break statement halts its execution during the fifth iteration (Zorn et al., 2013).

```
counter = 0;

While counter < 8

Output counter

If counter == 4

break counter += 1
```

7.7.2. Continue

The example demonstrates that the loop will produce output to the display on eight occasions, albeit the inclusion of the continue statement results in the omission of the fourth number (Bobrow & Raphael, 1974).

```
For counter = 0, counter < 8, counter += 1

If counter == 4

continue

Output counter
```

7.7.3. Return

The return statement serves the purpose of terminating a function's execution and resuming control of the statement that invoked the function (Levine et al., 1984).

```
Function DoSometing

statements
```

```
Return <optional return value>
```

7.7.4. Goto

Utilizing the goto structure is generally deemed unacceptable in well-organized programming. Certain programming languages can generate a label with an identifier name succeeded by a colon. The command "goto" is used with a label to direct program flow (Wulf, 1972).

```
code;
goto label;
code;
code;
code;
label: some statement;
code;
```

ACTIVITY 7.1:

Write a program that utilizes conditional statements to ascertain the parity of a number inputted by the user.

7.7.5. Exit

The function 'exit' is included in this discussion due to its frequent application in programming, despite its classification as a pre-defined function. An illustrative instance pertains to the act of initiating a file and subsequently evaluating its successful opening. If an error is present, it typically signifies a desire to halt program execution prematurely. The exit function is responsible for the termination of program execution and the subsequent return of an integer value to the operating system. The above-mentioned action can be classified as branching, which involves redirecting the program's flow to a different location (Roberts, 1995).

7.8. SUMMARY

Control structures refer to programming language constructs that allow programmers to manage the flow of program execution based on specific conditions. Control structures enable programmers to establish logical constructs that facilitate decision-making, iteration, and selective code execution based on specific conditions. The three primary categories of control structures in programming are conditional statements, loops, and control statements. Conditional statements assess a given condition and perform a set of instructions depending on whether the condition is true or false. Conditional statements encompass if/else statements and switch/case statements. Loops enable the software developer to iterate a code block multiple time. Instances of loop structures comprise loops, while loops, and do/while loops. Control statements enable the programmer to modify the sequence of program execution depending on particular conditions. Control statements, such as break and continue statements, are illustrative instances in programming. By utilizing control structures, programmers can develop intricate programs that execute various operations and react to different inputs and circumstances (Rasure & Williams, 1991).

REVIEW QUESTIONS

1. What are the different types of control structures in programming, and how are they used?
2. How do conditional statements work, and what are some common use cases in programming?
3. What is a loop structure, and how can it be used to repeat a block of code multiple times?
4. How do control statements work, and what are some examples of when they might be used in programming?
5. How do control structures relate to other programming concepts, such as functions and objects?

MULTIPLE CHOICE QUESTIONS

1. What is a control structure in programming?

a. A language construct that allows a programmer to control the flow of execution

b. A programming technique for organizing code

c. A data structure used for storing control information

d. None of the above

2. Which of the following is an example of a conditional statement in programming?

a. For loop

b. While loop

c. If/else statement

d. Break statement

3. Which of the following loop structures will always execute at least once?

a. For

b. While

c. Do/while

d. Switch statement

4. Which control statements can be used to terminate a loop prematurely?

a. Break statement

b. Continue statement

c. Return statement

d. Throw statement

Answers to Multiple Choice Questions

1. (a); 2. (c); 3. (c); 4. (a)

REFERENCES

1. Ahmad, R., (1999). Visual languages: A new way of programming. *Malaysian Journal of Computer Science, 12*(1), 76–81.
2. Al-Gherwi, W., Budman, H., & Elkamel, A., (2010). Selection of control structure for distributed model predictive control in the presence of model errors. *Journal of Process Control, 20*(3), 270–284.
3. Al-Gherwi, W., Budman, H., & Elkamel, A., (2011). A robust distributed model predictive control algorithm. *Journal of Process Control, 21*(8), 1127–1137.
4. Alpern, B., Wegman, M. N., & Zadeck, F. K., (1988). Detecting equality of variables in programs. In: *Proceedings of the 15th ACM SIGPLAN-SIGACT Symposium on Principles of Programming Languages*, p. 1–11.
5. Batrinu, F., Carpaneto, E., Chicco, G., De Donno, M., Napoli, R., Porumb, R., & Toader, C., (2004). New nested evolutionary programming approach for voltage control optimization with distributed generation. In: *Proceedings of the 12th IEEE Mediterranean Electrotechnical Conference* (Vol. 3, pp. 1007–1010).
6. Bobrow, D. G., & Raphael, B., (1974). New programming languages for artificial intelligence research. *ACM Computing Surveys (CSUR), 6*(3), 153–174.
7. Bowman, N. A., Jarratt, L., Culver, K. C., & Segre, A. M., (2020). Pair programming in perspective: Effects on persistence, achievement, and equity in computer science. *Journal of Research on Educational Effectiveness, 13*(4), 731–758.

8. Bria, A., Faber, W., & Leone, N., (2009). Normal form nested programs. *Fundamenta Informaticae, 96*(3), 271–295.
9. Burnett, M. M., & Baker, M. J., (1994). A classification system for visual programming languages. *Journal of Visual Languages and Computing, 5*(3), 287–300.
10. Ding, T., Qu, M., Huang, C., Wang, Z., Du, P., & Shahidehpour, M., (2020). Multi-period active distribution network planning using multi-stage stochastic programming and nested decomposition by SDDIP. *IEEE Transactions on Power Systems, 36*(3), 2281–2292.
11. Early, K., Hammer, J., Hofmann, M. K., Rode, J. A., Wong, A., & Mankoff, J., (2018). Understanding gender equity in author order assignment. *Proceedings of the ACM on Human-Computer Interaction, 2*(CSCW), 1–21.
12. Gebser, M., Schaub, T., & Thiele, S., (2007). Gringo: A new grounder for answer set programming. In: *Logic Programming and Nonmonotonic Reasoning: 9th International Conference, LPNMR 2007, Tempe, AZ, USA, May 15–17, 2007* (Vol. 9, pp. 266–271).
13. Henriksen, T., Serup, N. G., Elsman, M., Henglein, F., & Oancea, C. E., (2017). Futhark: Purely functional GPU-programming with nested parallelism and in-place array updates. In: *Proceedings of the 38th ACM SIGPLAN Conference on Programming Language Design and Implementation* , 11, pp. 556–571.
14. Hewitt, C., (1977). Viewing control structures as patterns of passing messages. *Artificial Intelligence, 8*(3), 323–364.
15. Hils, D. D., (1992). Visual languages and computing survey: Data flow visual programming languages. *Journal of Visual Languages & Computing, 3*(1), 69–101.
16. Kookos, I. K., & Perkins, J. D., (2002). Regulatory control structure selection of linear systems. *Computers & Chemical Engineering, 26*(6), 875–887.
17. Levine, L., Woolf, B., & Filoramo, R., (1984). *ACM SIGCSE Bulletin, 16*(1), 154–158.
18. Marcos, N. I., Forbes, J. F., & Guay, M., (2009). Coordination of distributed model predictive controllers for constrained dynamic processes. *IFAC Proceedings Volumes, 42*(11), 135–140.
19. Messac, A., (1998). Control-structure integrated design with closed-form design metrics using physical programming. *AIAA Journal, 36*(5), 855–864.
20. Meyer, R. M., & Masterson, T., (2000). Towards a better visual programming language: Critiquing prograph's control structures. In: *Proceedings of the Fifth Annual CCSC Northeastern Conference on The Journal of Computing in Small Colleges* (Vol. 1, pp. 181–193).
21. Narraway, L., & Perkins, J., (1994). Selection of process control structure based on economics. *Computers & Chemical Engineering, 18*, S511–S515.
22. Ni, Y., Menon, V. S., Adl-Tabatabai, A. R., Hosking, A. L., Hudson, R. L., Moss, J. E. B., & Shpeisman, T., (2007). Open nesting in software transactional memory. In: *Proceedings of the 12th ACM SIGPLAN Symposium on Principles and Practice of Parallel Programming* 10(2), pp. 68–78.

23. Pearce, D., Sarsakov, V., Schaub, T., Tompits, H., & Woltran, S., (2002). A polynomial translation of logic programs with nested expressions into disjunctive logic programs: Preliminary report. In: *ICLP* (Vol. 1, pp. 405–420).
24. Raftery, A. E., Niu, X., Hoff, P. D., & Yeung, K. Y., (2012). Fast inference for the latent space network model using a case-control approximate likelihood. *Journal of Computational and Graphical Statistics, 21*(4), 901–919.
25. Rasure, J. R., & Williams, C. S., (1991). An integrated data flow visual language and software development environment. *Journal of Visual Languages & Computing, 2*(3), 217–246.
26. Riccardi, G. A., (1981). The independence of control structures in abstract programming systems. *Journal of Computer and System Sciences, 22*(2), 107–143.
27. Roberts, E. S., (1995). Loop exits and structured programming: Reopening the debate. *ACM SIGCSE Bulletin, 27*(1), 268–272.
28. Rubin, M. J., (2013). The effectiveness of live-coding to teach introductory programming. In: *Proceeding of the 44th ACM Technical Symposium on Computer Science Education* 12, pp. 651–656.
29. Schaefer, R., (2011). On the limits of visual programming languages. *ACM SIGSOFT Software Engineering Notes, 36*(2), 7, 8.
30. Seidman, R. H., (1989). Computer programming and logical reasoning: Unintended cognitive effects. *Journal of Educational Technology Systems, 18*(2), 123–141.
31. Spector, L., (1996). Simultaneous evolution of programs and their control structures. *Advances in Genetic Programming, 2*, 137–154.
32. Syahidi, A. A., & Asyikin, A. N., (2018). Applying student team achievement divisions (STAD) model on material of basic program branch control structure to increase activity and student result. In: *IOP Conference Series: Materials Science and Engineering* (Vol. 336, No. 1, p. 012027).
33. White, L. J., & Cohen, E. I., (1980). A domain strategy for computer program testing. *IEEE Transactions on Software Engineering*, (3), 247–257.
34. Woodward, M. R., (1991). Concerning ordered mutation testing of relational operators. *Software Testing, Verification, and Reliability, 1*(3), 35–40.
35. Wulf, W. A., (1972). A case against the goto. In: *Proceedings of the ACM Annual Conference* (Vol. 2, pp. 791–797).
36. Young, M., Argiro, D., & Kubica, S., (1995). Cantata: Visual programming environment for the Khoros system. *ACM SIGGRAPH Computer Graphics, 29*(2), 22–24.
37. Zorn, C., Wingrave, C. A., Charbonneau, E., & LaViola, Jr. J. J., (2013). Exploring Minecraft as a conduit for increasing interest in programming. In: *FDG*, 1, pp. 352–359.

CHAPTER 8

FUNDAMENTALS OF OBJECT-ORIENTED PROGRAMMING

UNIT INTRODUCTION

To address a problem, we typically start by thinking about it in a broad sense, on a higher level of abstraction. We try to calculate the available resources, such as money; in other words, we dissect the issue. If resources are limited, humans have been known to resort to sleight of hand. For example, if we cannot find sufficient wallpaper, we might be unable to conceal some secret locations; however, things like furniture, photographs, and so on can help. It indicates that we try to organize the solution using the resources at our disposal following a plan. Together, abstraction, decomposition, and organization make up what we call a paradigm (Sanders & Dorn, 2003). These three steps are necessary for solving every problem. The functional paradigm was the foundation of the previous programmers' experiences (Xinogalos et al., 2006).

Assume that we will travel to Trieste by automobile, and at this point, we have begun to plan how we will do so. In accordance with the tenets of an outdated programming paradigm, we ought to have conceived of the problem as a matter of function operating on data:

- Please think of the issue despite a process that really can solve it, such as how to collect essential things, how to run a car, and so on. This is the first step in the abstraction level (Briot et al., 1998).
- At the deconstruction level, you should think about how to segment all processing in

smaller, more manageable processing components or functions, like the procedures involved in actually transferring an automobile from one location to another. We are aware that driving in cities differs greatly from driving on highways. We pay some thought to simple tasks like turning off and starting the car. So, we will create some functions;

- In terms of the organization, make sure that our functions are set up to communicate with one another following the regulations. We create iterations of function calls, sending various parameters to the functions, etc. (Wiener & Pinson, 1988).

This is the hint: Conventional programming practices tend to isolate data, and the processes that manipulate it, or at least do not actively advocate examining them together. This is an unusual strategy; we must create a number of information forms, then create a number of processes that work with these structures (Kanaki & Kalogiannakis, 2018) (Figure 8.1).

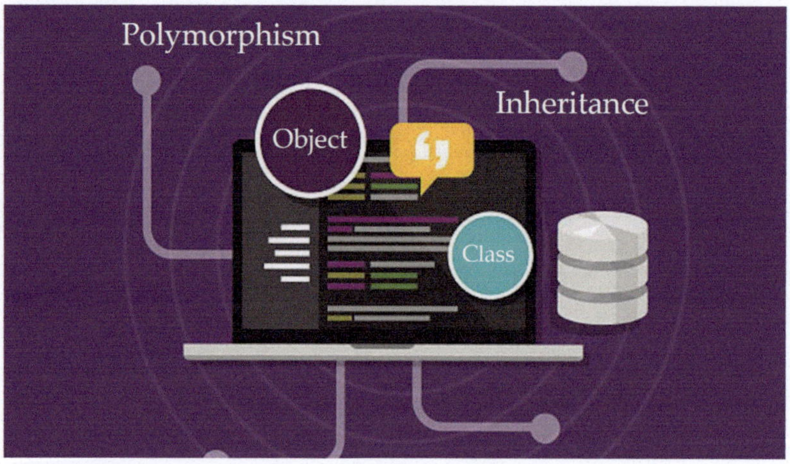

Figure 8.1. Object oriented programming with a real-world scenario.

Source: Hashim Lokasher, Creative Commons License.

In a real-world scenario, we first consider the general road before beginning to consider how to navigate the traffic of the many towns and cities pass through. After that, we might think about where would be the greatest area to stop for a meal, to rest, etc. Finally, we may consider the specifics of the trip, including how to plan the scheduler for this kind of adventure so that we arrive at a given restaurant at such a specific time. An example of an object-oriented way of thinking is the following: We look at things in terms of their connections to one another:

- On a higher level of abstraction, we think of several autonomous agents (objects) cooperating, such as the automobile, ourselves, goods to take, etc. (Cox, 1986).
- At the level of decomposition, we determine the categories of items on which to partition the overall project;

- At the organizational level, we produce the correct quantity of items of each type (Wu, 2006).

Learning Objectives

The information that the readers would be able to acquire after finishing this chapter is as follows:

- A world that is based on objects;
- The defining features of an item programming language;
- The idea of encapsulation comes in third;
- The idea of passing on a family business;
- An introduction to polymorphism's fundamentals;
- An introduction to the foundations of handling exceptions.

Key Terms

- Abstraction
- Class
- Distributed objects
- Encapsulation
- Inheritance
- Messages
- Object-oriented
- Programming
- Sample
- Variables

8.1. AN OBJECT-ORIENTED WORLD

An object-oriented language need to provide these three extremely crucial explicit qualities in order to adhere to the OOP paradigm (Uzakov et al., 2019). This is viewed from the perspective of a programmer. When we are seeking to find solutions to real-world problems using our object-oriented programming (OOP), we make considerable use of these notions as models for those difficulties. These three ideas are as follows:

- Encapsulation;
- Inheritance; and
- Polymorphism (Mylopoulos et al., 1999).

Abstraction can be thought of as an implicit quality. We utilize it in specifying ADT for short or new abstract data types.

Remember

Object-oriented programming (OOP) is a programming paradigm based on objects, which can contain data and code to manipulate that data.

8.1.1. Encapsulation Example

In the event that we decide to drive to Trieste, let's use the steering system of such a vehicle as an illustration of encapsulation. If we decided to take a car, this is what would happen.

When the initial models hit the roads, the function of a car's steering mechanism hasn't altered all that much. Users can start using it right away because of its uniform user interface. For instance, turning the steering wheel in a clockwise direction will cause the car to turn right, and doing it in an anticlockwise direction will cause it to turn left. So, in the framework of the object-oriented paradigm, this mechanism is viewed as an object. We don't know the implementation specifics; thus, we can use them without any technical knowledge. A select few of us have access to further information; they know that each automaker has a somewhat different way of implementing this strategy (Atkinson et al., 1990). The interface is conventional, but when the mechanism is altered by something like a rent trailer, we run into problems (Figure 8.2).

In exchange, the component that controls the vehicle's direction consists of many advanced subsystems, each with its own state, behaviors, interface, and implementation. The steering mechanism components that utilize these interfaces are the only ones with access to them, not the driver (Bergin et al., 2005). Encapsulation is a technique that is frequently used in OOP, and it is intended to conceal the implementation while exposing the interface (Yan, 2009).

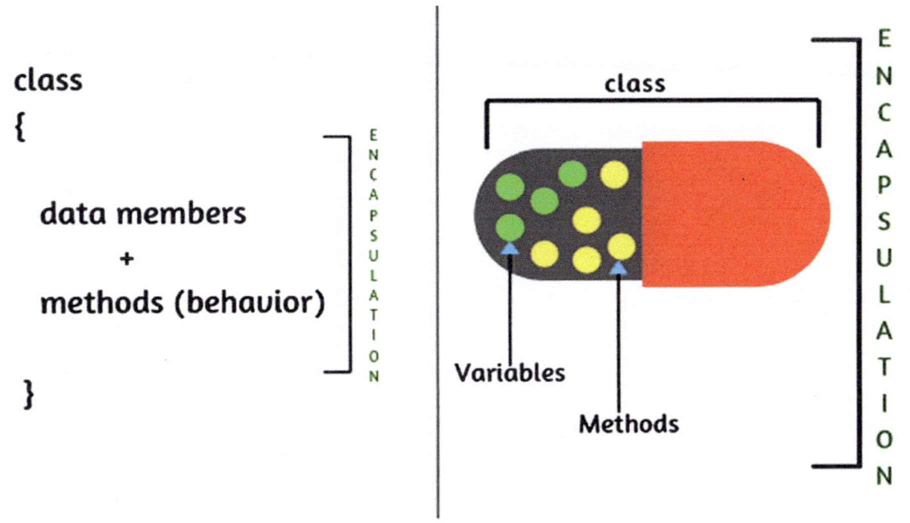

Figure 8.2. Illustration of the encapsulation.

Source: Scientech Easy, Creative Commons License.

8.1.2. Inheritance Example

Inheritance is another pointer in the direction of OOP (Smith & Robson, 1990). Consider the situation of a person who recently purchased an older home as an analogy. After purchasing the property, the individual does not typically tear down the old house and start from begin while constructing a new one; rather, he will typically make changes to the existing one. In OOP, this means that the individual derives from the home that already exists, or, to put it another way, that he extends it; hence, he is responsible for building subclasses of house that is already in existence. The characteristics of the old house have been carried over into the new one.

It is a highly typical technique to create new, enhanced things by employing new definitions that augment previously established definitions (Hirshfield & Ege, 1996). It is one of the sayings of OOP, which promotes the reuse of components already present in programs. Don't make the same mistake twice! Reuse the code, and don't start from scratch!

8.1.3. Polymorphism Example

Polymorphism, from the Greek (polys), means "one name, many shapes," which makes it arguably the most elusive idea to pin down, especially in terms of everyday speech. The Greek root for the polymorphism is morphe, meaning "name" (Sridharan et al., 2013). In keeping with our automobile theme, I'd like to compare polymorphism to the automatic transmission on your car. Imagine there are three modes: drive, neutral, and reverse (Figure 8.3).

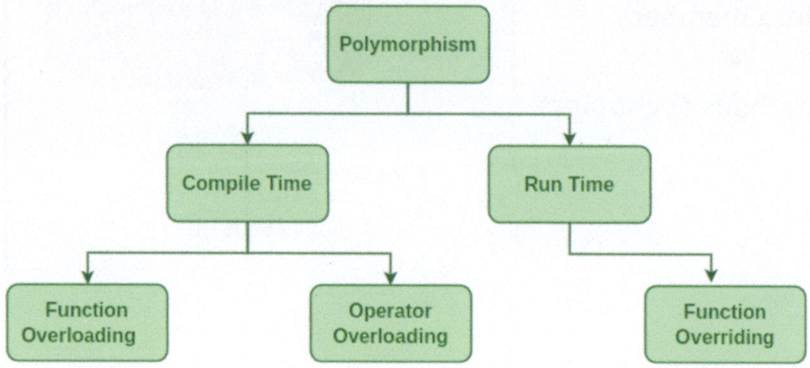

Figure 8.3. Polymorphism and its components.

Source: Geeks for Geeks, Creative Commons License.

We know that just one approach may be called the Reverse technique. When we put the gear selector into Neutral, the car's engine is severed from connecting to the transmission system.

We put the car in Drive to go forward while driving it. The mechanism of the automatic transmission system determines at runtime, based on various sets of conditions, which version of the Drive function to apply to every specific circumstance. The circumstances at hand will determine the particular implementation of the function that will be utilized. This is comparable to something that's known as runtime polymorphism (Srinath, 2017).

As a result, the automobile displays polymorphic behavior when moving in the direction of forward motion, but it displays non-polymorphic behavior when driving in the direction of backward movement.

Polymorphism is a technique that allows the behavior of an example of type to be altered depending on the present circumstances.

The use of OOP to construct a stacking class out of which stack items can be instantiated is an excellent illustration of this principle from the realm of computers (Stroustrup, 1995). Programmers familiar with queues, stacks, and other data structures analogous to stacks will be able to recognize them as a stack with no additional prior knowledge if a stack is applied as instantiated, as an object, a class, and described as suitable.

8.1.4. A Word of OOP Vocabulary

Languages before OOP and those after having different programming paradigms and vocabularies (Lange & Nakamura, 1997). Class methods have replaced procedures; you are a prime example of this shift.

Let's take OOP as an extra example. We can declare an abstract data type by encapsulating the data type's implementation type and the interface to a data type inside a class.

After that, the instantiation procedure can produce one or more instances of the class. An object is a term used to refer to an example of a class. Everything possesses a state and acts in a particular manner (Booch, 1994).

The current values which are recorded in the local variables are what determines the state of the system.

How the object behaves is established by the example methods of the classes from which it was instantiated.

The classes or subclasses that makeup inherited types of abstract data are derived from either the base classes or the superclasses (Joines & Roberts, 1999). While developing subclasses, we start by extending their parent classes.

The programmer creates instances of objects within the program and communicates with those objects by calling the methods associated with the class (or member functions). To "construct an instance of a class" is what is meant by "instantiate" an object.

OOP involves the definition of abstract data types, the encapsulation of those types of abstract data into classes, the creation of instantiations of objects, and the transmission of messages to objects (Andrianoff & Levine, 2002).

Nearly every action or object referenced in OOP terminology has evolved to be expressed by a multitude of distinct phrases, which further confuses the meaning of these words. These terms are usually ambiguous and frequently depend on the author or authors who first published the particular book you're currently enjoying reading. We can change the state of an object in a variety of ways, such as by sending it a message, using one of its ways, or using any of its member functions.

8.2. IMPORTANCE OF OOP

OOP, sometimes known as OOP, is a paradigm of programming that is utilized in the process of developing software applications (Sridharan et al., 2013). It is predicated on the idea of objects, which are packages that include information and function. The primary objective of OOP is to ease the process of developing software by partitioning complex issues into smaller, relatively manageable parts.

Modularity is a significant advantage that comes with using OOP. The ability to write and test code in separate modules is what we mean when discussing modularity (Hadjerrouit, 1999). This capacity makes it much simpler to manage huge software projects. The OOP modular method enables programmers to break down complex problems into smaller, relatively manageable components, making designing and maintaining code simpler.

Reusability is another significant advantage that comes with using OOP. The capacity to reuse code in various settings is what we mean when we talk about reusability (Gottlob et al., 1996). This can help programmers save both time and effort. OOP makes it possible to reuse code by introducing the idea of inheritance, which permits the construction of new classes that are derived from existing courses and inherit the attributes and operations of the base class from which they are derived.

Another essential advantage of OOP is its flexibility (Kölling, 1999). The capacity of an item to behave in a manner dependent on the circumstances in which it is utilized is called flexibility. This enables the object to assume a variety of different shapes. The OOP makes this flexibility possible by introducing the idea of polymorphism, which permits things to take on various distinct forms (Salvaneschi et al., 2014).

Scalability is also another significant advantage that comes with OOP. The capacity to remove or add objects without disrupting the rest of the code is what we mean when we talk about scalability. OOP is a scalable programming method, meaning that objects may be added to or removed from a program without introducing unexpected side effects (Zimmermann et al., 1992).

Encapsulation is the key to OOP's provision of a safe programming method, which brings us to the conclusion of this chapter (Kölling, 1999). The internal data of an object can only be accessed once it has been encapsulated, which makes it harder for unauthorized code to change the object's properties or gain access to its data.

In general, OOP is a significant programming paradigm that gives a method for creating software that is scalable, modular, reusable, flexible, and safe. As a result, it is a crucial tool for developing reliable and effective software applications.

8.3. THE CHARACTERISTICS OF AN OOP

After going through the fundamentals of what makes an object-oriented program tick, let's dive into the specifics of the inquiry at hand.

8.3.1. An Object

Let's take a look at these three overarching inquiries:

- What exactly are objects when talking about OOP?
- What kinds of things should serve as the program's objects while designed to be object-oriented? and
- What is OOP that distinguishes it from conventional procedural programming and suggests that it might be superior to the latter?
- An example of data type is referred to as an object.

The two objects are declared in the JAVA code piece that follows.

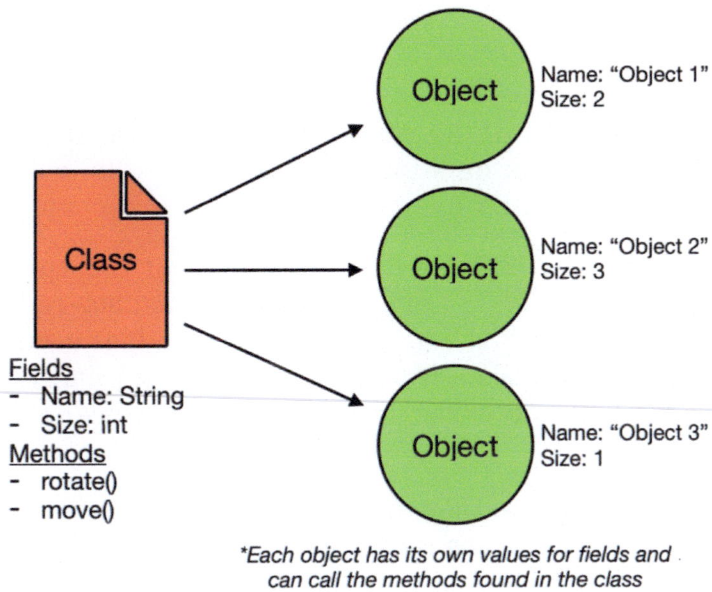

Figure 8.4. Illustration of an object.

Source: Jordan Burroughs, Creative Commons License.

The very first thing is an example of a straightforward integer variable that goes by the name tired. Some people in the field of computer science do not believe this to be a real object. They believe that an object ought not to be an essential part of the language itself. This may be true in general but remember that we are interpreting things quite broadly (Figure 8.4).

The other object is an example of an abstract data type called a Person. The thing in question is called man, and the data type is Person (Pokkunuri, 1989).

```
...
int tired; // an example of an int type
Person man; // an instance of abstract data type
// recognized as a Person
...}
```

The integer data type derives from so-called primitive types, which are built into the language. You might already be conscious of this or be able to infer it.

It is expected that you established and declared an abstract type of person Named in your code. From a linguistic perspective, this is a novel type of data (Rahnev et al., 2014).

8.3.2. Abstraction

The declaration of an abstract type of data containing a specification of t behavior and data representation of the class is referred to as abstraction. It demonstrates the different types of data that may be stored with new kinds of data and the various ways it can be manipulated.

JAVA programmers use the keyword "class" to present the specification of a new type to the compiler, which entails defining the data represented by the behavior of a new variant (Kölling, 1999). It means that a new type's specifications are converted into a form that the programmer can know and operate with by using the keyword class. This allows the compiler to produce more accurate results.

After the new type has been specified, one or more examples of that type of object can be transitioned from the abstract to the concrete state of existence. Put another way, an instance of such an object can be created (Figure 8.5).

After the object has been instantiated, it is referred to as having a state and behaving in a certain way. The behavior of an item is governed by the methods it possesses, while the status of an object is identified by the values that are now stored in its data variables (instance methods or member functions) (instance variables) (Nygaard, 1986).

As a graphical user interface (GUI) component, the button is the most common example. If a button is considered an object, its behavior and state can be readily envisioned by us (Xinogalos et al., 2006). It can exist in various shapes, including sizes, positions, captions, etc. At any particular point, the information held in the local variables of the button object determines which of these states the button will be in. A property of an object is a collection of one or even more local variables that describe the object's current state.

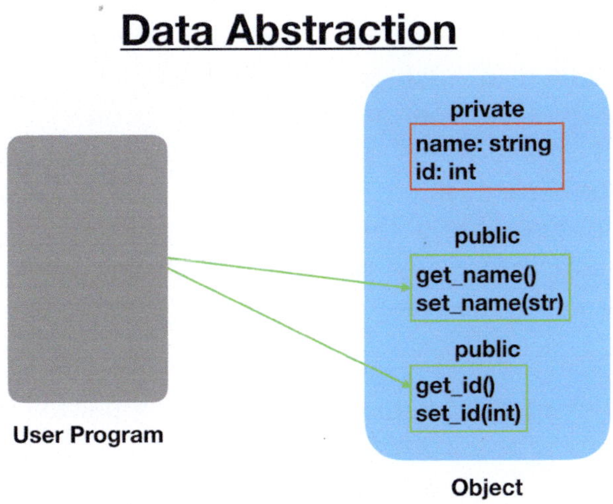

Figure 8.5. Schematic of the abstraction.

Source: Pankaj, Creative Commons License.

Similarly, an action predefined for the button will typically be triggered whenever it is clicked using a mouse.

On the one hand, each independent button object possesses instance variables, values that define the condition of the button anywhere at a given time. On the other hand, each button object contains a particular fundamental behavior to react to a click or other event, which can then be used in conjunction with an action (Agarwal et al., 1996).

8.3.3. Sample Class Definition

Let's create a working example now by trying to construct the code to model a human being. Many will say it's like their daily routine when they alternate between working and resting. Every member of the group must report their current state, whether they are awake and able to work, sleepy, or overjoyed. There will be three instance variables in this class: an integer for weariness, a string for name, and a second string for origin (Embley et al., 1991).

```
This is what the line that corresponds to it looks like:

class Human {// code of the class

...

}
```

The word "class" is the most crucial term in the definition, and its full name is Human (Concas et al., 2006).

The three instance methods of the new type define the behaviors of the new type. Data can be saved in such an object of unknown type, given the name setPerson. This feature can be used. The second one, which retrieves data from an object and is known as getHumanInfo, can access previously saved information (Wiedenbeck et al., 1996). The final one is known as Work, and it is responsible for putting into action changes to an object called weary, which belongs to the class Human. The code also isn't displayed now; we will look at it later. These are the lines that correspond to each other (Lange & Nakamura, 1997):

```
// data storage instance method with a void setPerson parameter (int state, String na, String orig) {...

}

// display information about a person String using an instance method getHumanInfo() {...

}

// Work on the instance method String Work() {...

}
```

This new type can be expanded by including other behaviors through the setting up of different methods, and this is something that we can do.

After the new type has been specified, we can construct examples of this type, also known as objects. We may interact with those objects as we interact with the other variables produced from primitive data types.

8.4. ENCAPSULATION

Encapsulation the first of three key ideas that influence the creation of object-oriented software (Santos, 2014). On a conceptual level, we consider the cooperation of distinct agents. Lastly, we put a representation of data and behavior into a class, allowing us to describe both the implementation and interface of the course.

An enclosed design is one that, by standard procedures for OOP, typically conceals its execution from the class user and reveals just its interface (Gatziu & Dittrich, 1992). After going through these steps, a clementine seed was produced. Realization of all of its behavior is obscured from us; all we know is how to cultivate it, and we are familiar with its user interface.

Because of the experiences of human beings, we are aware of the seeds' interface, and we have class documentation that describes the interface. But God did not offer detailed documentation on how sources are implemented. An average user typically does not need to understand how well the steering system of an automobile is developed, and most people are unaware of the specifics of the mechanism's implementation. To produce and perhaps alter the user-level documentation, a class designer needs to have documentation on the commission.

In passing, I should mention that JAVA has a specialized method for producing documentation, which will be discussed in the following courses.

Java employs the terms public, protected, and private to restrict access to a class's constituent components. The meanings of the initial two phrases can be determined with little effort (Hogg, 1991). The final period, protected, confers exclusive access privileges to the members of derived classes from the base classes to the members of the inherited classes.

Typically, users who use an attractive class are unable to modify the values of its local variables without using the class's interface (Banciihon, 1988).

Can you recall the code fragments that we provided? Now, let's examine the source in its entirety.

```
class Human {
int tired; // instance variables
String name; // of the class
String origin; //
// instance method for storing and retrieving data
void setPerson (int state, String na, String orig) {
tired = state; name = na;
```

```
origin = orig;
} // end method setPerson
// instance method to display info of a human
String getHumanInfo() {
String info;
info = (“My name is ” +
name + “ and I am ” +
origin + “ ”);
if (tired > 1)
info = info +
(“I am very tired.”);
else
info = info +
(“and I am ready to work.”);
return info;
} // end method showHumanInfo
void drinking(){
System.out.println(
“I like drink with friends”);
}//end drinking()
// instance method Work
String Work() {
if (tired < 2) {
tired ++;
```

```
return
("Ouff… working again…");
}
else
return
("Sorry can't work, being too exhausted.");
} // end method Work
String rest() {
if (tired < 1)
return
("Not very tired, so going to a party.");
else {
tired --;
return
("Sleeping, hhhharrarrrdrrhhhh…");
}
}
} // end class Human definition
// Driver program
class ex1 {// defining the controlling class
public static void main(String[] args) {// define main
Human obj = new Human ();
obj.setPerson(0, "Olexiy," "Ukrainian"); //store data
```

```
// Get info about Olexiy
System.out.println (obj.getHumanInfo());
} //end main
} //end ex1 class
```

In general, the class should consist of public methods for them to be accessible to a user. All of the classes and techniques in our software are, by default, accessible to the public. Invoking those methods allows the class to save, read, and modify values (Korson & McGregor, 1990). The setPerson method was used in the software that was just shown to insert data about me, and then the getHumanInfo function was used to retrieve information about me.

The program that we are looking at does not have any *secret implementation*. This isn't a well-designed program from an OOP perspective, but at the same time, it is too simplistic! (Civello, 1993).

Please note that we utilized the setPerson and getHumanInfo methods in our program. There is a remark of special significance regarding the names of procedures that begin with set and get (Chidamber & Kemerer, 1991):

In Java, the keywords "set" and "get" at the beginning of the names of methods have a specific significance. Specifically, the JAVA Beans Application Programming Interface (API) introspection feature considers such names to indicate design patterns to alter the object's properties...

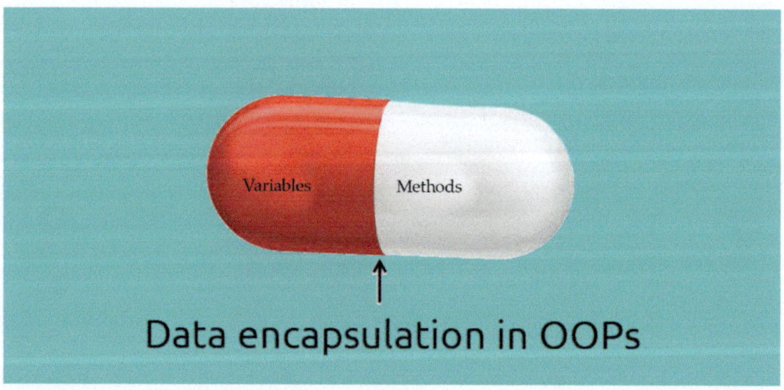

Figure 8.6. Illustration of the encapsulation, class, methods, and variables.

Source: Geek Bot, Creative Commons License.

Object-oriented styles are not considered to be good design by default. There has been widespread agreement upon basic design standards for classes in an effort to improve the quality of designs created. Typically, the data members are held in confidence (Canfora et al., 1999). Typically, the interface comprises solely of methods and has relatively few member functions, if any. This is a mechanism for hiding the in-question implementation (Figure 8.6).

On the other hand, the data members intended for use as symbolic constants are publicly disclosed and defined in a way that prevents their values from being modified. This is the only exception to the general rule.

The methods provided by the interface should either be used to control access to the private local variables or offer a means to reach them. The interface ought to be as general as is humanly possible, meaning that it shouldn't be tied down to a specific implementation in any way (Schultz & Axelsen, 2016). It indicates that from a functional standpoint, the method's arguments should have the same significance. If, for whatever reason, it becomes necessary to change the implementation, the change should be carried out in such a way as to prevent the interface from being altered.

In our software, the only variables and methods we use are example variables and example methods. The class methods and class variables are the following topics for discussion.

Did you Know?

Instance and class variables are types of variables used in OOP to store data and state information for objects and classes, respectively.

8.4.1. Instance and Class Variables

Our program exclusively employs exemplary variables and procedures. A discussion of class procedures and class variables is required. Just what are you trying to say? What purpose do they serve for us?

Each example of such a type or object stores its data in a collection of variables known as "instance variables" that are defined in a certain manner. These variables are handled as distinct entities and are stored in distinct memory regions (Sarcar, 2022). A single period specifies the required connecting operator for object instance access. With our software, you may access the name of the object obj by putting obj.name into the field.

It is feasible to speculate about it (Sanders et al., 2008):

All objects that belong to a class share the same set of variables. They are pretty comparable to the concept of global variables. There is only one instance of such a class variable stored in Memory, and all of the objects that belong to that class have access to it.

Class variables have a beneficial property in that they can be accessible even if no item of the type has been instantiated. This is a very significant aspect of class variables. You may get to them by using the dot operator, which is used to link the variable name with the class name.

8.4.2. Instance and Class Methods

Two distinct types of methods can be assigned to a class:

- Procedures specific to instances; and
- Methods specific to categories (Alrashidi et al., 2014).

Suppose you are familiar with the circumstances surrounding instance variables and class variables. In that case, you can readily speculate that methods that are designated as static belong to the class, whereas ways that are not static belong to the instance.

Instance methods are "tied" to the objects to which they are applied since they require a thing of the class to be invoked (Guidec et al., 1996). Using the illustrative method on a particular object will have accessibility to the object's instance variables.

Class methods cannot access members outside of the class. They have no access to the instance's data or methods (Ågerfalk, 1999).

The incredible quality of class methods is that you can call them by just referring to the class name rather than needing first to create an instance of the class. Using the right joining operator on the name of lass and the name of the method, one may retrieve class methods in the same way as class variables can be accessed.

8.4.3. Sample Program

A significant portion of what we've been talking about is probably going to be easier to comprehend when it is viewed in the context of an actual application (Freeman-Benson & Borning, 1992). The following Output will be generated by the software and shown on a standard output device:

```
---------------

This cat has child(ren): 100

This cat has legs: 4

---------------
```

This cat has a child(ren): 1220. This cat has legs: 4

Let's look at some of the fascinating snippets of code that make up the program before we move on to the listing of it.

The declaration of 2 member variables of class is displayed in the first intriguing piece of code that we will look at. The first is an example variable with the name legs, while the second is a class variable with the name child.

int child; // declare an example variable 'child' static int legs; // declare a class variable 'legs'

The declaration of variables in Java typically looks something like this, with the name of the type coming first, then the Variable's name is declared (Clark, 2006). The point of interest in the discussion setting is that we use the fixed keyword in the statement of the class variable.

The following code demonstrates the definitions of two distinct approaches (with the bodies of methods deleted for brevity). The class method is referred to by its shorthand name, classMethod, whereas the instance method is referred to by its shorthand name, instanceMethod (Kosbar & Schneider, 1992).

```
void {instance method() {// define an instance method
……. // body of method deleted for brevity
} //end instance method()
static void class method() { //define} a class method
……. //body of method deleted for brevity
} //end class method()
```

Most procedure or member function declarations in Java look like this: first comes the name of the return type (void indicates that nothing is returned), next comes the name method, and then comes the formal parameter list. The method's body is subsequently wrapped in a corresponding set of curly braces and returned to its original state {} (Jacobson, 1993).

You may probably anticipate correctly at this point: utilizing static keywords inside the specification of the class method is the crucial point to consider.

The following snippet of code is a single sentence extracted from the main structure of one of the procedures. This statement will cause the Output to be shown on the device designated as the standard Output. This single phrase exhibits some of the syntax complexity present in an object-oriented program using overloaded operators, classes, class variables and instance methods (Voigt et al., 2010).

```
System.out.println("This cat has legs: "

+ legs);
```

This assertion is comprised of three parts that are connected with periods. The first component is the word System, the name of one of the classes included in the standard JAVA class library. To provide context, the System class is immediately loaded into Memory whenever a new Java program is started.

A period serves as the connection between the term out and the name of the System class. The System class contains a member variable whose name is "out," and "out" is the name of that Variable (Kniesel & Theisen, 2001).

The public class variable is being used for the member variable named out. Because of this, it is now feasible to access this Variable by combining the name of the class with the name of the Variable and then separating the two words with a period.

It is important to note that the joining operator used is a period, and the class uses two types out is attached to the phrase println (Sutcliffe, 1991). In addition to being a class variable, the Variable out is also a references Variable, and it stores a reference to an instance of PrintStream class.

An instance method with the name println can be found in the PrintStream class (). There are 10 different overloaded variants of the println() procedure contained within the PrintStream class. The version being used in this instance has a behavior that causes its strings argument to be shown on the device designated as the standard Output.

Now think about the String that is passed to println method like it is given below (Xianzhong & Zhenyu, 1991):

```
("This cat has child(ren): "

+ child)
```

The literal strings in Java are enclosed in quotation marks, much like in C. Java loads the plus sign in this way because it has the ability to concatenate texts as well as the addition operator in arithmetic (Boyapati et al., 2002). Also, despite the fact that their right operand has never been and isn't already a string, the overloaded plus operations have the ability to push it into the string representation. If the correct operand is not already a string, then this is the case. In this case, the right operand is the example variable, also known as an instance variable, rather than a string. The sample variable's value is first converted to a reticulation by overload plus operators, and then it is concatenated with the left operand. The stages are carried out in the sequence they are given above.

Now, let's take a second look at the two identical techniques as before, but this time, let's keep the bodies of methods intact for additional research.

```
// instance method void instanceMethod () {

System.out.println("This cat has child(ren): "

+ child);

} // end instanceMethod static void classMethod () {

System.out.println("This cat has legs: "

+ legs);

} // end classMethod
```

The code that allows access to the class member may be seen in the bodies of the methods, as shown above. It is essential to remember that one member is an example variable denoted by the name child. In contrast, the other membership variable is a class object represented by the name legs (Howard, 1988).

The class method known as the class Method is only permitted to display and access the class variable. In contrast, the instance method known as a child can access and display both the provided to make and the class variable. Class methods can't access instance variables.

class ex2 {// defining the controlling class public static void main(String[] args) {// define main............ // code

```
} //end main

} //end ex2 class
```

Now have a look at the breakdown of the primary approach that is provided down below. The governing method of a JAVA application must be referred to as the "main method" or "function." This requirement does not apply to applets (Skoglund, 2003). In the straightforward application that we are developing, the process of instantiating an object and accessing its instance and class method will be handled by code located in the ex2 function.

Remember that to use an instance method, you need to contact it via an object of a class. This is required to gain access to an instance method. The following snippet of code is found in the main procedure, and it creates an instance of an object with the name "mour" that belongs to the class "cat."

```
cat mour = new cat();
```

This is a standard statement used in Java for creating an instance of an object. The new operator requests the operating system to provide memory "from the heap" to store one instance of an object with the typical cat (Lau & Taweel, 2007).

Suppose the necessary amount of Memory is properly allotted. In that case, the address of the memory block in question will be put into a reference variable that goes by the name of mour. If the operation cannot be completed, the JAVA run time engine will throw an error. There is a subtype of exception known as this one, and it can be either ignored or captured by the application so that it can be processed. If it is disregarded, the runtime environment will terminate the program. Later on, we will talk about handling exceptions.

As soon as we have direct access to an item of a class (access to an object instance that refers to an object of a class), we seem to be capable of making use of this instance variable to obtain the ability to access the public member's factors of course and also to invoke a general procedure that is associated with a class. This is possible because that instance variable refers to an item of a class. An instance of this principle can be seen in the code snippet below.

This Bit of code contains two statements and may be found here. These statements utilize a reference variable known as mour in conjunction with the period to gain access to the instance variable and instance method of an object (Bansiya & Davis, 2002). The period is also required. It's indeed important to remember that the object of a class is the only way to access the instance methods and variables.

```
// access instance variable via objects: mour.child=100;

//access instance method via the object mour.instanceMethod();
```

It is crucial to note that it is unnecessary to utilize an instance of the class to access either the class variable or the class method. This accessibility is of equal significance (Menzies & Haynes, 1996). The following code contains two statements, both of which use the class name to gain access to the class variable or the class method associated with the class.

```
// access class variable via the class mour.legs = 4;

// access class method via the class mour.classMethod();
```

Access to class variables and class methods could be gained in one of two ways: through an object of the class or simply by referring to the class by its name (Singh & Kahlon, 2011). Please note that we do not assign a new value to the class variable "leg" because this value is used by both of the objects in the class. Cat: mour and meow.

At long last, we finished putting everything together using the JAVA program.

```
/* Copyright 2001, O.Ye. Tykhomyrov
The second example, ex2.java
Illustrates instance and class variables along with 4
instance and class methods.
*/

class cat {
int child; // instance variables ‘child’
static int legs; // class variable ‘legs’

// instance method
void instanceMethod () {
System.out.println(“This cat has child(ren): "
+ child);
} // end instanceMethod
static void classMethod () {
System.out.println(“This cat has legs: "
+ legs);
} // end classMethod
}
// Driver program

class ex2 {// defining the controlling class
public static void main(String[] args) {// define main

// instantiate an object of the class cat
cat mour = new cat();
```

```
cat meow = new cat();
// access instance variable via objects:
mour.child=100;
meow.child=1220;
// access class variable via the class
mour.legs = 4;

System.out.println("---------------");
// access instance method via the object
mour.instanceMethod();
// access class method via the class
mour.classMethod();
System.out.println("---------------");
meow.instanceMethod();
meow.classMethod();
} //end main
} //end ex2 c
```

8.4.4. Messages

Messages are also referred to as member functions at times. "A method or membership function can be invoked at any time and thus constitutes a message" (Atkinson et al., 1990).

A message is sent from the computer program to an object, instructing the object to use the method, and the program may also pass parameters to the method for use.

Someone wrote lately that an object-oriented program is nothing more than a collection of objects scattered around and communicating via messages (Schäfer & Rauch, 2004). This is perhaps a bit of an exaggeration, but it's not far off from the actual situation (Figure 8.7).

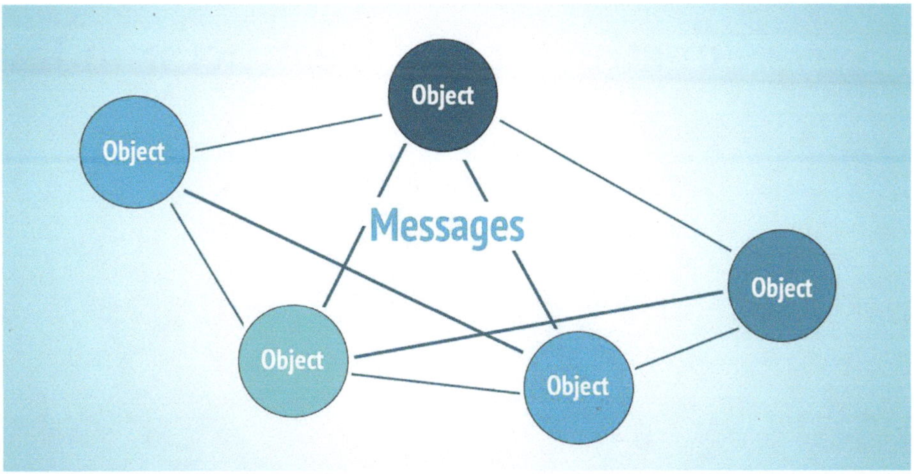

Figure 8.7. Schematic of the messages in OOP.

Source: Branko Babić, Creative Commons License.

8.4.5. Constructors, Destructors, and Garbage Collection

The majority of object-oriented systems, as well as some non-object-oriented programs, place a significant emphasis on using dynamic Memory, allocation, and reclamation from the heap (Bugliesi & Jamil, 1994).

Any specific language or language system, such as the Java virtual machine (JVM), ought to carry out at least one operation in memory:

- to ensure that memory is made available to the program only when it is required;
- to ensure that memory is made available to the program only when it is required;
- reusing it as necessary (Kifer et al., 1995).

Failing to address this crucial problem leads to a problem known as "memory leakage."

Constructors are employed to create and perhaps initialize objects (Voigt, 2009):

```
// instantiate an object of the class cat mour = new cat();
```

In Java, constructors, like other methods, can be overloaded with additional functionality. The issue of overload will be tackled after this (Bracha & Ungar, 2004). In a nutshell, method overloading refers to multiple methods with the same name. The listing of actual parameters is what the compiler uses to decide which version to operate (Figure 8.8).

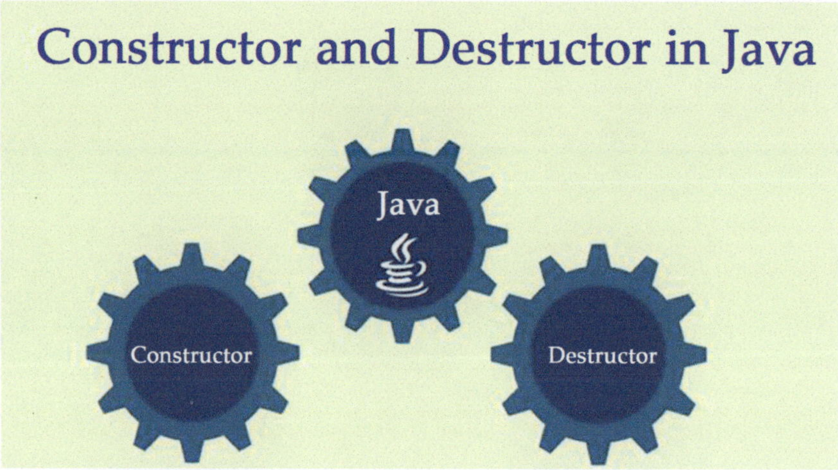

Figure 8.8. Example of constructor and destructor in Java.

Source: Educba, Creative Commons License.

In this particular line, the new operator serves two purposes: first, it allows dynamic Memory from the heap; second, it acts as a function Object() {[native code]} to build the object in the memory space that was allotted for it. The memory location address where the thing is stored is the value returned and given to the reference variable that goes by the name mour (Narayanan et al., 1998). An error will be generated if the Memory cannot be allocated.

When you create a new class in Java, you do not have the option to provide a function Object() {[native code]}; instead, Java defines a default function Object() {[native code]} for you that does not require any parameters.

Another option is to define your function Object() {[native code]}, which does not require any arguments (Lu & Potter, 2006). The process of defining a function Object() {[native code]} is very similar to the operation of defining a method; however, constructors must share the same name as the class, they cannot include return statements, and they cannot have a return type.

The following snippet of code illustrates the essential components of a Java program, which is analogous to the one that was just discussed but has been updated to make use of a parameterized function Object() {[native code]} (Wiedenbeck et al., 1999).

```
...

String name;

// Parameterised constructor cat (String n)
{name=n;}
```

```
...
System.out.println("This cat named " +
name +
" has child(ren): "
+ child);... cat mour = new cat("Pirat");...
```

- *Destructors:* When the program no longer requires an object, the software will often call on a specialized method called a destructor to execute cleanup on the object. C++ supports destructors, while JAVA doesn't support destructors (Clarke & Drossopoulou, 2002).

When an object no longer requires a certain amount of Memory, JAVA supports an additional mechanism that returns the Memory to an operating system.

Reclaiming Memory That's No Longer Required by Objects Utilized in the Program (Boyapati et al., 2003). The sanitation worker is a component of the runtime running in a low-priority thread. It is responsible for reclaiming Memory that's no longer required by objects utilized in the program. If no longer reference variables refer to the object, an object in Java is said to be in a state where it is eligible for garbage collection.

8.5. INHERITANCE

Encapsulation is the first important trait distinguishing an object-oriented program from other types. The other one is passing down family traditions. Let's take a look now, shall we?

After purchasing an older home in which to reside, a person can consider tearing it down and rebuilding it to combine it with another, more contemporary home that is also cosier, all without destroying the original folder structure. So, following the completion of the renovation, the house would be classified as a subclass of the house that previously existed. The characteristics of the old house have been carried over into the new one (Figure 8.9).

The same is true for the OO program: in most cases, a class can inherit the properties and capabilities of another class (Singh, 1995). Yet, one can circumvent this system by employing a variety of strategies.

Many people refer to the original class as the "base class" or the "superclass," whereas the newly created class is sometimes referred to as the "derived class" or the "subclass." Expanding base class or the superclass is another name commonly used to refer to inheritance.

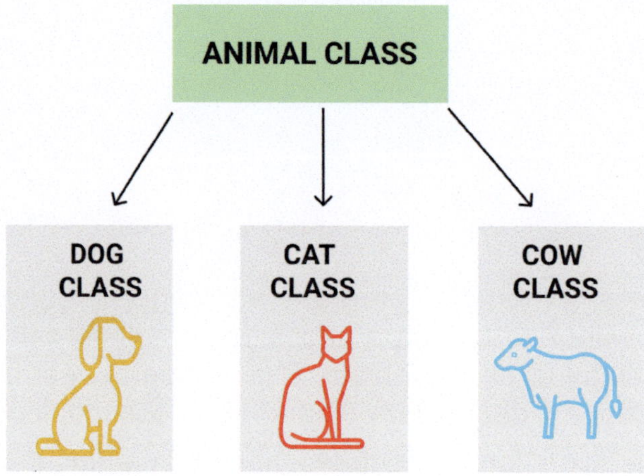

Figure 8.9. Example of inheritance in OOP.

Source: Patrick, Creative Commons License.

There is a clear order to inheritance (Oren et al., 2007). To put it another way, a class has the potential to be both a subclass and a superclass of other courses.

The derived class takes on behavior and the data representation of the base class, except for situations in which the derived class overrides some of the base class's methods to alter the behavior. Additionally, the derived class can introduce additional data representations and behaviors specific to the needs of the derived class.

Generally speaking, a program can instantiate instances of a base class in addition to objects of a class derived from the base class. By designating the base class as abstract, it is also feasible to prevent instances of the class name from being instantiated in certain circumstances. Suppose the base class is indeed an abstract base class, which is a class that does not exist independently of its ability to be derived from other classes. In that case, the program cannot instantiate objects of the base class itself but implement objects of classes derived from a base class (Figure 8.10).

The inheritance mechanism in Java makes constructing an organized hierarchy of classes possible (Rahnev et al., 2014).

When numerous abstract types of data share characteristics, you can build their similarities into a single location class and divide their unique qualities into distinct derived categories. This allows you to design your abstract types of data more efficiently. One of the functions of inheritance is to do this. Remember that we have established a class Human, yet not everyone is the same. We have different races, sexes, cultures, religions, and other things that distinguish us from one another. Yet, we all share quite a few characteristics, such as having two legs, upper limbs, and one head. We all can study, sleep, etc. The developed class Human is equipped with methods to signify a human state regarding the possibility of working. Because of this, the Human class we have developed uses this as its shared parameter.

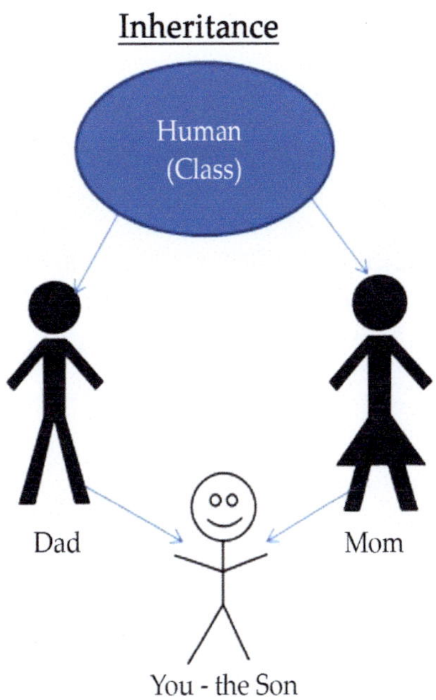

Figure 8.10. Example of inheritance.

Source: Mukesh Chaudhary, Creative Commons License.

We can derive a Gentleman or Woman class from this introductory class. They indeed enjoy their relaxation in quite different ways: the Lady enjoys chatting with her neighbors over a cup of tea, while the Gentleman spends much of his time enjoying a pint of beer in his local watering hole.

After this, objects of classes will be able to work with all of the Human parameters and the new ones (Halbert & O'Brien, 2000).

With this hierarchical class system, you may have noticed that inheritance develops the structure from one of the most general to the least general. This is because inheritance works in Reverse. This is standard practice.

You serve as an illustration here. In the next section of code, there is a single line that must not be skipped; it is the line that defines the Lady & Gentleman subclasses (Joines & Roberts, 1999):

class Lady extends Human {...} class Gentleman extends Human {...}

The Lady & Gentleman classes are demonstrated to be subclasses of the Human class by the usage of the keyword extends.

Let's look at the subsequent portion of the changed code if you don't mind.

```
...

// a new method public void drinking(){System.out.println

("Drinking tea with my neighbors");}
```

We announced the addition of a new method of drinking. Naturally, the Gentleman uses the same precise strategy, but this time pertaining to beer!

Another potentially sensitive section of the code demonstrates manipulation with a method declared in a base class, Human (Ducournau & Habib, 1987). To access that technique, you must first type the term super, then the period, sometimes known as the dot operator.

```
// changing mathod getHumanInfo public String getHumanInfo() {String info; info=super.getHumanInfo(); info=info+"and I am a lady."; return info;

}
```

The final portion of the code illustrates how to use newly created classes. This is nothing new.

```
...

Gentleman me = new Gentleman(); Lady anne = new Lady();

me.setPerson (0, "Olexiy," "Ukrainian"); //store data you.setPerson(0, "Anne," "Russian"); //store data

System.out.println(me.getHumanInfo()); System.out.println(you.getHumanInfo());...
```

8.5.1. Single and Multiple Inheritance

Multiple inheritances are a feature supported by OOP languages like C++ (Lieberman, 1986). This indicates that a new class could be derived from far more than one class name to achieve the desired results (Halbert & O'Brien, 1987). In certain circumstances, this is an advantage, yet, in other cases, it can lead to issues. Although JAVA does not provide multiple inheritances, the same result can be achieved using a specialized mechanism known as an interface. This is only offered to let you know that OOP languages may or may not have the tools to accomplish the same goals and that this is a possibility.

8.5.2. The ISA Relationship

You could overhear folks talking about their ISA connections every once in a while. The origin of this language goes back further to more fundamental concepts than you might initially expect (Singh, 1994).

Object-oriented designers frequently work hard to perfect inheritance as a modeling technique for situations where a derived class "kind of" corresponds to the base class (Baclawski & Indurkhya, 1994). For instance, a lady "sort of" qualifies as a human. A wife "sort of" fits the bill for a lady, etc. (Figure 8.11).

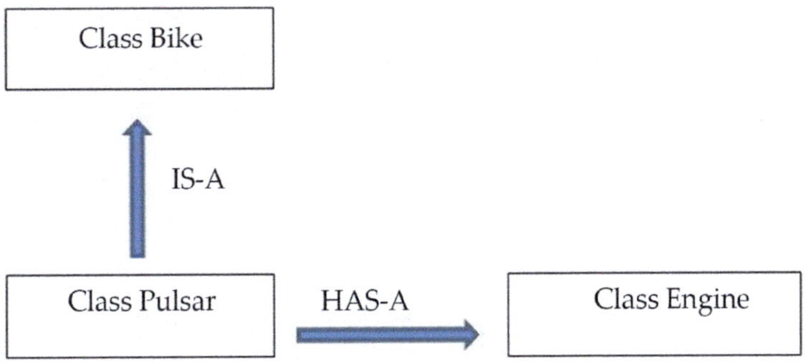

Figure 8.11. Difference between IS-A and HAS-A.

Source: Satendra Singh Bhati, Creative Commons License.

The acronym ISA is often used to refer to this kind of connection.

8.6. POLYMORPHISM

Polymorphism is the final property that must be present in an object-oriented language (Alkazemi & Grami, 2012).

The word "polymorphism" comes from the Greek language. It signifies "one thing, many shapes" or something along those lines. In OOP, polymorphism refers to "one interface, numerous methods" and indicates that the compiler does not intuitively recognize some functions or operators (Muntean et al., 2018). The JAVA programming language does not support operators' overloading, yet it facilitates the overriding and overloading of methods.

8.6.1. Overloading Methods as a Form of Polymorphism

The ability to replace any one of the three C functions is perhaps the most well-known example of polymorphism:

```
1. abs()
```

```
2. labs()

3. fabs()

by a solitary JAVA function referred as ABS().
```

C calls for using three distinct functions, the specifics of which are determined by the data types (Ducournau, 2002). In Java, you need to remember one name for the function, regardless of the data type, whether int, long, or float. When referring to this scenario, the term "overloaded function or method" is typically used. A compiler can recognize this scenario, and the polymorphism that occurs during compile time is given the name compile time polymorphism. Several authors also mention static binding or early binding when discussing this particular scenario. Most of the time, they do not regard function overload as a "real" form of polymorphism.

8.6.2. Overloading of Operators

Polymorphism of this sort is possible in so many non-OOP languages (Bruce et al., 1995). For example, the "+" operator adds any form of data when working in the C programming language. This polymorphic activity has always been an inherent part of the language, and the programmer cannot change it or exercise any control over it (Figure 8.12).

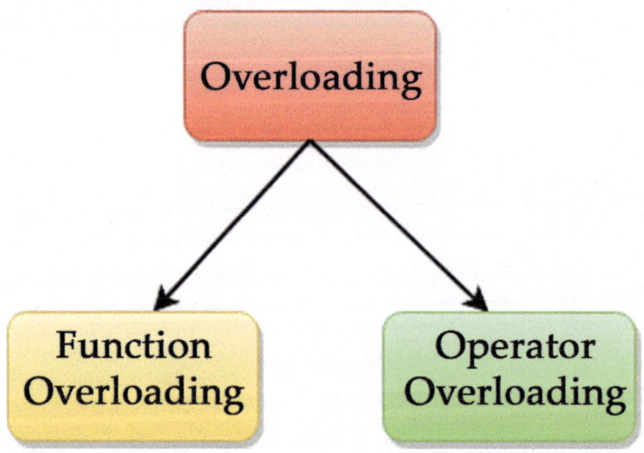

Figure 8.12. Overloading and its types.

Source: Java Point, Creative Commons License.

C++ gives the programmer the option and, including one or two exceptions, the obligation of defining the behavior of practically any operator that can be applied to an item of a new category. This can be done only if the class is written in C++ (Wong et al., 2017).

JAVA does not provide operator overloading, but in many circumstances, overloaded operators will give a much clearer and more intuitive syntax (Åkerblom & Wrigstad, 2015).

8.6.3. Overriding Methods as a Form of Polymorphism

The words override and overload is not interchangeable, including how they are written or spoken or the meanings they convey. The concept of overloading a method is unrelated to the practice of overriding a method (Sandhu & Singh, 2008).

There is more to the story than just the methods of overloading and the operators who engage in it. Runtime polymorphism is the term used to describe the situation in which a derived class modifies the behavior of procedures specified in a base class, typically to meet the unique requirements of the derived class (Wilde & Huitt, 1992).

The concept of overriding a procedure in a base class in Java is supported, which allows objects of a derived class to force the base class method to act differently relative to those objects (Binder, 2000). In other words, the behavior of a process called drinking() described in the base class but overwritten within the derived class would change based on whether it was invoked by an item of a base class or by an item of the derived class. The drinking() method is defined in the base class but overruled in the derived class.

Reference variables of such a base-class type in Java can reference an item of any class obtained from the same base class as the base class.

Suppose an overruled method is called utilizing that evidence consistently. In that case, the system can determine, at the running time, which edition of the method is based on the object's true form rather than the local type of variable used to call the process. This determination will be based on the fact that the system can decide which version the method can use based on the true object type. The following piece of Java code illustrates this fact.

In the first step, an overridden method with the same name is called drinking() while referring to an object of the base class. In the second step, an overridden method with the same name is called drinking() while referring to a thing of the derived class.

In the first scenario, the drinking() method from the base class is the one that is called. In the second scenario, the drinking() method from the derived class is the one that is called. This is of no importance (Wilde et al., 1993).

Finally, as the third step, an overridden method with the name drinking() is called upon a base-class reference that points to an obtained object. When something like this is carried out, the implementation of the invoked method is defined within the derived class rather than the one defined within the base class. This is the crux of what runtime polymorphism is all about (Nordlander, 2002).

```
// This program illustrates the runtime polymorphism.
// Output of the program should be as followed:
// My name is null and I am null and I am ready to work.
// I like drink with friends
// My name is Olexiy and I am Ukrainian and I am ready to work.
// and I am a Gentleman.
// I like drinking beer in my favorite pub
// My name is Olexiy and I am Ukrainian and I am ready to work.
// and I am a Gentleman.
// I like drinking beer in my favorite pub

class ex4 {
public static void main(String args[]) {
// Human class ref to Human class object
Human obj = new Human();
// Gentleman class ref to Gentleman class object
Gentleman me = new Gentleman();
// set information about me:
me.setPerson (0, “Olexiy,” “Ukrainian”);

// Display information about obj:
System.out.println(obj.getHumanInfo());
// invoke method named drinking:
obj.drinking();
```

```
// Display information about me:
System.out.println (me.getHumanInfo());
// invoke method named drinking:
me.drinking();

// Human class ref to Gentleman class object
obj = me;

// Display information about obj:
System.out.println (obj.getHumanInfo());
// invoke method named drinking:
obj.drinking();
}
}
```

In practically all JAVA programming, the concepts of inheritance and method overriding are utilized. Even the well-known "Hello World" Java applet needs to have the Applet class expanded, and it also needs to override the paint() method.

8.7. EXCEPTION HANDLING

Exception management is essential to the operation of JAVA, even though OOP does not consider it to be a core notion (Weimer & Necula, 2004). As a result, it would be beneficial to talk about it for a bit in a more generic way.

We shall make an effort to take a cursory glance at the following subjects (Figure 8.13):

- What does it mean to make an exception?
- How do we raise exceptions and catch them when they occur?
- Once we have identified an exception, what steps should we take next?
- How can we take advantage of an exception class hierarchy the development environment makes available to us?
- Would the management of exceptions provide any benefits for us?

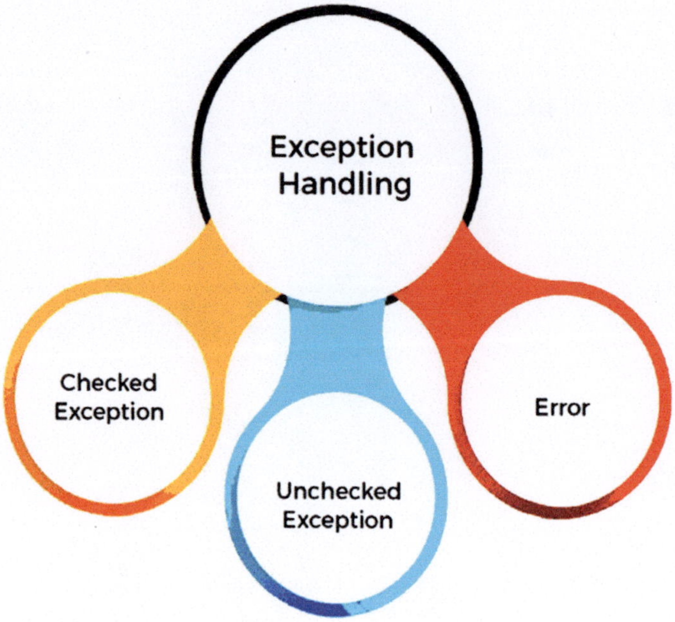

Figure 8.13. Illustration of the exception handing.

Source: Java Point, Creative Commons License.

8.7.1. Exception Hierarchy

One possible definition of exception is presented in the following sentence:

An occurrence during a program that deviates from the typical order in which instructions are carried out is an exception.

Monitoring exceptional conditions inside a program and automatically switching control to specialized exception-handling code created by a programmer are made feasible by exception-handling capability (Romanovsky et al., 2003).

Then, we attempt to run the statements in a block of code enclosed in braces. Following that, a programmer's code or even the runtime system directly raises this exception item of a certain kind of uncommon condition found within that block. The Java exception is an object directly or indirectly descended from the class Throwable (Poo et al., 2007).

There are two subclasses of the Java Throwable class (Xu, 2013):

- An error signifies a non-catchable error that should not have happened. The JAVA interpreter typically exits after displaying a message in response to errors (O'Grady & Seshadri, 1991); and
- An exception denotes a strange circumstance that needs to be handled carefully to avoid program termination.

There is a subset of the possible exceptions which Java can automatically throw for which capturing and processing are optional. The compiler permits you to disregard the exceptions in this subset (Holmes & Joyce, 2001). If it happens, the runtime system will catch an ignored exception and end the program.

To compile your program, the application's code must automatically recognize the remaining exceptions that Java can throw.

Recognized implies that the program's code will catch the exception and handle the object to use another piece of code or pass it to the next level of the method-invocation tree (Kienzle, 2000).

After that, the JAVA application can execute a block of code denoted by finally. This code block is typically employed to carry out some required cleanup regardless of the probability of an exception.

It is required that the throws keyword be included in the declaration of a method's signature if the method can pass an exception on to the subsequent level of the invocation hierarchy (Bloom & Zdonik, 1987).

If your program detects and handles an exception, the code used can be as complex or straightforward as you choose to make it. The reality is that you can satiate the requirements of the compiler by simply ignoring it once you've found it. Depending on the kind of exception, this might be a good idea, or it could be that it's not a good idea at all. A Throwable JAVA class provides the methods inherited by all exception objects.

8.7.2. Advantages of Using Exception Handling

In comparison to "conventional" methods of error management, exception handling offers several benefits, including the following:

- Separating error handling code derived from the "regular" one provides a mechanism to isolate the specifics of what to do if something unusual happens from a normal logical way of the computer code; in other words, it is a way to handle exceptions (Campéas et al., 2005).
- Spreading errors up the call stack makes it possible to take corrective action at a higher level in the program (Miller & Lennox, 1991). This makes it possible for the corrective measures to be still executed in the procedure that calls that one whenever there is an error;
- The ability to establish a comparable hierarchical system for exception handling is enabled by grouping Types of errors and error differentiation, which then groups them logically (Cabral & Marques, 2007).

8.8. FINAL REMARKS OF OOP

OOP needs a different approach to the design of computer programs (Filman et al., 2000). Multiple class hierarchies must have their shared behaviors and features recognized and explained. Most of the work is finished once class hierarchies have been outlined. Some objects have new instances generated for them, and their methods are called. The benefits of OOP are as follows:

- The ability to reuse code while maintaining its individuality through inheritance and encapsulation;
- Maintainability: modifications made to a superclass are propagated to all of the classes that inherit from it (Meyer, 1997);
- The ability to maintain code's independence through encapsulation. The implementation details are hidden from view, and the only part of the object that the outside world may see is its interface.
- An extremely high level of code organization and modularity is especially crucial for projects of a substantial scale; 8 prompts you to think before you code.

The following are the drawbacks:

- So, because the inheritance mechanism should be implemented at runtime, compiled programs are typically larger than their uncompiled counterparts.
- Compilated programs are typically slower than their uncompiled counterparts since subclasses need to look up inherited code before calling it (Enrich et al., 1994).

ACTIVITY 8.1:

Write a simple program using an object-oriented programming language such as Java or Python to demonstrate the basic principles of OOP, including classes, objects, and inheritance.

8.9. SUMMARY

Introduction to OOP is a chapter that provides an overview of the world of OOP. The chapter begins by defining OOP and its primary objective, making programming more object-oriented. It then discusses the characteristics of an OOP language, which include data abstraction, encapsulation, inheritance, and polymorphism. The concept of encapsulation is then explained in detail, along with its primary advantage of improved code maintainability. The purpose of heritage in OOP is also discussed, which is to reuse code and reduce redundancy. The basics of polymorphism are then introduced, which involves the ability of an object to take on many forms. The chapter also covers the fundamentals of exception handling: catching and responding to errors. Furthermore, the chapter provides an overview of distributed objects and how they can be enabled using CORBA and RMI. Finally, the chapter introduces the concept of object-oriented design and its importance in programming.

Overall, the chapter provides a comprehensive understanding of the world of OOP and its essential concepts, making it a necessary read for anyone interested in programming.

REVIEW QUESTIONS

1. What exactly is meant by the term "object-oriented programming," and what are its fundamental goals?
2. What distinguishes an entity programming language from other types of languages?
3. Please define encapsulation and explain the key benefit it offers.
4. What is inheritance, and how does it function in object-oriented programming?
5. Please provide an overview of polymorphism and discuss the significance of this concept in object-oriented programming.

MULTIPLE CHOICE QUESTIONS

1. What is the primary objective of Object-Oriented Programming?

a. To reduce the size of the program
b. To simplify the code
c. To make programming more object-oriented
d. To make programming language easier to learn

2. Which of the following is a characteristic of an Object-Oriented Programming Language?

a. Functional programming
b. Imperative programming
c. Object-oriented programming
d. Both a and b

3. **Which of the following is the primary advantage of encapsulation?**
    a. Improved program performance
    b. Improved code readability
    c. Improved code reusability
    d. Improved code maintainability
4. **What is the purpose of inheritance in Object-Oriented Programming?**
    a. To reduce the size of the program
    b. To simplify the code
    c. To make programming more object-oriented
    d. To reuse code and minimize redundancy
5. **Which of the following best describes polymorphism?**
    a. The ability to create objects from classes
    b. The power of an object to take on many forms
    c. The ability to define types with multiple methods
    d. The ability to define various classes with the same name

Answers to Multiple Choice Questions

1. (c); 2. (c); 3. (d); 4. (d); 5. (b)

REFERENCES

1. Agarwal, R., Sinha, A. P., & Tanniru, M., (1996). The role of prior experience and task characteristics in object-oriented modeling: An empirical study. *International Journal of Human-Computer Studies, 45*(6), 639–667.
2. Ågerfalk, P. J., (1999). Encapsulation or availability. In: *Seminar in Scandinavia (IRIS 22): Enterprise Architectures for Virtual Organizations* (Vol. 1, p. 37).
3. Åkerblom, B., & Wrigstad, T., (2015). Measuring polymorphism in python programs. In: *Proceedings of the 11th Symposium on Dynamic Languages* (Vol. 1, pp. 114–128).
4. Alkazemi, B. Y., & Grami, G. M., (2012). Utilizing BlueJ to teach polymorphism in an advanced object-oriented programming course. *Journal of Information Technology Education: Innovations in Practice, 11*(1), 271.
5. Alrashidi, M., Callaghan, V., & Gardner, M., (2014). An object-oriented pedagogical model for mixed reality teaching and learning. In: *2014 International Conference on Intelligent Environments* (Vol. 1, pp. 202–206). IEEE.
6. Andrianoff, S. K., & Levine, D. B., (2002). Role playing in an object-oriented world. In: *Proceedings of the 33rd SIGCSE Technical Symposium on Computer Science Education* (Vol. 1, pp. 121–125).

7. Atkinson, M., Dewitt, D., Maier, D., Bancilhon, F., Dittrich, K., & Zdonik, S., (1990). The object-oriented database system manifesto. In: *Deductive and Object-Oriented Databases* (Vol. 1, pp. 223–240). North-Holland.
8. Baclawski, K., & Indurkhya, B., (1994). The notion of inheritance in object-oriented programming. *Communications of the ACM, 37*(9), 118–119.
9. Banciihon, F., (1988). Object-oriented database systems. In: *Proceedings of the Seventh ACM SIGACT-SIGMOD-SIGART Symposium on Principles of Database Systems* (Vol. 1, pp. 152–162).
10. Bansiya, J., & Davis, C. G., (2002). A hierarchical model for object-oriented design quality assessment. *IEEE Transactions on Software Engineering, 28*(1), 4–17.
11. Basili, V. R., Briand, L. C., & Melo, W. L., (1996). A validation of object-oriented design metrics as quality indicators. *IEEE Transactions on Software Engineering, 22*(10), 751–761.
12. Bergin, J., Stehlik, M., Roberts, J., & Pattis, R., (2005). *Karel J. Robot: A Gentle Introduction to the art of Object-Oriented Programming in Java* (2nd edn., pp. 1–10). Redwood City: Dream Songs.
13. Binder, R., (2000). *Testing Object-Oriented Systems: Models, Patterns, and Tools* (3rd edn., pp. 2–6). Addison-Wesley Professional.
14. Bloom, T., & Zdonik, S. B., (1987). Issues in the design of object-oriented database programming languages. In: *Conference Proceedings on Object-Oriented Programming Systems, Languages and Applications* (Vol. 1, pp. 441–451).
15. Booch, G., (1994). Coming of age in an object-oriented world. *IEEE Software, 11*(6), 33–41.
16. Boyapati, C., Lee, R., & Rinard, M., (2002). Ownership types for safe programming: Preventing data races and deadlocks. In: *Proceedings of the 17th ACM SIGPLAN Conference on Object-Oriented Programming, Systems, Languages, and Applications* (Vol. 1, pp. 211–230).
17. Boyapati, C., Liskov, B., & Shrira, L., (2003). Ownership types for object encapsulation. *ACM SIGPLAN Notices, 38*(1), 213–223.
18. Bracha, G., & Ungar, D., (2004). Mirrors: Design principles for meta-level facilities of object-oriented programming languages. *ACM SIGPLAN Notices, 39*(10), 331–344.
19. Briot, J. P., Guerraoui, R., & Lohr, K. P., (1998). Concurrency and distribution in object-oriented programming. *ACM Computing Surveys (CSUR), 30*(3), 291–329.
20. Bruce, K. B., Schuett, A., & VanGent, R., (1995). PolyTOIL: A type-safe polymorphic object-oriented language. In: *ECOOP'95—Object-Oriented Programming, 9th European Conference, Åarhus, Denmark* (Vol. 1, pp. 27–51). Springer Berlin Heidelberg.
21. Bugliesi, M., & Jamil, H. M., (1994). A logic for encapsulation in object oriented languages. In: *Programming Language Implementation and Logic Programming: 6th International Symposium, PLILP'94 Madrid, Spain, September 14–16, 1994 Proceedings 6* (Vol. 1, pp. 215–229). Springer Berlin Heidelberg.

22. Cabral, B., & Marques, P., (2007). Exception handling: A field study in java and. net. In: *ECOOP 2007–Object-Oriented Programming: 21st European Conference, Berlin, Germany, July 30-August 3, 2007; Proceedings 21* (Vol. 1, pp. 151–175). Springer Berlin Heidelberg.
23. Campéas, A., Dony, C., Urtado, C., & Vauttier, S., (2005). Distributed exception handling: Ideas, lessons and issues with recent exception handling systems. In: *Rapid Integration of Software Engineering Techniques: First International Workshop, RISE 2004, Luxembourg-Kirchberg, Luxembourg, November 26, 2004. Revised Selected Papers 1* (Vol. 1, pp. 82–92). Springer Berlin Heidelberg.
24. Canfora, G., De Lucia, A., & Di Lucca, G. A., (1999). An incremental object-oriented migration strategy for RPG legacy systems. *International Journal of Software Engineering and Knowledge Engineering, 9*(1), 5–25.
25. Chaumette, S., (1998). JEM-DOOS: The java/RMI based distributed objects operating system of the JEM project. In: *Computing in Object-Oriented Parallel Environments: Second International Symposium, ISCOPE 98 Santa Fe, NM, USA, December 8–11, 1998 Proceedings 2* (Vol. 1, pp. 135–142). Springer Berlin Heidelberg.
26. Chidamber, S. R., & Kemerer, C. F., (1991). Towards a metrics suite for object oriented design. In: *Conference Proceedings on Object-Oriented Programming Systems, Languages, and Applications* (Vol. 1, pp. 197–211).
27. Civello, F., (1993). Roles for composite objects in object-oriented analysis and design. In: *Proceedings of the Eighth Annual Conference on Object-Oriented Programming Systems, Languages, and Applications* (Vol. 1, pp. 376–393).
28. Clark, D. R., (2006). Overview of object-oriented programming. *Beginning Object-Oriented Programming with VB 2005: From Novice to Professional* (2nd edn., pp. 3–9).
29. Clarke, D., & Drossopoulou, S., (2002). Ownership, encapsulation and the disjointness of type and effect. In: *Proceedings of the 17th ACM SIGPLAN Conference on Object-oriented Programming, Systems, Languages, and Applications* (Vol. 1, pp. 292–310).
30. Coleman, D., Hayes, F., & Bear, S., (1992). Introducing objectcharts or how to use statecharts in object-oriented design. *IEEE Transactions on Software Engineering, 18*(1), 8, 9.
31. Concas, G., Marchesi, M., Pinna, S., & Serra, N., (2006). On the suitability of Yule process to stochastically model some properties of object-oriented systems. *Physica A: Statistical Mechanics and its Applications, 370*(2), 817–831.
32. Cox, B. J., (1986). *Object Oriented Programming: An Evolutionary Approach* (Vol. 1, pp. 2–8). Addison-Wesley Longman Publishing Co., Inc.
33. Ducournau, R., & Habib, M., (1987). On some algorithms for multiple inheritance in object oriented programming. In: *ECOOP'87 European Conference on Object-Oriented Programming: Paris, France, June 15–17, 1987 Proceedings 1* (Vol. 1, pp. 243–252). Springer Berlin Heidelberg.
34. Ducournau, R., (2002). "Real world" as an argument for covariant specialization in programming and modeling. In: *Advances in Object-Oriented Information Systems:*

OOIS 2002 Workshops Montpellier, France, September 2, 2002 Proceedings 8 (Vol. 1, pp. 3–13). Springer Berlin Heidelberg.

35. Embley, D. W., Kurtz, B. D., & Woodfield, S. N., (1991). *Object-Oriented Systems Analysis: A Model-Driven Approach* (2nd edn., pp. 2–4). Yourdon Press.
36. Enrich, H. D., Engels, G., Paredaens, J., & Wegner, P., (1994). *Fundamentals of Object-Oriented Languages, Systems and Methods* (Vol. 95, pp. 5–10). In Dagstuhl Seminar Report.
37. Filman, R. E., Friedman, D. P., & Norvig, P., (2000). *Aspect-Oriented Programming is Quantification and Obliviousness* (Vol. 1, pp. 3–9).
38. Freeman-Benson, B. N., & Borning, A., (1992). Integrating constraints with an object-oriented language. In: *ECOOP'92 European Conference on Object-Oriented Programming: Utrecht, The Netherlands, June 29–July 3, 1992 Proceedings 6* (Vol. 1, pp. 268–286). Springer Berlin Heidelberg.
39. Gamma, E., Helm, R., Johnson, R., & Vlissides, J., (1993). Design patterns: Abstraction and reuse of object-oriented design. In: *ECOOP'93—Object-Oriented Programming: 7th European Conference Kaiserslautern, Germany, July 26–30, 1993 Proceedings 7* (Vol. 1, pp. 406–431). Springer Berlin Heidelberg.
40. Gatziu, S., & Dittrich, K. R., (1992). SAMOS: An active object-oriented database system. *IEEE Data Eng. Bull., 15*(1–4), 23–26.
41. Gottlob, G., Schrefl, M., & Röck, B., (1996). Extending object-oriented systems with roles. *ACM Transactions on Information Systems (TOIS), 14*(3), 268–296.
42. Guidec, F., Jézéquel, J. M., & Pacherie, J. L., (1996). An object-oriented framework for supercomputing. *Journal of Systems and Software, 33*(3), 239–251.
43. Hadjerrouit, S., (1999). A constructivist approach to object-oriented design and programming. *ACM SIGCSE Bulletin, 31*(3), 171–174.
44. Halbert, D. C., & O'Brien, P. D., (1987). Using types and inheritance in object-oriented programming. *IEEE Software, 4*(5), 70, 71.
45. Halbert, D. C., & O'Brien, P. D., (2000). Using types and inheritance in object-oriented languages. In: *ECOOP'87 European Conference on Object-Oriented Programming: Paris, France, June 15–17, 1987 Proceedings* (Vol. 1, pp. 20–31). Berlin, Heidelberg: Springer Berlin Heidelberg.
46. Hibbard, W., Rueden, C., Emmerson, S., Rink, T., Glowacki, D., Whittaker, T., & Anderson, J., (2002). Java distributed objects for numerical visualization in VisAD. *Communications of the ACM, 45*(4), 160–170.
47. Hirshfield, S., & Ege, R. K., (1996). Object-oriented programming. *ACM Computing Surveys (CSUR), 28*(1), 253–255.
48. Hogg, J., (1991). Islands: Aliasing protection in object-oriented languages. In: *Conference Proceedings on Object-Oriented Programming Systems, Languages, and Applications* (Vol. 1, pp. 271–285).

49. Holmes, B. J., & Joyce, D. T., (2001). *Object-Oriented Programming with Java* (Vol. 1, pp. 2–9). Jones & Bartlett Learning.
50. Howard, G. S., (1988). Object oriented programming explained. *Journal of Systems Management, 39*(7), 13.
51. Hyde, R. L., & Fleisch, B. D., (1998). A case for virtual distributed objects. *Int'l. Journal on Parallel and Distributed Computing, 1*(3), 1–11.
52. Jacobson, I., (1993). *Object-Oriented Software Engineering: A Use Case Driven Approach* (Vol. 1, pp. 5–10). Pearson Education India.
53. Joines, J. A., & Roberts, S. D., (1999). Simulation in an object-oriented world. In: *Proceedings of the 31st Conference on Winter Simulation: Simulation—A Bridge to the Future* (Vol. 1, pp. 132–140).
54. Kanaki, K., & Kalogiannakis, M., (2018). Introducing fundamental object-oriented programming concepts in preschool education within the context of physical science courses. *Education and Information Technologies, 23*(6), 2673–2698.
55. Kienzle, J., (2000). Exception handling in open multithreaded transactions. In: *Workshop on Exception Handling in Object-Oriented Systems at ECOOP 2000, Sophia Antipolis, Cannes, France, June 12–16 (No. CONF)* (2nd edn., pp. 3–6).
56. Kifer, M., Lausen, G., & Wu, J., (1995). Logical foundations of object-oriented and frame-based languages. *Journal of the ACM (JACM), 42*(4), 741–843.
57. Kniesel, G., & Theisen, D., (2001). JAC—Access right based encapsulation for *Java. Software: Practice and Experience, 31*(6), 555–576.
58. Kölling, M., (1999). The problem of teaching object-oriented programming, Part 1: Languages. *Journal of Object-Oriented Programming, 11*(8), 8–15.
59. Kölling, M., (1999). The problem of teaching object-oriented programming, Part 2: Environments. *Journal of Object-Oriented Programming, 11*(9), 6–12.
60. Korson, T., & McGregor, J. D., (1990). Understanding object-oriented: A unifying paradigm. *Communications of the ACM, 33*(9), 40–60.
61. Kosbar, K., & Schneider, K., (1992). Object-oriented modeling of communication systems. In: *MILCOM 92 Conference Record* (Vol. 1, pp. 68–72). IEEE.
62. Lange, D. B., & Nakamura, Y., (1997). Object-oriented program tracing and visualization. *Computer, 30*(5), 63–70.
63. Lau, K. K., & Taweel, F. M., (2007). Data encapsulation in software components. In: *Component-Based Software Engineering: 10th International Symposium, CBSE 2007, Medford, MA, USA, July 9–11, 2007; Proceedings 10* (Vol. 1, pp. 1–16). Springer Berlin Heidelberg.
64. Lieberman, H., (1986). Using prototypical objects to implement shared behavior in object-oriented systems. In: *Conference Proceedings on Object-Oriented Programming Systems, Languages and Applications* (Vol. 1, pp. 214–223).
65. Lu, Y., & Potter, J., (2006). Protecting representation with effect encapsulation. *ACM SIGPLAN Notices, 41*(1), 359–371.

66. Menzies, T., & Haynes, P., (1996). *Empirical Observations of Class-Level Encapsulation and Inheritance* (Vol. 1, pp. 6–9). Technical report, Department of Software Development, Monash University.

67. Meyer, B., (1997). *Object-Oriented Software Construction* (Vol. 2, pp. 331–410). Englewood Cliffs: Prentice Hall.

68. Miller, D. J., & Lennox, R. C., (1991). An object-oriented environment for robot system architectures. *IEEE Control Systems Magazine, 11*(2), 14–23.

69. Muntean, P., Wuerl, S., Grossklags, J., & Eckert, C., (2018). CastSan: Efficient detection of polymorphic C++ object type confusions with LLVM. In: *Computer Security: 23rd European Symposium on Research in Computer Security, ESORICS 2018, Barcelona, Spain, September 3–7, 2018, Proceedings, Part I 23* (Vol. 1, pp. 3–25). Springer International Publishing.

70. Mylopoulos, J., Chung, L., & Yu, E., (1999). From object-oriented to goal-oriented requirements analysis. *Communications of the ACM, 42*(1), 31–37.

71. Narayanan, S., Bodner, D. A., Sreekanth, U., Govindaraj, T., McGinnis, L. F., & Mitchell, C. M., (1998). Research in object-oriented manufacturing simulations: An assessment of the state of the art. *IIE Transactions, 30*(9), 795–810.

72. Nordlander, J., (2002). Polymorphic subtyping in O'Haskell. *Science of Computer Programming, 43*(2, 3), 93–127.

73. Nygaard, K., (1986). Basic concepts in object oriented programming. In: *Proceedings of the 1986 SIGPLAN Workshop on Object-oriented Programming* (Vol. 1, pp. 128–132).

74. O'Grady, P., & Seshadri, R., (1991). X-cell—Intelligent cell control using object-oriented programming (part I). *Computer Integrated Manufacturing Systems, 4*(3), 157–163.

75. Oren, E., Delbru, R., Gerke, S., Haller, A., & Decker, S., (2007). ActiveRDF: Object-oriented semantic web programming. In: *Proceedings of the 16th International Conference on World Wide Web* (Vol. 1, pp. 817–824).

76. Plášil, F., & Stal, M., (1998). An architectural view of distributed objects and components in CORBA, Java RMI and COM/DCOM. *Software-Concepts & Tools, 19*(1), 14–28.

77. Pokkunuri, B. P., (1989). Object oriented programming. *ACM Sigplan Notices, 24*(11), 96–101.

78. Poo, D., Kiong, D., & Ashok, S., (2007). *Object-Oriented Programming and Java* (2nd edn., pp. 1–7). Springer Science & Business Media.

79. Rahnev, A., Pavlov, N., Valchanov, N., & Terzieva, T., (2014). *Object Oriented Programming* (Vol. 2, No. 1, pp. 7–9). Lightning Source UK Ltd., London.

80. Raptis, K., Spinellis, D., & Katsikas, S., (2001). Multi-technology distributed objects and their integration. *Computer Standards & Interfaces, 23*(3), 157–168.

81. Rentsch, T., (1982). Object oriented programming. *ACM Sigplan Notices, 17*(9), 51–57.

82. Romanovsky, A., Dony, C., Knudsen, J. L., & Tripathi, A., (2003). *Advances in Exception Handling Techniques* (Vol. 1, pp. 4–8). Springer.

83. Saleh, K., Probert, R., & Khanafer, H., (1999). The distributed object computing paradigm: Concepts and applications. *Journal of Systems and Software, 47*(2, 3), 125–131.

84. Salvaneschi, G., Hintz, G., & Mezini, M., (2014). REScala: Bridging between object-oriented and functional style in reactive applications. In: *Proceedings of the 13th International Conference on Modularity* (Vol. 1, pp. 25–36).

85. Sanders, D., & Dorn, B., (2003). Jeroo: A tool for introducing object-oriented programming. In: *Proceedings of the 34th SIGCSE Technical Symposium on Computer Science Education* (Vol. 1, pp. 201–204).

86. Sanders, K., Boustedt, J., Eckerdal, A., McCartney, R., Moström, J. E., Thomas, L., & Zander, C., (2008). Student understanding of object-oriented programming as expressed in concept maps. In: *Proceedings of the 39th SIGCSE Technical Symposium on Computer Science Education* (Vol. 1, pp. 332–336).

87. Sandhu, P. S., & Singh, G., (2008). Dynamic metrics for polymorphism in object oriented systems. *International Journal of Computer and Information Engineering, 2*(3), 697–700.

88. Santos, A. L., (2014). Novel interaction metaphors for object-oriented programming concepts. In: *Proceedings of the 14th Koli Calling International Conference on Computing Education Research* (Vol. 1, pp. 117–126).

89. Sarcar, V., (2022). Encapsulation using properties and indexers. In: *Test Your Skills in C# Programming: Review and Analyze Important Features of C#* (Vol. 1, pp. 183–211). Berkeley, CA: Apress.

90. Schäfer, J., & Rauch, D. I. N., (2004). *Encapsulation and Specification of Object-Oriented Runtime Components* (2nd edn., p. 89).

91. Schultz, U. P., & Axelsen, H. B., (2016). Elements of a reversible object-oriented language: Work-in-progress report. In: *Reversible Computation: 8th International Conference, RC 2016, Bologna, Italy, July 7–8, 2016, Proceedings* (Vol. 1, pp. 153–159). Cham: Springer International Publishing.

92. Shalloway, A., & Trott, J. R., (2005). Design patterns explained: A new perspective on object-oriented design, 2/E. *Pearson Education India, 4*(1), 6–10.

93. Singh, G. B., (1994). Single versus multiple inheritance in object-oriented programming. *ACM SIGPLAN OOPS Messenger, 5*(1), 34–43.

94. Singh, G. B., (1995). Single versus multiple inheritance in object-oriented programming. *ACM SIGPLAN OOPS Messenger, 6*(1), 30–39.

95. Singh, S., & Kahlon, K. S., (2011). Effectiveness of encapsulation and object-oriented metrics to refactor code and identify error prone classes using bad smells. *ACM SIGSOFT Software Engineering Notes, 36*(5), 1–10.

96. Skoglund, M., (2003). Practical use of encapsulation in object-oriented programming. In: *Software Engineering Research and Practice* (Vol. 1, pp. 554–560).

97. Smith, M. D., & Robson, D. J., (1990). Object-oriented programming-the problems

of validation. In: *Proceedings, Conference on Software Maintenance 1990* (Vol. 1, pp. 272–281). IEEE.

98. Sridharan, M., Chandra, S., Dolby, J., Fink, S. J., & Yahav, E., (2013). Alias analysis for object-oriented programs. *Aliasing in Object-Oriented Programming. Types, Analysis and Verification* (2nd edn., pp. 196–232).
99. Srinath, K. R., (2017). Python–the fastest growing programming language. *International Research Journal of Engineering and Technology, 4*(12), 354–357.
100. Stal, M., (1999). Distributed objects from a patterns perspective. In: *Proceedings of Technology of Object-Oriented Languages and Systems-TOOLS 30 (Cat. No. PR00278)* (Vol. 1, pp. 445–449. IEEE Computer Society.
101. Stroustrup, B., (1995). Why C++ is not just an object-oriented programming language. In: *Addendum to the Proceedings of the 10th Annual Conference on Object-Oriented Programming Systems, Languages, and Applications (Addendum)* (Vol. 1, pp. 1–13).
102. Sutcliffe, A. G., (1991). Object-oriented systems development: Survey of structured methods. *Information and Software Technology, 33*(6), 433–442.
103. Sventek, J., (1998). Guest editor's introduction: Selected papers from the 4th USENIX conference on object-oriented technologies and systems. *Distributed Systems Engineering, 5*(4), 139–140.
104. Uzakov, Z., Mamatov, F., & Begulov, O., (2019). Implementation of object-oriented programming technology in the one-dimensional oil displacement problem. In: *2019 International Conference on Information Science and Communications Technologies (ICISCT)* (Vol. 1, pp. 1–5). IEEE.
105. Voigt, J., (2009). *Characterizing the Use of Encapsulation in Object Oriented Systems* (2nd edn., pp. 2, 3).
106. Voigt, J., Irwin, W., & Churcher, N., (2010). *Class Encapsulation and Object Encapsulation: An Empirical Study, 1*, 2–6.
107. Weimer, W., & Necula, G. C., (2004). Finding and preventing run-time error handling mistakes. In: *Proceedings of the 19th Annual ACM SIGPLAN Conference on Object-Oriented Programming, Systems, Languages, and Applications* (Vol. 1, pp. 419–431).
108. Wiedenbeck, S., Ramalingam, V., Sarasamma, S., & Corritore, C. L., (1999). A comparison of the comprehension of object-oriented and procedural programs by novice programmers. *Interacting with Computers, 11*(3), 255–282.
109. Wiener, R. S., & Pinson, L. J., (1988). *An Introduction to Object-Oriented Programming and C++* (Vol. 1, pp. 2–7). Addison-Wesley Longman Publishing Co., Inc.
110. Wilde, N., & Huitt, R., (1992). Maintenance support for object-oriented programs. *IEEE Transactions on Software Engineering, 18*(12), 1038.
111. Wilde, N., Matthews, P., & Huitt, R., (1993). Maintaining object-oriented software. *IEEE Software, 10*(1), 75–80.
112. Wirfs-Brock, R. J., & Johnson, R. E., (1990). Surveying current research in object-oriented design. *Communications of the ACM, 33*(9), 104–124.

113. Wirfs-Brock, R., & Wilkerson, B., (1989). Object-oriented design: A responsibility-driven approach. *ACM Sigplan Notices, 24*(10), 71–75.

114. Wong, Y. S., Hayati, M., Yatim, M., & Hoe, T. W., (2017). A propriety game based learning mobile game to learn object-oriented programming—Odyssey of phoenix. In: *2017 IEEE 6th International Conference on Teaching, Assessment, and Learning for Engineering (TALE)* (Vol. 1, pp. 426–431). IEEE.

115. Wu, C. T., (2006). *An Introduction to Object-Oriented Programming with Java TM* (Vol. 1, pp. 2–7). McGraw-Hill Incorporated.

116. Xianzhong, L., & Zhenyu, W., (1991). Ada-based support for abstraction, encapsulation and unit hierarchy. In: *Proceedings of the Conference on TRI-Ada'91: Today's Accomplishments; Tomorrow's Expectations* (Vol. 1, pp. 116–126).

117. Xinogalos, S., Satratzemi, M., & Dagdilelis, V., (2006). An introduction to object-oriented programming with a didactic microworld: Object Karel. *Computers & Education, 47*(2), 148–171.

118. Xu, G., (2013). Resurrector: A tunable object lifetime profiling technique for optimizing real-world programs. In: *Proceedings of the 2013 ACM SIGPLAN International Conference on Object Oriented Programming Systems Languages & Applications* (Vol. 1, pp. 111–130).

119. Yan, L., (2009). Teaching object-oriented programming with games. In: *2009 Sixth International Conference on Information Technology: New Generations* (Vol. 1, pp. 969–974). IEEE.

120. Zimmermann, T., Dubois-Pelerin, Y., & Bomme, P., (1992). Object-oriented finite element programming: I. Governing principles. *Computer Methods in Applied Mechanics and Engineering, 98*(2), 291–303.

INDEX

B

C

G

H

I

J

Q

R

S